MW01687246

# From Sheep to

# SHERO

Transforming the Face of Tribal BS

to live a life of spirituality, humanity, enlightenment, responsibility and opportunity

# From Sheep to
# SHERO

Transforming the Face of Tribal BS

to live a life of spirituality, humanity, enlightenment, responsibility and opportunity

Dear Nania jan,
Thank you for
your support.
Be a Shero,

Rebecca Moradoghli

[tuum est]

Tuum Est
Vancouver, Canada

Library and Archives Canada Cataloguing in Publication

Moradoghli, Rebecca, 1970-

From sheep to SHERO: transforming the face of tribal BS to live a life of spirituality, humanity, enlightenment, responsibility and opportunity / Rebecca Moradoghli.

ISBN 978-0-9813408-0-7

1. Leadership. 2. Self-actualization (Psychology). 3. Responsibility. 4. Self-culture. I. Title.

BF637.S4M666 2010 158.1 C2010-900367-5

Tuum Est
141-757 West Hastings St.
Suite #750
Vancouver, BC
V6C 1A1

Printed in Canada

## Dedication

*To my parents Ashot and Vartoohi,*
*and my brother Raymond*
*for their unconditional love and support.*

# TABLE OF CONTENTS

# ACKNOWLEDGEMENT

"I have never met a man so ignorant that I couldn't learn something from him." Galileo Galilei

I sit here with pen and paper in hand about to present to you my innermost ideas. It was my grandmother's vision that I would reach out to others and make a difference in our local community and the global community at large. Her favourite Armenian folklore poem, which she would recite at family dinners, was called "Angraged." Literally translated it meant illiterate. The following is the translation in English and although it does not do the poem justice the main theme of the poem becomes self-evident.

**Illiterate (Angraged)**

I am never jealous of anyone
On the surface of this planet
Except, you educated Sirs
I am jealous of your good fortune
Take pity on this humble person
And please teach me how to write
Give me one sheet of blank paper
Give me a feathered pen
So I can present to you my vision
What thoughts are in my mind
An incredible world I can show you
That you have never imagined
Right now they are disappearing
Those thoughts and dreams

I'm illiterate, I'm without education
Please teach me dear Sirs
It's a noble job, for man to write
To be able to pass along words
Everything that one is thinking
Everything that is in one's soul
To be able to tell the story with a pen
Whatever has heaped in ones heart
To be able to preach the truth
And the enormousness of good deeds
Oh dear duck with your white feathers
I have given you food
I have loved you now return the favour
From your wing give me a feather
You beautiful duck, please give me
Two feathers so my mind can fly
I'm illiterate and uneducated
Please teach me dear sirs.

My grandmother was never formally educated but she knew how to bring people together with love, laughter, humility, and compassion. I am honoured that events have come to pass exactly as they should in that I have been given an opportunity to do what she always wanted to do; have a pen and paper and share my thoughts.

# INTRODUCTION

Where did this concept of shero come from? The term shero came across my path in the late 90s. I remember hearing about it on the Oprah Winfrey Show and it was used to describe a heroine. While this word shero resonated with, I felt it was a universal rather than a female concept. Despite my reservation, the word somehow stuck with me. Seeds were sown and something bigger than me was taking place. Events happened in my life such that I became very clear as to what shero stood for and I wanted to share the concept with a story. It was important for me to show shero, not just talk about it. Text books are great, 'how to' books are great, but my experiences with people have showed me that nothing makes a greater impact than a story one can relate to. I wanted to show how you can walk the shero walk. I remember Grade 11 Algebra class, in which my favourite teacher Mr. Morgan would, with pain-staking effort and in great detail describe Algebra equations and ways in which to solve the problem. I would sit and listen but in the back of my mind, I would think, 'enough of this already, I get it.' But then that night at home, tackling the homework, I couldn't do it. He had made it seem so easy yet I could not apply it. The only thing I could remember was my smartass thoughts that I had had in class. The point is I knew how I could apply the rules to the example he had on the overhead but I didn't get the bigger picture to be able to apply it to other equations. The same with all self-help books and seminars, it makes complete sense when we are given the tools but when it comes to applying it to our everyday living we don't know how and we end up going back to our old patterns. Why? BS! Belief Systems. That's what holds us back. It doesn't matter what tools you learn if you do not change your BS you're not going to change anything. In the words of an amazing mind:

"You can not solve the problems of today, thinking the way you did when you created them." Einstein.

So what is a shero? Who is a shero? And finally, how does it tie into BS and the tribe? Simply put, shero stands for spirituality, humanity, enlightenment, responsibility and opportunity. These are five universal principles. Spirituality in that we realize that there is something bigger than oneself. Humanity, in that giving becomes our number one priority and not getting. Enlightenment in that we constantly need to learn and grow realizing if we don't grow we perish. This applies to personal growth as much as it does to business growth. Responsibility in that we are in charge of making choices for ourselves and thus are empowered in doing so. Although we may not be able to control all the events that occur around us, we are solely responsible for how we react to the events. Opportunity in realizing there is no such thing as failure there is opportunity for learning and growth in every situation. Simply put these five words are principles in which we hold close to us. These are constructive and positive principles by which we define ourselves with our environment. It is what gives our lives meaning and inspires us to keep moving forward. If you show ownership of shero then you will naturally commit to it and it will become as natural to you as breathing.

Belief systems are usually based on the past. They come from something that was passed on from generation to generation. They are usually a sentence long and are generalizations about people and the world. They are perceptual filters in that when we believe something we walk, talk and act as if it's true. The irony is that we consider beliefs true without positive proof. They are generalization we make about the world around us. They are maps we have made in order to help us figure out where it is we need to go, have to go, must go. Sometimes the belief is so embedded in our psyche that we don't own it anymore, the belief owns us. Beliefs have the power to create or destroy. Think 9/11 and the beliefs held by the pilots flying into the building. Think Kamikaze and the beliefs held by the pilots as they smashed into navy ships. Now think Mother Theresa or Ghandi and the beliefs associated with them.

In this story I have made many references to Armenian tribal beliefs. I am very proud that both my parents are Armenian and direct descendants of the Armenian Diaspora as a result of the 1915 Genocide. The significance of this is that although my parents were born outside of Armenia, they maintained their culture, language, and their BS. That is in part what shaped me and brought me to this point to be able to share this book with you. It was difficult for me to question tribal BS as it was what defined me in the bubble that I was raised in. But it is important to further define what I refer to when I speak of tribal. It is not just an Armenian concept. Tribal can be applied to Italians, Indians, Greeks, Japanese, and to all tribes of the world. Tribal can be broken down or built up. What I mean is that you can say the global tribe as a way of looking at the bigger picture or you can break it down and call your immediate family your tribe. The tribe could be people with common ethnic and cultural or simply a group of persons in a corporation. Anytime there is a group of people that identify themselves with each other that becomes a tribe. Depending on the context tribal mentality is used, it can be either constructive or destructive. Depending on the beliefs associated within that tribe, it can cause a person to either appreciate or depreciate in the way they perceive the world around them. There are beliefs that keep us from living fully. They separate us from other cultures as opposed to merge us in humanity. Beliefs sometimes turn into 'us versus them' dogma. As an example, the principle of spirituality brings people together. However the dogma in how we perceive the path to spirituality separates us. In other words, we consider ourselves spiritual by thinking we are Christian, Muslim, Jewish, or Buddhist, yet we don't embrace the fundamental point of spirituality in terms of coming together as we are too busy separating each other by man made rules and regulations. Throw into that equation mistrust, fear, paranoia, and rally around the flag complex and we have the state of the world as we see it today. By leaving the destructive tribal BS that only serves to divide us and embracing the five principles of shero no matter what tribe were in, we become closer to living a life of fulfillment. We do not have to give up our uniqueness and backgrounds only destructive beliefs. We must find peace within ourselves as individuals prior to expecting peace from an outside source. Real lasting change begins from the inside out, not outside in.

I see human beings as pieces of a puzzle that make up the world. If you imagine the earth as a giant jigsaw puzzle and think of all the people as a piece of the puzzle you will realize that we are all individual and unique, yet without any of us the picture would not be complete. It doesn't matter your gender, race, nationality, economic background, religion, or age. You can break down this list to finite details but the result is the same. The principles that spell out the word shero explain the power everyone has to evolve.

If we incorporate the five principles of spirituality, humanity, enlightenment, responsibility, and opportunity in our daily lives, we will improve the quality of our own lives and unlock our true potential and authentic selves. By walking the walk and talking the talk, we will have a rippling effect within our immediate families, community, cities, states, and countries.

The reason this book is titled *sheep to shero* is to show the difference between being a sheep-like follower and not questioning things to evolving into someone who questions the status quo incorporating shero principles for a constructive solution to all beliefs. Many people reading this will identify with the BS and may even relate it to the way in which they look at themselves and the world. So how does this differentiate between all the excellent books that are out there? Only in that I am not giving you tools you do not already have, as I believe we all have the answers within ourselves if we sit still to listen. I am simply giving you five principles packaged in a word that you can carry with you as a guideline in which you approach this time you are given on this planet. I am introducing the word shero as one principle. Being aware of the concept of shero will enable you, with a snap of a finger, to be shero.

This book has been inspired by actual events yet interpreted as seen through sherovision. Certain points and conversations have been glorified or toned down to make the point. The characters are fictitious. The main characters are Arka (Armenian for King) and Takouhi (Armenian for Queen). There is significance to the names. Not necessarily that it ties in with my cultural heritage, but more in that it represents that each and every one of us are our own Kings and Queens. We are ultimately in charge of ourselves. This is a story about a person who took on a chapter of her life with shero principles as she questioned and adjusted the tribal belief systems she was raised with. This is a story about all that is shero and all that is and can be you! I hope the following pages resonate with you in some way. I hope that by reading the story you realize how we have so many things in common. We all share the same nervous system after all. Where I have smiled in the book I hope you will too. Where I have cried in the book I hope you can feel it with me. The rest of the map, the belief system, is in our hands. We can either create an amazing map that will get us to exactly where it is we want to go with ease, comfort, and love, or we can choose the status quo eat what we're fed and in doing so constantly spin our wheels out of control not knowing where we're going or what we're doing. I'm here to invite you to entertain the notion that 'Tuum Est,' Latin for it's up to you. If done right, the sun will never set when living the principles that make shero! Enjoy!

# 1

# GOING HOME: ARMENIA?

"You're going where?" said her father with his heavy foreign accent.

"To Armenia, dad!" Takouhi said with a sheepish smile. In a split second she felt like the little girl that used to be fearful of her fathers big brown eyes.

"Why?" he asked in a stern voice.

Why indeed she thought to herself, why indeed! It was time to embark on a journey back to the mother ship. She had lived in many countries and met different people in her life but had never felt at home anywhere because of the belief systems she was raised with. Of the many beliefs that influenced her one of them was her grandmother always telling her that nobody would understand her better than her own tribe. For this reason, she had married what had seemed the best-suited bachelor from a very small population of Armenians in Vancouver. Another belief had been that she couldn't leave the parental home until she was married. This belief was significant in that it showed the tribe that the girl came from a respectable family. She followed through with these beliefs because at the time they were as real to her as having to stop at a stop sign on the road. Then her marriage fell apart in spite of beliefs that there is no such thing as divorce. The pain of divorce was accompanied by piercing solitude. If it was true that nobody understood her better than her own tribe, then no one was going to understand her because her tribe sure didn't. To top it all off, there was the BS of 'do not hang around her, she is a divorced woman, and she might give you ideas.' 'Wow' she had thought when she had heard that, 'pretty soon they will let me read and vote too!' Those were just few examples of belief systems that had influenced her tremendously throughout her teens and twenties. She called that period her sheep days. What had it meant to be a sheep? A good follower of the belief system that was fed to her and that she hungrily accepted. At the time, compliance to the beliefs meant acceptance, fitting in, and ultimately feeling loved. Forget the boat, do not rock the Ark! (The Ark was significant to Armenians, as allegedly Noah's Ark had landed on Mount Ararat) She had concluded that this was a common human condition; to want to feel like you are good enough and that you are loved. Surely it wasn't just applicable to her tribe but to all members of the human race. Now, she wanted to investigate the source of the BS. Was it still real at the source or did the Diaspora carry it with them when they left? Like an archeologist, she was going to do some digging, but unlike Indiana Jones or Lara Croft, she was embarking on a mental archeological adventure. The only tools she needed were her pen, her notebook, and an open mind and heart.

Takouhi was in Heathrow Airport, London, looking at gate 22 and waiting for BA flight 6585 on route to Yerevan. She didn't think she would ever want to go but her gut told her that if you want to stop being a sheep you have to hand in your pink slip directly to the Sheppard. Her loving aunt's extreme nationalistic views on Armenia had unknowingly caused a resistance within Takouhi to make the final decision to go. The more people had insisted the more she had resisted. That being said, she wanted to find out if going back to her heritage would resolve her angst of facing the beliefs and wanting to fit in.

Takouhi had heard so many horror stories about luggage being lost on route to Armenia and she had planned to bring a carry on with extra clothes. However, as a result of recent terrorist threats towards international airports, she was only allowed to carry her passport and wallet. She had to beg the security personnel back in Vancouver to allow her to bring her pen and notebook. She was never without those two items. Seeing that liquids of any sorts were also disallowed she couldn't wear her contact lenses. There she was wearing glasses, green cargo pants, white t-shirt and about to begin her archeological dig at the airport. Oddly enough she was humming the Indiana Jones theme song but she figured somewhere in the mix she would throw in a Duduk solo, the duduk being a very famous Armenian instrument. Her first archeological observations as she recorded in her notes were of the people around her waiting to board the same plane.

> *I am perplexed with my first impressions of my comrades. I have never been around so many Armenians in an airport before. Some of them look like gangsters, projecting the typical BS of money and power. Some of them are blond with blue eyes. Not your usual dark haired woolly mammoths I have seen in North America. I am one of them so I don't mind saying that.*

And she started smiling. She put her pen down and observed. Her eye caught the attention of two men sitting in the corner by the gate. After a few minutes of studying them in a covert manner she changed her role from archeologist to profiler and continued to write.

*There are two intriguing men in disguise sitting about ten rows ahead of me to the right. Their disguise is the persona of being armed and dangerous. It's a persona, the outer protective barrier. My experience has been that the cooler they appear on the outside the more like marshmallows on the inside. Who knows what you'll find when you crack open the walnut. Nuts? The first gentleman has really short black hair, clean cut, and wears designer shoes. I'm guessing he is the bad boy who is undercover. He takes great care of his appearance, including some very unique jewelry. He's possibly an artist of sorts. A con artist perhaps?*

Takouhi started laughing out loud at what she had written so much so that the person next to her looked at her puzzled as if she was crazy.

*No but seriously...he appears to be the strong silent type. I think I will name him Asbed, knight in Armenian. Maybe he is a knight about to go rescue a young damsel in distress from a challenging life in Armenia? The other gentleman sitting directly across from him has not stopped talking... He has lighter coloured hair, is very skinny and tall. He is so low key that he actually stands out. He seems very chatty and opinionated. I'll name this character Vrej, revenge and vengeance in Armenian. He seems so passionate about what he is talking about even from a distance that it seems like he has something to prove.*

*However, that being said, I realize that these are just generalizations. Who knows what Asbed and Vrej are really like?*

She started laughing again because not only had she just named them but also she was now referring to them by their new names.

She looked up to see Asbed looking at her with curiosity, as if he was wondering, what is she writing? Thank God he wasn't a mind reader otherwise she would be in trouble. The more he looked the more she looked. His curiosity brought out hers. Then he got up and started walking her way. What did he want? She though she knew what he was up to, but he simply crossed in front of her and dropped something in the garbage.

The announcement came to board the plane. In her usual manner, she held back to board the plane last. She preferred to let the crowds go ahead. She knew she would be sitting at an aisle seat so she wouldn't be inconveniencing anyone when she did finally board the plane. When she did board, she sat down and noticed that the two men sat about ten rows behind her. Well, that was that. She thought she wouldn't have an opportunity to speak to either of them and figure out if her profiling was correct. As soon as she finished that thought, an African American gentleman approached her and asked her, in Armenian, if she would change seats with him. He wanted to sit with his friends who were sitting next to her. BS challenge 101. What? How did this African-American learn to speak in Armenian? When did this happen? Did he take a course in the language? Or maybe someone dared to break away from the BS of marrying outside the tribe. But didn't that mean that the language and the customs would disappear? So why was he going to Armenia and how come he spoke Armenian? She almost wanted to say no in that she wished one of his friends would move so she could sit next to him and explore this further. But she looked at him and said, 'why not, as long as your seat is an aisle seat.' He responded, 'yup.' And off she went, and ended up sitting one row behind Asbed and Vrej to the left. She ended up sitting by the emergency exit with another girl who was going to the American Embassy in Yerevan. Once Takouhi was seated, she called her mom to tell her that the plane was on time, that they had boarded, and for her mother to tell her aunt in Armenia that all is as it should be. As she was speaking, she noticed that Asbed was leaning into the aisle with his ear to her conversation. She couldn't believe how obvious he was. Or was she just very aware of her surroundings thanks to the four years of hell she had recently gone through with the stalker? As soon as she put the phone down the announcement came over the intercom. 'Ladies and gentleman, there was an accident with the last passengers boarding the plane. The gentleman fell and has broken his leg. We have to remove his luggage from the flight.'

Asbed turned his head looked directly at Takouhi and said, 'You jinxed the flight,' the most unique opening line she had ever heard and proof that he was listening in on her conversation. Who does that? She picked up her cell phone and phoned her mother again and told her what some stranger had just said and broke out laughing. They sat on the runway for about four hours, a delay that tired all the passengers. They dozed on and off, waking up in the hope that the plane had arrived. Finally, the plane took off and they were on route to Armenia.

Takouhi began to converse with her neighbour Sarah.

"If you don't mind me asking Sarah, why are you going to the American Embassy in Yerevan?" Takouhi asked with curiousity.

"No worries. My Armenian boyfriend works there and I'm coming from Greece to visit him," she said.

Oh my God, if Takouhi's grandmother were alive, what would she say? She couldn't help but think about the belief systems that were being challenged already and she hadn't even set foot on Armenian soil yet.

"When I go to Armenia I really stand out. Even though there are some blue eyed blond Armenian girls, my dress and mannerism make me unique," continued Sarah.

All of a sudden Vrej, who had dozed off during the four-hour delay, came back to life and jumped into the conversation taking Takouhi off guard.

"Noooo…." He said with a smartass smirk on his face. He had been eyeing Sarah the entire time and had been waiting for the opportune moment to jump in. His timing was perfect and they all started laughing. Vrej was interested in Sarah so the conversation continued between them across the aisle. Takouhi was happy to listen in on the conversation and getting to know Vrej based on what he was saying. At one point she heard Vrej say 'Why would anyone choose to vacation in Armenia of all places in the world?' What would he think if he knew Takouhi was going to be there for two and a half weeks by choice?

After nine hours of being on a plane it was time to disembark. Takouhi went straight to the immigration area. The terminal was chaotic and unorganized. Exactly as she had expected.

"Where is your husband?" asked the female immigration officer.

"I don't have one," replied Takouhi.

"Why are you here? What is the purpose of your trip?" asked the Immigration officer.

It occurred to Takouhi that the idea of a woman traveling by herself all the way from North America and single might be a rare one here.

'That was a good question' Takouhi thought. 'What is the purpose of my trip?' What were Takouhi's expectations? Why did this trip seem so worthwhile right now? She definitely needed a plane ride, a culture shock, and she wanted to meet her family that she had never met before. But more importantly she wanted to come to the source of the belief systems that had shaped her way of living and thinking all the way on the other side of the world. She came in however, with preconceived notions, insecurities, and a whole lot of BS of her own, especially the concern about how they would react to her being a 'spurkahay,' an Armenian not born in Armenia. Maybe they'd think, 'look at her traveling on her own, on an expensive ticket to come all the way to Armenia. That means she must be rich and thus spoiled.' For whatever reason, that seed was placed in her mind at one point of her evolution as a person and had woven itself into the fabric of her personality. It was as though it had become her life's mission to prove that she was a hard worker and not spoiled whether she was considered Armenian, Canadian, a single, or a married woman. Was it her insecurity, stubbornness, or pride speaking?

Another one of her preconceived beliefs was that Armenian men born and raised in Armenia were rough in demeanor and saw women as second-class citizens. The belief was that the men saw themselves as real men and women as knowing their roles of motherhood, cooking, and never speaking back. Yet another belief that Takouhi had heard was projected towards the younger Armenian women in Yerevan. The premise was that instead of spending time studying they were constantly dressed up looking for the rich Armenian Knight to come from the other side of the world and rescue them. Wasn't that why she had named a complete stranger Asbed? Takouhi realized that these were just thoughts. Yet what drove her crazy when she was in North America was the fact that some people would speak of this as if they were examined and inalienable truths. She knew that thoughts and beliefs could always be changed as long as there was a want, will, and desire.

The problem she always had was that she had felt out of place in North America. She hadn't been allowed to fully assimilate with North American culture due to the belief systems with which she was raised, so she wasn't sure where she belonged. But, what if she felt the same way here? What if she was part of the limbo generation. Not Gen X or Gen Y but the first wave of immigrants who were not born in the country they were raised but still felt detached from the same country. Where did she fit in the great big jigsaw puzzle of the world theory that she believed in?

All these thoughts ran through her mind when the immigration officer was simply asking her 'Why are you here?' She said the basics, "I am visiting my aunt." The officer said with a friendly smile, "enjoy your stay." That was easy! Once again she thanked God that nobody could read her mind. She walked down to the baggage claim awaiting her luggage. Looking around she did not see the two boys from the flight. There were numerous men there with carts. They didn't look familiar to her in terms of having been on the plane. She assumed they were baggage handlers. Finally, after her standing there for five minutes, the baggage handlers came up to her one at a time and offered to help her with the luggage which had not arrived yet. She didn't realize at the time that was the routine way of doing things. Being Ms. Independent, she said, "no thank you, I can manage on my own." She got some attitude with that remark from the baggage handlers. She didn't mean to come across as arrogant. She didn't realize that was the way they made their livelihood otherwise she would have been more than happy to help them. The other problem was she didn't have any Armenian money to give them. So she went to grab herself a trolley, which also cost money but all she had to give to the trolley attendant was Canadian dollars. He looked at her and snarled under his breath and said, "like this is worth anything." That comment opened her eyes a little. Here she was thinking that she may be perceived as coming from the land where the sheep graze on money and she's spoiled, and here's a man looking at her and telling her that her money is worthless to him. She was laughing in her mind. It once again proved to her the power of BS and how it makes you see the world. Having convinced the man that yes, Canadian dollars are in fact worth something; she grabbed her trolley and went to the carousel awaiting her bags. The carousel turned and turned and nothing came out. She looked up and there was Asbed and Vrej with an entourage. They had a few pieces of luggage. Yup, she had been right. They must have been gangsters with connections. Nobody else was allowed to have family and friends inside the airports luggage area. But these guys did. She guessed this meant they were important and special? She walked by them and said "nice meeting you," thinking she wouldn't see them again and remembering that she hadn't said goodbye to them on the plane. They said *Hajoghootchoon*; good luck. A common phrase used in Armenian. She walked to a corner and stood there with her trolley. Still no sign of her luggage or anyone else's for that matter except for a few pieces. Then they heard the announcements. The remainder of the luggage was either left behind in Heathrow or was not unloaded in Yerevan. And then she saw human nature at its worst. One poor airline agent was put in charge of writing out descriptions of lost luggage. The agent had a flood of people coming at her and blaming her for the lost luggage. What opened Takouhi's eyes yet again was that most of these people were from North America having been raised and lived there for a long time. Would they have behaved the same way in North America had their luggage been lost? Or did the fact that they were in a developing and unsophisticated country give them a self-imposed authority to act in an unrefined manner?

She heard comments such as "they are all thieves." "Our luggage is in the back and they are probably going through our stuff." Takouhi refused to be part of the unruly mob. "Every bone in my body wants to get up there, stand next to the agent, and make the mob line up in an orderly fashion." She said under her breath. At home she was a leader and a manager but she chose not to get involved here. The crowd was too overbearing for her and her energy was too low. She knew that her involvement when her pistons weren't fully firing would do more damage than good. The last thing she would have wanted to do was snap back at the people. As soon as she said that a voice next to her said, "and what is it that you do?" She looked up and there standing next to her was Asbed. Where did he come from? She had lost all track of him. In fact both of them were there. She looked at him and replied, "I manage a commercial diving company. I organize and send crews all around the world for ship repairs. You can imagine the organization required for such jobs! So organizing this chaos would normally not be an issue but I'm so tired!"

He looked at her with surprise.

"You're Canadian?" asked Asbed with curiosity as he saw her holding the passport.

"Yes, I'm from Vancouver!" Takouhi replied. It was so interesting to see the reaction on both of their faces. She could tell she was an anomaly to them. She wondered how they were now profiling her. Or had they already done so and were now comparing their notes?

"Where are you guys from?"

"We both live in Los Angeles but we're originally from Armenia. Last time I was here was in 1990. And he was here in 1996" replied Vrej as the now designated spokesman for the two.

"So you were born in Armenia?"

"Yes," replied Vrej with a heavy sigh. Takouhi right away realized why he had such a heavy sigh. Vrej was struggling with the BS of how Armenians born in Armenia are seen a certain way by Armenians who were raised in the Diaspora. Isn't that funny? Takouhi was afraid of being judged by the Armenians born in Armenia whereas Vrej was afraid of being judged by the Diaspora. Takouhi's BS and his BS were very different in the way in which they translated the world around them yet their BS made them feel unhappy and unsure.

All three of them had pulled back from the chaos. They couldn't believe the behaviour of the rest of the passengers. It was now Asbeds turn to continue the conversation.

"Wow; I've never even thought about Canada."

"So you're telling me you only see east west and not north south?" He started laughing.

"Do you come to LA a lot?"

"I used to" she said "but not recently because of my demanding and hectic work schedule."

"Well, when you do come to LA give us a call we'd love to take you around."

She thought 'well, that's great but it would be even better to have new friends to show me around here.'

As she had envisioned it, she was the last person to give the information about her missing luggage. As the airline agent was completing Takouhi's luggage info there was a tug on her shirt. It was Vrej.

"Listen, I have a lot of friends and contacts here so if you need anything call me." He gave her his local number. Great minds think alike! She wondered if she would contact them and see them again or for that matter her luggage.

By this time it was 6:00 a.m. Yerevan time. She walked out with only a passport, wallet, pen, and journal. There was her aunt and her cousin from Germany waiting for her outside the gates. She was so happy to see them. There was also a tidal wave of Armenian men offering to help her with her luggage. Did anybody take the time to look to see if she had any? Or was it the pen and journal they wanted to carry for her? In spite of all the challenges thus far she skipped her way through the crowds towards her family. Her family took her upstairs to the airports departure area for a surprise. In front of her stood the woman who was supposed to have been her mother-in-law in 1994. It was the love Takouhi had had for her that made her stay in a relationship with her son. She thought she could overlook the great differences between her and her fiancé because she had the love of a great mother. The hardest part about breaking up with her fiancé at the time was the knowing that she would never be close with her again. But there she was. The last time Takouhi saw her was in San Francisco, and now here she was before her in Yerevan. This was a good sign. What a wonderful way to start her journey. If there was a contest to see who had the biggest smile or gave the biggest hug Takouhi wondered who would have won at that moment. It probably would have been a tie. No matter what had gone on in the past, the mother was such a genuinely loving person that when she hugged a person that person felt the authenticity. She was a spiritual being in that she was a giver. Not just of things but of her time and effort. Perhaps another mother would have not even looked twice at Takouhi after having given back the engagement and after the so-called shame Takouhi had caused (another BS). It was her dream to have a mother-in-law like her but instead when she got married years later she got.... Well the opposite! Takouhi remembered one incident where she had taken a decorated Christmas tree to her in-laws house to ring in the festive season. "We don't do Christmas trees anymore. Christmas is just for kids." Takouhi watched as her Christmas tree was tossed on the balcony.

Finally they all arrived at her aunt's apartment and Takouhi fell asleep at 8:00 a.m., knowing that in a few hours they were supposed to be attending a wedding of a cousin she had never met. She woke up at 1:00 p.m. with the realization that her outfit for the wedding would end up being green cargo pants, runners, a white shirt, and glasses. She started laughing. It really didn't matter. Had she been in Canada or the States she probably would have been stressed out over this but this weird feeling came over her. She felt that there was something bigger happening here. As she was sitting on her aunt's balcony writing in her journal she looked up. Right across from her was the outline of Mount Ararat. She made it. Every time she had looked up from her marble desk in her executive office at work she would look to see a framed limited edition print of Mount Ararat on a clear sky day across the wall from her. All of a sudden there it was, live and real. When she had put up the print two years ago she had wondered what it might feel like to actually view it in person. It was a surreal and emotional moment for her. She didn't know why. She wasn't born in Armenia; she had never set foot there. And technically speaking, Mount Ararat is not on Armenian soil. So what was it? Was it remembering all the stories she had heard about her heritage and culture? Was it because she remembered the stories her ex father-in-law told about losing his entire family during the genocide? Was it the knowing what Armenia meant to the Diaspora as a result and the historical significance of Mount Ararat to Armenians? She didn't know. But she knew it was more than one thing. And she knew it wasn't just her. She had seen other people from different cultures go back to their homeland whether they were born there or not and having the same emotional experience. Some of her friends were grandchildren of holocaust survivors. The grandchildren went to Israel for the first time and had the similar emotional experience as she was having. Takouhi also had friends who weren't born in India but when they went back to meet their grandparents for the first time they also had a connection to the land and people. In fact living in Canada allowed Takouhi to have connections with so many cultures. She had Armenian, Iranian, Syrian, Jordanian, Indian, Serbian, Croatian, Italian, Greek, Chinese and Japanese friends and the list of friends went on. All of which had their own kinds of BS. Was it right? Was it wrong? Takouhi thought it can be neither, only the power you give it and how you let it steer your life's course.

She went to the wedding and she thought she had disappointed everyone in that they had certain expectations. But there she was in all her military glory. She did discover one thing though. It was a sheer joy dancing in running shoes. She loved to dance and usually at the end of the night her feet would be killing her as she also had a love for high heels. But hey, she got to boogie in runners. Thus far, this had been an amazing vacation and 24 hours hadn't even passed yet. She had already met two great people that she would most likely not have met when going to visit family in LA. She had great conversations with the person sitting next to her on the plane. She got to see a woman she admired from the past. She met a part of her family tree that she had only heard about. Like the changing autumn leaves, the colourfulness of the characters old and new beautified her new surroundings. And the icing on the cake… dancing with her running shoes and she could get away with it. The Queen was now in her kingdom… or was she?

# 2

# TAKOUHI THE TOURIST

Over the course of the next few days she did the typical tourist events. She was fortunate enough to have her aunt as her tour guide and her loving cousin from Germany. She also had her mother's cousin from LA there with his wife and friends. The group of them would load up in the sturdy four-wheel rental SUV and they would go to various ancient and historic sites. They went to Garni, Khorvirab, and Noravank. The incredible architecture and history were spiritual for her, as she felt small in the great sphere of things. For Takouhi, spirituality meant knowing that there is one universe and one almighty force, something bigger than her and that she was an important part of it. The world and its inhabitants were like a giant jigsaw puzzle in which each individual is a puzzle piece. All pieces were individual and unique and without any of them, the picture was not complete. She believed that we are constantly evolving and growing as spiritual beings who happen to be experiencing life within the parameters of a human shell. There were people who disagreed with passion with her thought. She had learned to accept that. It wasn't that Takouhi thought she was greater than nor less than. She just felt that she had evolved from the man made religious belief systems used to control the masses as it wasn't constructive and it only served to divide and instill fear in people. The one thing she was grateful for in terms of all the religions of the world was the way in which they aspired to show their greatness and power by inspiring art and architecture. The most beautiful mosques, churches, temples had been built due to the desire for and belief in something greater and bigger than individuals. These buildings were a direct result of spiritual inspiration but also had trickled inspiration of thought by their presence. For instance, when Takouhi was at Khorvirab she was awe struck by the structure of this monumental church that had withstood so many wars and battles. And no matter what the initial intention of building the church, it had inspired her to sit on its walls and write in her journal in August of 2006. She wrote:

*Spirituality transcends all cultures, nations, races etc. We can be different! I am not thinking that we should all be the same. How boring would that be? Isn't ultimate goal of spirituality the knowing that inspite of being a unique piece of the global puzzle there is something bigger than just the one piece.*

She put her pen down, took a deep breath and looked behind her at the majestic Mount Ararat.

One day she decided to head out on her own and explore. She liked venturing out on her own and creating her own exclusive tour. She had come to realize over the years of traveling on her own and the many road trips she had taken that you meet more people that way. She got in a taxi and decided to head to downtown Yerevan. Only when exploring alone had she had the opportunity to meet incredible people who would not normally approach her if she were with a crowd. She was still in her military outfit. Every night she would wash it, and leave the house in clean clothes each day. As she stepped into the taxi, the driver looked at her and started up a conversation.

"Where are you from?"

She considered telling him the truth and put aside her suspicious BS. The little voice inside her head was telling her to be careful, but she responded with the truth.

"I'm from Vancouver, Canada."

"So are you married?"

Oh my, she thought, she knew where this was going.

"Nope."

"It's a shame," he said "you're a young beautiful woman. You should get married and have children."

And before she could answer, he continued.

"So how long does it take to get working papers in Canada if you marry an Armenian?"

Oh my God! This was a scene from a movie where it was the typical BS of men and women in Armenia looking for a way out by marriage. She had walked into a BS scene.

"Oh this is my stop," she said quickly.

"But that's not where you said you wanted to go" he exclaimed in a surprised tone.

"I know but I forgot there was a store I wanted to go see and it is right here," she tried to explain in a calm and cool voice.

So she said her goodbyes and off she went. Phew. That was close. She had heard of this belief system and she knew some people who had actually simply married a stranger with foreign credentials to leave the country. However, she refused to apply this BS on the entire population. She didn't think all Armenians wanted to leave their country for the hopes of a so-called better material life. Just as she didn't believe that other people from less affluent cultures wanted to leave their countries either.

Yes there were those who would give anything to leave. But there were others who choose to stay to improve their culture and their heritage in spite of the difficulties. Of course the ones that left weren't necessarily doing so because they wanted to have the opportunity to have fancy cars and diamond rings. Some of them left so they could send money back home. This opened up another BS whether this was a correct way of conducting affairs within Armenia or not. Takouhi thought it wasn't her place to credit or discredit this BS she was simply thinking about the ways in which decisions were made based on them. As for the taxi driver, he wanted a way out and he may have seen her as an opportunity. But it wasn't his lucky day.

Takouhi's employer and friend came across this BS as well. He wasn't Armenian and the countries that he was going through weren't Armenia. He was on a great motorcycle journey and crossed many economically challenged Eastern European countries. The stories he told her made her head spin. So many women had approached him, hoping that he would put them on the back of his motorcycle and carry them off into the sunset. She had told him what the possible motivations were. Not that she wanted him to think that he wasn't a catch or good looking, but he needed to be aware of certain BS before he made life altering decisions. Being his right hand person and never seeing herself as just an employee she had shared the common BS. It was amazing to her how in speaking of the particular belief systems as they applied in this case were as real to her as knowing that you should stop at a red light. Only after sharing the possible BSs with him and seeing his eyes pop open did she realize how foreign it was to him. A foreign BS to one person and real BS to someone else.

Having left the taxi, Takouhi was in the midst of an unknown place. It wasn't like she had never been in an unknown place before. She remembered all the road trips she had taken by herself in the last six years and all the amazing people she had met as a result. As she walked down the street, she came across a motorcycle store. Being an avid fan of motorcycles, she went into the store, almost out of spite. She knew how they would react to her. She walked in and went straight towards the one bike that was in the showroom.

"Can I help you?" asked the gentlemen looking up from behind his desk.

"I'm looking at this dirt bike you have. Is it this year's model?"

"No it is last years and it's actually mine" the worker replied.

"Oh so it's not for sale?" Takouhi asked.

"Everything is for sale if the price is right. Is your husband coming by?" he asked with curiosity.

"What do you mean by that question?" she said with a smile.

"Well I'm assuming the bike is for him right?' he asked in a condescending tone.

Takouhi remembered that she had read somewhere that in communicating with someone words only represent approximately 7% of communication, the tone of a person's voice about 38% and a person's body language 55%. Put that all together and it was very clear why Takouhi was ready for verbal dual-loge. For Takouhi a dual-logue meant when two people were speaking to each other but neither of them was listening. She had a vision of two rams striking each other with their powerful horns. Both strong, both right? 'Okay my kind sir, bring it on,' she thought.

"Actually I'm comparing bikes from Armenia to Canada" she said very calmly.

"What do you mean you're comparing bikes?" his arms crossed his chest and his horns faced her ready to strike.

"What I mean is that I wanted to see what kinds of motorcycles are carried in stores in Armenia in comparison to the ones in Canada," she said.

"Why would that make a difference to you?" he said with his horns getting closer.

"Because I ride them!" she said with a grin on her face.

He was stunned. The ram was confused and shook its head.

"You ride bikes? Are you serious?" The adult ram turned into a cute little baby ram in 2.3 seconds. Still mighty yet approachable.

"Are you kidding me? You're joking right? That is so cool! I can't believe it! It's rare that guys ride bikes in Armenia, but a girl? No way? Really?"

Now it was Takouhi's turn to be taken aback because she thought she was going to go to war with this guy and all of a sudden she's the coolest girl on the block for him. The conversation just went on from that point. In thirty minutes she went from walking into the store and investigating a belief system expecting the worst, to coming out feeling absolutely energized and refreshed. She had walked in thinking the worst because of the belief system that had been passed down to her during her sheep days. In the past she had heard that bikes are not for girls, especially for Armenian 'good' girls. Yet she loved her motorcycle and the old belief system didn't apply but she was quite aware of all the people that still looked at it that way. She had adjusted that BS, but had not considered that others might do the same. She was guilty of assuming that only she had adjusted those beliefs. The question she was now asking herself was at what point do we stop being sheep and start to question? At what point do we realize that the BS that we hold true isn't even ours but it was somehow passed on to us? And how many BSs do we use in our day-to-day life to navigate ourselves and make the decisions that we do? We do it all without any question. What she wasn't realizing was the fact that she was already thinking all this meant she was well on her way. In fact she had already come a long way but if only she knew how far she had yet to go.

# 3

## VREJ FOR VENGEANCE

After a few more days of exploring the city on her own and with her cousin, she decided to phone the two boys from the plane. She managed to get a hold of Vrej and they arranged to meet at a very famous monument called Mother Armenia. As she waited for him she stood at the foot of the monument. It was a statue of a women standing with a sword in her hand protecting the city below her feet. Takouhi was the size of an ant in comparison to the Amazon woman behind her, strong, proud, and ready to fight for her city and her beliefs. Yup. She had come to the right place. Just as she had tilted her head looking as high as she could at the statue Vrej came along and caught her off guard by tugging on her shirt.

"What are you so fascinated by?" he asked and looked to see what she had been looking at.

"I love this statue. It has been placed on this hill overlooking Yerevan for a reason. I am assuming to inspire the feeling of protection."

"Isn't it interesting that you see that and all I can see is the condition of the statute and its surroundings," he said kicking away some garbage.

"What do you mean? It seems okay?"

"I know what you're thinking. It seems okay for a third world country right?"

"Well that's not exactly what I meant, but I do know they don't have the money and resources to spend on the upkeep of these monuments around the city and that's why they depend on tourism I suppose."

"Well you should have seen it during communist times. It was pristine and clean."

"Sure, it was clean and they took care of everything but you also gave up a lot remember?" she winked at him and smiled.

They walked through a surrounding park and found a bench to sit on. It was surrounded by the most graceful willow trees she had ever seen. She loved the way their branches just gracefully danced with the gentle breeze. She looked over to Vrej. It occurred to her that the timing of meeting him and Asbed had been amazing. She was fully embracing the moment hearing the words of the gentleman as she was sitting on the bench under the hot summer sun. She didn't do much speaking. Instead she listened. It was her way of getting to know him. She figured he'd know who she was when the time is right. He had his own set of very serious belief systems about how things should be. Two hours had passed as he spoke of relationships with short and frustrated sentences. He had broken up with his girlfriend prior to taking this trip to Armenia. As she was fully engaged and listening to every fiery word, she knew that there were many reasons why they broke up which he chose not to discuss. Yet one thing became very clear. Vrej's ex-girlfriend had not been Armenian and that had caused a problem within the family. She knew it! The classic Armenian belief that you should not marry an odar, a person outside the tribe. This had applied to her so many times in the past. If you dared to go against your family, you were destroying your tribe by not carrying on the traditions. If you did as your family says, then your friends would think you weren't open minded. If you did get married outside of your tribe but the marriage failed, then you heard nothing but I told you so. Further, if you were going to marry outside your tribe they better be a doctor, lawyer or someone prominent to make up for the shame. Takouhi had sensed a fiery vengeance in Vrej. If he were a dragon, Armenia would have lost its favourite statue and surrounding park. He was being pulled in two directions. His heart was pulling him one way and his family's belief systems the other. But the part that made this so beautiful and classic, Takouhi had thought, was when any tribal family pressed forward with the all or nothing way of thinking, in this case all Armenian or nothing, the individuals did not have an opportunity to think of what their values and beliefs were. What was the point of having a large number of Armenian couples that didn't understand each other and didn't have a clue about the real joys of life? What? Did the tribe just want quantity and not quality? Was it beneficial to get married for the sake of families? Takouhi wasn't deciding for or against the belief systems. She was trying to think of all the angles of the argument. She knew many Armenian girls in North America who didn't know anything about their culture, the country, or the language. Were they Armenian by default? And yet these friends were expected to marry Armenians. So Takouhi wondered what that meant to them. Was it the fear of the unknown that kept the parents pushing? For the time being, Takouhi decided that she would just listen to Vrej because it wasn't time yet to share her thoughts. She wasn't ready to venture into the dragon's lair.

On that same day they met with Asbed. It was so nice seeing him and he had such a sweet smile when he saw her. She noticed their different clothes, it was day ten and she was still in her military outfit. There was a joke going around in town that if you saw people wearing the same clothes a few days in a row it meant they were on that particular flight. The three of them went to see the new Church that was built in Yerevan. It was beautiful but new. The old churches spoke more strongly to Takouhi. To her, the modern churches, here or in North America, had no history and no soul.

Vrej and Asbed decided that they wanted to light candles to make a wish or special request. Asbed took the candles, Vrej and Takouhi followed. Takouhi noticed that Asbed was in another world when he was lighting the candles. She wondered what he was thinking. He was there physically but was lost in thought. Vrej on the other hand was still talking. Takouhi figured it was best to let him ramble and get the venom out of his system. Asbed turned and instinctually gave Takouhi some candles to light, assuming that's what she would want to do. But she couldn't do it. She didn't know why. Of the many thoughts she had had prior to arriving to Armenia, one of them was that she didn't want to light a candle and make a wish at any church. It had to be the one. She wasn't sure which one and she had already seen so many that were beautiful but it didn't speak to her soul. All the churches had become tourist attractions. Another reason was that she wanted to light a candle privately and not with the boys as her witnesses. She wanted a private moment with God in her church of choice in what was perceived as her homeland. So she left and gave the candles to an old woman who was on her way in.

The next few days were followed again by more tourist attractions with Takouhi and her family. And then there was Lake Sevan. Takouhi and her cousin had gone there with the family. There was a beautiful church that overlooked the lake. The lake had historic significance for Armenians. At one point in the country's history, Armenia had ports all the way from the Caspian Sea, the Black Sea, and the Mediterranean. But now it was a landlocked country with Lake Sevan as its great vacation spot. As Takouhi looked down from the cliff she noticed a very shiny, brand new hotel. Then the boys phoned to say that they, along with a few friends, had rented a bungalow at the hotel for a couple of days. Takouhi and her cousin were invited to join. And so they did. What an amazing place and yet it stood out from the rest of the environment. The hotel was just as a four-star hotel should be in that it was clean, beautiful, and the service was great. However, the hotel had fences around it. Those staying at the hotel were predominantly tourists who were there to have a great time. The money they were spending at the hotel most average Armenians couldn't make in a month at their jobs in Armenia. But here they were having fun, playing in waterfalls and going on boats on the lake. Next to the chain linked fence were Armenians from Armenia who were there camping by the lake with their tents and cars. It was a very big distinction between have and have nots. It occurred to Takouhi that it was no wonder that Armenians thought that all foreigners were rich. This is what they saw.

That night all of them were gathered by a small coffee shop within the hotel grounds, having dessert and coffee. Takouhi was getting antsy sitting there as most of them were speaking Russian and she didn't understand.

She wanted to go for a walk by the lake. There was a beautiful full moon and she wanted to be near the glistening Sevan shore. As she was walking towards the water she felt another tug on her shirt. That had become the customary way for Vrej to get her attention it seemed.

"So what do you think of our Armenia thus far?" asked Vrej.

"Well, I've seen many beautiful monuments, churches, historic sites."

"I bet you've seen more than we have and we used to live here."

"Yeah you're probably right! I know how it is to take your home for granted but as a tourist you end up seeing more. People come to Vancouver so they can go skiing in Whistler but I haven't gone for five years" exclaimed Takouhi knowing exactly what he meant.

"So what do you think of our friend from Kazakhstan?" he asked.

"What do you mean? I don't know her enough to say anything about her. She seems nice I suppose" Takouhi saw a blimp on the radar, something was coming.

"It just frustrates me," he said with a snarky tone.

Takouhi knew that the tea pot had reached its boiling point and it was about to spill.

"What frustrates you?" she said.

"The fact that she is hanging out with us, is our friend and everyone thinks she's beautiful and very nice," he said as steam was beginning to come out of the dragon's nostrils.

"I don't see your point yet. What does this mean to you?" She knew exactly what he meant but wanted to hear it from him.

"Well it's just that everyone in my family says she's nice and stuff even if she's not Armenian. But when I was dating my girlfriend who wasn't Armenian, nobody took the time to figure out if she was nice or not. They just said right away no," he blurted out.

"So if I understand you correctly, you are telling me if this girl right here dates you or Asbed then your family would change their story about her from being nice to forget it she's not Armenian?" she asked knowing exactly where he was going

"Yup, probably, and it pisses me off!"

"I hear you, brother. This has happened to me and to many others who left our respective countries whether it's Armenia, Serbia, Croatia, Italy you name it. It's a common theme. Our parents got so focused on maintaining their culture that they forget spirituality and humanity. I think it stems from way back when our tribes were really small and we didn't have the opportunity to assimilate. There was no mode of transport let alone emails or texts. Now we're global and the concepts of borders are disappearing. We have come a long way and yet we have so far to go. I'll give you an example. Even within our Armenian community there used to be distinctions. After the genocide, my grandparents went to Iran; other people's families went to Lebanon or Syria. I like to think of it as a spaceship. The mother spaceship of Armenia sent out little pods of survivors to all these different countries. Once these pods landed, they didn't have much contact with the mother ship as she was under the iron curtain. So the pods rebuilt with what they knew from the past and not really advancing. They kept all the same belief systems and didn't allow for much evolution. There was some assimilation within the areas in which they landed. In fact, they picked up the habits of the local areas but still didn't fully integrate. It was very important for them to maintain their identity with the mother ship. The next stage of evolution was that now the pods saw themselves different from the other pods. The pod generations in Iran saw themselves different than the pod generation in Lebanon. The concept of marriage between these two pods was rare because although they were Armenian now they were from different parts of the world. To make it even more interesting, there was division internally within the pods themselves. An Armenian from Tehran would not necessarily mix with an Armenian from Tabriz, which was in the same country. Same country, same pod, more dissecting. And we're doing the same thing now. Break down Armenians as you know them in the greater LA area."

"Oh I see what you're saying" he said having listened intently "The Armenians from Beirut are in Pasadena, the ones from Iran are in Glendale, and last but not least the ones who are directly coming from Armenia are in Hollywood or Van Nuys."

"You got it! You see where I'm going with this" she said all excited as she was in her element.

"But I don't understand what you're saying with this. I understand the pattern but how does this relate to what I'm speaking about when it comes to my ex-girlfriend?" he asked a bit confused.

"I'm simply trying to make a point in that things have changed slowly yet surely. You see in spite of differences in Armenians due to where their initial pods landed, today we are okay with the concept of an Armenian from Iran marrying with an Armenian from Beirut. This would have been very rare even thirty years ago. Realizing that the world is shrinking, borders are disappearing and we are not as distant and different as we once thought we were," she continued. "If I understand our parents' belief system correctly, it's not that they don't appreciate or value other cultures. I believe they are simply trying to protect what they know. This applies for those parents who are active Armenians. What I mean by this is that they read, write, and know about politics within Armenia, the rich history. Our culture and people have gone through so much in the course of humanity. There aren't many of us left. So I think they are simply trying to keep the race alive. But you know what I find extremely interesting?"

"What's that?" he asked with great intent.

"The Armenians that marry outside of the tribe become more Armenian" she said.

"What do you mean by that?" he asked with great curiosity.

"Well, it seems that all of a sudden they want to make sure that their children know about their identity and heritage. I've seen this within my family and friends. In the past they really didn't think twice about what it means to be Armenian but as soon as they get married to a non-Armenian and have kids, they start learning and hence passing it on. They become more Armenian whereas the offspring of two Armenians getting married take things for granted. It almost seems that as the DNA pool changes, the need for knowledge increases. Of course I'm speaking very, very generally here. This is not based on any scientific research. It's just my opinion based on some observations," she finished with a humble tone.

"I get all that you are saying but how does this go back to my ex-girlfriend," he said.

Takouhi realized there was something deeper here.

"Tell me about your ex" she asked with great curiosity.

"What's there to tell? I did everything for her and she kept breaking up with me. It was her mother. She hated Armenians" he said, his voice dripped in venom.

Interesting, Takouhi thought, a situation where the parents on both sides were not in agreement. But she continued with the questions.

"So are you telling me that you broke up because of your parents and hers?"

"Well we didn't understand each other and it didn't help that we didn't have support," he said.

"But if you did understand each other would it have mattered if you had support or not?"

"Hmmm I guess not because all that would have mattered was that we get along and have things in common."

"So did you get along and did you have things in common?" she asked.

"Well there was definitely the attraction and I did so much for her and her family," he said.

"Vrej, I am sure that you did so much and that what you say is true. However, I asked you did your characteristics click and did you have things in common?"

And out of nowhere came a beautiful belief system that she had heard so many times before. This belief system crossed all tribes and borders.

"Takouhi, a perfect relationship does not exist. In fact, love does not exist. If I could have a kid without having to deal with a wife I would. And time is ticking. I want to be a father by the time I'm thirty," He said with the strength of conviction in his voice.

"Wow! Where did that come from?" she said startled. This was much deeper than she thought. This was a deep belief system.

"Look at your parents and my parents and all the other people you know. They all got married out of necessity. It was what they were supposed to do at the time. If they didn't get married by a certain age, then their life was over. So they didn't have the luxury of thinking about love. They were only thinking about survival and about who was going to be the best provider at the time. The prettier girls got, the richer the guys. Nobody cared about who had what belief systems or about humanity or giving. They didn't have the luxury to think beyond survival. In fact, the same thing is happening today to some degree within Armenia and all the communist block countries. It's about survival of the fittest." He was pretty intense and deeply believed in what he was saying.

"I understand your theory however; we are talking about you right now." She said calmly.

"What do you mean?" he said.

"You still didn't answer my question. Did you have things in common with her?" she was bringing him back to the question at hand.

"But I just told you love doesn't exist" he was getting agitated.

"Okay, listen to me. Have you heard the quote from Einstein where he says 'You can't solve the problems of today thinking the way you did when you created them'?" she said.

"Nope" he looked perplexed.

"Well, you live in California right?" she said.

"Yup!" he was trying to figure out where she was taking him.

"Do the rules of your or my parents' generation apply to you as per your explanation of love? What I mean is do you need to get married due to survival?" she said.

"I suppose not!"

"So you do have the luxury of thinking about what love means right?"

"Well yeah but..." and Takouhi interrupted him.

"Listen, you have lots of BS pulling you in many directions. Let me list what you've told me so far. A) Marriage is about survival not love B) Love doesn't exist anyway C) Can't marry a non-Armenian D) Time is of the essence for having a child. Would you say that sounds right?" she asked with a smile.

He started smiling too because the thoughts that he had had all this time in his head were now formulated by someone else in front of him.

"Well I guess so, but are you saying I'm wrong?" he asked puzzled.

"I just look at things differently. You're not wrong. You just carry along a list of beliefs that do not necessarily apply to you and have been carried forward to you from your parents, their parents, and their parents before that. I'm not saying our parents were wrong. They did the best they could with what they knew. I'm challenging you to think about and dissect your beliefs. Toss out the ones that don't serve you and replace them with more powerful ones that take you as first and foremost a human being. You see, if you were to take care of yourself and have a healthy viewpoint that is truly yours then when you do have a child, no matter how old you are, you will be much more qualified as a parent. As opposed to having kids because you think the time is ticking. As much as I love my heritage and my tribe if you will, humanity is whole. Regardless of where we're from, we all have the same nervous system, and we have the same fears in common."

"What's that?" he asked.

"That we won't be enough and that we won't be loved," she said "so I find it very hard to believe that you do not believe in love. In fact I know you are saying this because you are hurt that your relationship didn't work out. It has nothing to do with whether she was Armenian or not. It had to do with you not finding the right piece of your puzzle."

"What do you mean?" he asked.

"Just like pieces of a puzzle I believe we all have certain matches. I believe that love does exist but it is fear that pulls us apart. Fear of vulnerability, fear of rejection, and the list goes on. Love isn't just about gazing into each other's eyes as important as that is as well. To me, love is looking in the same direction and valuing each other's goals and dreams. Being a team with the same motto whatever that motto or mantra may be. You would do anything necessary for her, and she would do anything necessary for you. There is no dominance of one over the other. Your core values have to be the same. It seems to me that you didn't have much in common except for she liked you for buying her things and taking her places. That's not a firm foundation. But as opposed to taking responsibility for realizing that wasn't the right match for you, you are placing the blame on your parents, saying she wasn't Armenian."

Takouhi could not believe that Vrej was speechless. The dragon had no fire left in him. There were a few moments of dead silence, which was broken by the small ripples of the lake washing up on the shore. Takouhi realized that she had just met this man ten days ago and now she was speaking with him about deep beliefs. Did she offend him? Was he pissed off?

"When did you start thinking this way? Or rather, have you always thought this way?" He looked at her and for once spoke with a whispering tone.

"Oh God no! It took a lot of being beat up emotionally to finally come to these conclusions. There was a rumble in the foundation of my beliefs when I was first engaged to a man in San Francisco. He was Armenian and everything on the outside was perfect. His parents were warm and loving. Our families had known each other for many years. But I just didn't click in that my beliefs were so different than his. It was so hard for me to break that engagement because I was giving up what seemed to be perfect on the outside, for my spiritual needs as a human being on the inside. I couldn't relate to him as a person. We had the love of stuff in common but then what happens if you take the stuff away? I didn't understand what was happening at the time but I'm proud to say I had the courage to keep going. And then I did get married to another Armenian guy. At first I thought he was spiritual and we shared the same values. It didn't matter to me if we had stuff or not. But somehow along the way we both fell into our belief systems of the way things should be and weren't strong enough to do something about it. It's that classic thought of had I known what I know now back then perhaps things would have been different. But at the same time I have absolutely no regrets because I wouldn't be the person I am today had I not gone through that. But in all honesty my biggest growth came the eight years since my divorce. They say the greatest period of growth comes from a time of great pain and discomfort. I took full responsibility for the situations I had put myself in but I also took the opportunity to learn from all of them. As painful as they were there was so much to learn. I believe in the bigger picture and that everything happens for a reason you just need to figure out the lesson and use it to improve and fine tune yourself."

She stopped for a moment and took a deep breath and slowly breathed out as if to relive and release the entire summary she had just described. It was as if she had been sent there to tell her story at the shores of Sevan as the full moon glistened and the universe listened.

"You know Takouhi, I would never have guessed that I would be having this conversation all the way at the banks of Lake Sevan. Do you know that I was supposed to come to Armenia with her to show her my country? So I decided to come here to think and here we are having this conversation. Go figure…"

"The universe works in mysterious ways. If this conversation has been of value to you then I am very grateful. But I have to say it has been a win-win situation in that sharing my belief systems makes me fine tune it and adjust it as required. And it definitely makes me feel great when I can make a difference in a person's life by putting things in perspective. It's about giving and sharing. There is nothing more important to me than giving because I truly feel that by doing so you are getting." She was so overwhelmed with emotion at that moment that she felt her eyes well up. It wasn't due to the fact that she was saying what she was saying. She was touched because of the location in which she was saying it and the irony of saying it to someone she had just met that was from a different pod. Both pods had come to the mother ship looking for answers. The conversation was beautiful, genuine, and full of love. And he said love doesn't exist! Ha! They walked back to the rest of the gang who were still deeply engrossed in conversation. Takouhi took a long look at Asbed and wondered if he shared the same BS as his friend Vrej. She wanted to find out.

# 4

# THREE PEAS IN A POD

The next morning it was time to go. Takouhi and her cousin got in their taxi and went off on another tourist attraction while the two boys and friends stayed behind; they had family coming to meet them at the hotel. The ride to the next city where she was to meet family she had never met was beautiful. The taxi was run down and rattled but the driver drowned out the mechanical sounds by playing Armenian pop music. The countryside on that warm August day, with the lush rolling hills was absolutely majestic. The music seemed like a soundtrack in a movie. She was in a movie as far as she was concerned. All the things that had happened thus far seemed beautifully scripted. Takouhi went back in time and wondered how much war and bloodshed had these lands seen. And it was a miracle that all the beautiful church's had survived. In fact they had survived because they were built in such remote places in mountain-sides and valleys away from main cities. She envisioned Alexander's Army going through these lands and yet somehow the church's stood. And yet she still hadn't found a church she wanted to light a candle in.

Two days before departure from Armenia Takouhi received a call first thing in the morning.

"Can you guys be ready in 20 minutes?" It was Vrej phoning.

"Why? What's going on?" she asked.

"I'm getting baptized in the city of Aparan," he almost sounded like he was singing.

"You're what? Getting baptized? I thought you were baptized already?" she asked.

"It's a long story but can you be ready?" he asked, the urgency in his voice palpable.

Takouhi looked at her cousin who wasn't feeling well.

"Well, my cousin can't come but I guess I will!"

It was to be a road trip but with more people she hadn't met. That's when she was in her element. Just as he had said 'in twenty minutes,' Vrej was at the door. She took a seat in the taxi and went to meet Asbed. Takouhi didn't realize that she was meeting Asbed's family. Up until that day she really hadn't had much conversation with Asbed, at least nothing like the conversations she had had with Vrej. But she was touched that they thought of her enough to invite her to come along this journey. What made it different this time was that her cousin wasn't there and neither were the boys' friends who had come from out of town. It was the three North American tourists Asbed, Vrej, and Takouhi on route to Aparan with Asbed's family. She would not have been able to plan this so perfectly had she been in charge of operations. And how did events happen as they did in that she felt so comfortable around these guys. Was it her trusting nature that brought down their defenses? Was it simply luck or fate? Were events happening as they should in the right time, place, and sequence? And was the universe speaking to her?

## THREE PEAS IN A POD

Two cars were on route to Aparan. And the three of them were in the back of one of those cars. They shared one Ipod between the three of them. There was competition between the two boys about which Frank Sinatra song was the best one: *If You Go Away* or *My Way*. Who would have imagined that Takouhi would be in Armenia talking about blue eyes? They arrived in Aparan and headed straight to the church where Vrej was to be baptized. Takouhi stepped out of the car and observed the architecture of the walls and wondered how many pages could these walls write if she lent them her pen. As she was observing it was announced by Vrej that Asbed was to be his godfather and Takouhi was to be the witness.

"My son, are you here to be baptized?" asked the priest who appeared to be in his forties. Takouhi had envisioned a much older bearded priest.

"Yes sir" replied Vrej.

"All of you sign the baptism registration book please" instructed the priest.

The three of them went to sign the book and returned to the front of the church.

"My son, have you been baptized before?" asked the priest.

At that moment they all looked at each other but said nothing. But the priest sensed something was up based on their slow response. He asked again with a sharpness in his tone.

"Well, have you been baptized?"

"Uh… well yeah, but" replied Vrej sheepishly.

"My son, can a man be born of the same woman twice?" he said sternly

They all looked at each other in shock but with devilish smiles. Takouhi assumed what he was trying to say was that once you have been blessed with what the church says as the holy spirit you are born so you can't do it twice? She was perplexed but didn't question it. She was not in a position to get into a dual-logue with an Armenian priest.

The priest turned to him and said that he would take him and his cross and bless it for him. Vrej and the priest disappeared into a special room.

"He could have lied and said he hadn't been baptized before" said Asbed with his perfect bratty smile and sparkling brown eyes.

"Yeah but it wouldn't be the same" replied Takouhi with the same mischievous smile.

"I guess if we want to make sure Vrej is telling the truth in the future we have to make him come to church" said Asbed and they both started cracking up with laughter. By the time Vrej came back with his blessed cross, Asbed and Takouhi were in tears outside because they had been laughing so much, yet Vrej was very quiet as they drove towards Asbed's family's house. The priest had belittled him with his comments in front of his friends.

In honour of the baptism that was supposed to have taken place, Asbed's family was throwing a big gathering at the family house. What Takouhi loved about this day was how open and loving the people were. They were sitting around a large family table that accommodated over fifteen people surrounded by a lush orchard of fruit trees. There was an abundance of food and drink. The barbeque was endless and she wondered if there was a slaughterhouse nearby. The vodka was being poured, and people raised their glass and made toasts. She looked to her right where Asbed was sitting and noticed that he wasn't drinking. That's when she heard 'Only in North

America where the woman drinks and the man doesn't' announced one of the older gentleman who had been given the title of uncle. Now that was an interesting BS. She raised her glass to that comment and made sure she confirmed the uncle's observation. She was a stranger to them but they took her in with open arms. They were very loving people and definitely opinionated. Conversations around the table ranged from politics, to family members in Armenia and abroad and back to internal family jokes and mischief around the table. It wasn't her place to say much. She just wanted to observe. Takouhi was an outsider just like Vrej. This was Asbed's territory as it was his family. At one point Takouhi overheard Asbed's grandmother asking about his brother. Up until that point she had no idea that Asbed had a brother.

"I didn't know you have a brother?" she asked Asbed "Why didn't he come with you guys?"

"He couldn't make it this year." He replied quietly as his eyes met his grandmother's eyes.

She turned to go for a walk and noticed that Vrej was in the garden where all the beautiful apple trees were. He looked deep in thought. And she knew what and who he was thinking about. She went up to him and asked about Asbed's brother.

"I didn't know Asbed had a brother?" she asked with curiosity.

"You mean Arka? Ah, if only you knew," he said with a huge and heavy sigh.

"What do you mean?" she asked.

"We were all shocked when we found out. He has a brain tumour!" his head hung low as he kicked the pebbles in front of his feet.

"Oh my gosh, I had no idea!" she was startled. "Is he okay? What's the prognosis?"

"Well this summer is exactly a year since he's had it. We found out last summer when Asbed and I were on vacation in Hawaii. We didn't know what to do. We wanted to cut our vacation short to come and be with him but he told us not to as there was nothing urgent or immediate that anybody could do. He's fighting it. It's affected his eyes right now but we'll see what happens."

He went on to say what a smart person he was and that he had just finished law school. They had anticipated an amazing future with him. The idea of him being sick was traumatic for all of them. Apparently, Asbed, Vrej, and their brothers and a few others were a tight bunch back in LA. The thought of one of the brothers being ill had devastated them. Takouhi looked at Asbed's grandmother with her heart as only at that moment she understood the gravity of the woman's question.

A short while later all three of them got in the back of the car and this time they were driven to a place on top of what was between a mountain and a hill. At the top was what appeared to be a shack of sorts. It was a very small, one-room dwelling. Inside, there was nothing but lit candles and pictures of loved ones. It was a place to make a wish, to speak to God. This was the place! She had found it. Two days prior to returning home and she had found the place where she wanted to light her candle and make her wish. The location was majestic. The dwelling was majestic in its simplicity. All three walked in at the same time. The family that brought them there were already prepared with candles as they knew where they were headed. Asbed, Vrej, and Takouhi were given candles. While the other two family members who had brought them there waited outside the three friends stepped into another paradigm. Even though Takouhi was in the company of the two boys it didn't bother her. It was as if she wasn't there at the moment and had transported herself to another dimension. She thought about all her blessings. She was thankful for her parents, her brother, their health and hers, and all the events that had brought her here. She also thought about her grandmother who had passed away in February of that same year and how much she missed her.

She looked up to notice Asbed lighting the candle and just as she had noticed that first time in the church at the beginning of their journey, he was once again distant. He was physically standing in front of her but he wasn't there. She imagined that was how she must have looked only moments ago. But this time she knew who he was thinking about and she envisioned what his reaction would be if she stood beside him and simply put her hand on his shoulder. They all stepped outside one by one and started to explore the lush mountainside. Takouhi started taking pictures randomly. She noticed Asbed had walked away and was looking toward the valley. It was a beautiful moment with the lush green background and a trickle of light blue reflecting from the sun in what was once a large river. She snapped a few more photos.

Time came where they loaded up in the back of the cars and once again like three peas in a pod sharing an Ipod they headed back. It was truly an amazing day. It took her three weeks to find the exact place where she wanted to talk to the universe. It was worth the wait.

Just as they had arrived in Yerevan together, the three amigos were heading back to their homes together. Once again they were on the same flight. The difference was that this time Takouhi ended up sitting with Vrej whereas Asbed lucked out and got a first class seat all the way to London. Takouhi was disappointed as she was hoping that just like in the car they would all be together until the moment where they had to go their separate ways in London. During the flight the two of them went to the first class cabin and hung out with Asbed.

"I never even thought about Vancouver or Canada before I met you" said Asbed.

"Well, I guess you guys now have another place to visit. And you keep talking about snowboarding and skiing so that is the right place to be." said Takouhi.

"Yeah we'll definitely figure out a way to come up to Vancouver during the ski season" said Vrej. "Now we have a contact in Vancouver!"

"I would love to show you guys around. You both made my trip here so memorable I would love to be able to be as gracious a host as you have been," said Takouhi.

Vrej went back to his seat and Takouhi and Asbed continued in conversation.

"You know I had a complete different image of who I thought you were when I first saw you" she said.

"Oh yeah? What was it?" he asked with a little bratty smile.

"I thought you fit the profile of the wanna be Armenian gangsta" she said as she looked away unsure of his reaction.

"And what do you think now?" he asked.

"Well, there's more to you than meets the eye that's for sure" she said as she smiled and went back to her seat.

The difference between the flight from London to Yerevan and the flight from Yerevan to London was amazing. When they got off the flight in Yerevan all three of them wanted to run off the plane. This time when the plane landed in London they didn't want to get off as it meant the trip and the friendship as they had known if for the last three weeks was ending. They walked her to her gate as they were flying to Los Angeles and she was flying home to Vancouver. She gave both of them a big hug. She reached into her carry on and pulled out two envelopes that she had prepared for both of them. It was a poem she had written the night before that summed up their last few weeks together.

*Flight from Vancouver to London to Yerevan*
*Gate 22 is where I ran*
*Took out my journal and started to write*
*Gave mention to the boys sitting to my right*
*Got on the plane, sat in my seat*
*Switched seats with a man so his friends he could meet*
*To my surprise I now sat behind the boys*
*Who were playing with their gadgets and toys*
*Grabbed my phone and called my mom*
*That we're on time so she'd be calm*
*Put my phone down and there it came*
*Announcement of a delayed plane*
*He turned around cause he was eavesdropping*
*Said I jinxed the plane and started laughing*
*And from there started a journey without plan*
*From Sevan to Aparan and Yerevan*
*And let's give mention to our hang out Jazzve*
*The food the drinks and Armenian Café*
*In the back of the car like 3 peas in a pod*
*My way, If you go away and the IPOD*
*Waterslides, Baptism, Barbeque*
*How could I have had a greater trip without you?*

She walked away not knowing which weighed more: her carry on or the pressure in her chest. She stopped, turned around and saw Asbed was looking as she was walking away. He gave her a peace sign over his heart. It was a sign of friendship and camaraderie. Although she had had so many more conversations with Vrej that one gesture brought her closer to Asbed. He made a statement without saying a word. There was a connection with that man. She couldn't explain it. It was camaraderie on a higher level. She turned away and as she was walking the pressure in her chest was replaced with calmness and balance. Those few moments equaled thirty minutes of meditation. There was an unspoken understanding. She needed to find out more.

# 5

# BEGINNING A BEAUTIFUL FRIENDSHIP

The Takouhi who returned to Vancouver was different than the Takouhi who had left three weeks prior. The immediate noticeable difference was that she had lost weight. The entire BS that she had carried with her in her invisible heavy carry on, she had left in Armenia. Certain beliefs had become clear to her and she wasn't as traumatized by them. The concept of being seen foreign, or spoiled or any of the things that she had thought on her route to Yerevan were no longer applicable.

One of the main things on her agenda was to make sure she kept in touch with her newfound friends. She wanted to show her appreciation to the boys for taking her around the city and country and welcoming her into their families. It was very important to her that they understood how much she truly valued their efforts and that it was not taken for granted. She put together little thank you packages and sent it off to the boys. The one she sent to Asbed was very special to her. When she had come back she had reviewed all her pictures. There was one particular picture of Asbed overlooking the valley of Aparan. That was one of the moments where she felt he was deep in thought. In hindsight she now knew he must have been thinking of his brother. It was a majestic photo with vibrant blue skies and green lush landscape with him looking away in the distance. Takouhi had that picture transferred onto a cup. On the back of the cup she simply had them write Armenia 2006. She sent it with priority post so that he would receive it by his birthday. A few days later she received her very first call from Asbed.

"Hi Takouhi, how are you?" It took a moment for Takouhi to realize who was on the phone.

"Hi! How are *you*? How is everything?" she had been reading a book and dropped it on the floor as she jumped up surprised.

"I received your package. I don't know what to say!" His voice reminded her of the pre-recorded automated answering machine messages. Without a hint of emotion he went straight to the point. She was quickly trying to assess the situation in her mind. 'Was that a sign that he was nervous or that he didn't like the package?' In seconds, she started pacing her apartment with the phone in her hand. She needed to focus on something to ground her and collect her thoughts. She stopped pacing, took a deep breath, and looked at the beautiful calm Vancouver Harbour.

"I hope you like it" she looked in the mirror behind her and her wrinkled up nose and squinted eyes showed her lack of confidence.

"You don't understand. Geez, I love it!" The monotony that had been in his voice was gone. But there was awkward silence.

"I have never received a gift that has made me react that way. I can't describe that reaction or that feeling!" he said as he fumbled for words.

Takouhi took a deep breath and stuck her tongue out in the mirror at herself for fun, as if to say to herself 'you were worried because?'

"Asbed I wanted to show my appreciation for all that you and Vrej did," she said calmly. "I know it's not much. It's nothing fancy but it was just such a beautiful picture and the moment I can't even describe. I wanted to capture that for you."

"Takouhi, I don't even have a clue what I could possibly ever give to you that would make you feel the way I did when I saw this gift. Does that make sense?" The energy level in his tone of voice had changed and she imagined him speaking to her with his hands waving around. Very animated and full of motion, she assumed that he was probably pacing around whatever room he was in.

Yeah it made sense she thought. It absolutely made sense. Takouhi and Asbed were both on the same radio frequency.

Takouhi had a business trip to attend to in Long Beach. She had suggested the trip to her employer as a means for her to meet the alliance members they were working with. It was her intention that during this trip the members in the LA office would understand the key role she played at the Vancouver office and how her contributions directly benefited all alliance members. Up until that point all her efforts were silently done in the background and there was little or no understanding of her contribution to the alliance members other than a simplified version of being an assistant. Being a leader, she knew that the only way perceptions about her contributions were going to change was if she brought the change to light herself. Her employer wasn't going to do it for her.

If that were his intention he would have acted on it already. Yet there was another great opportunity here.

Takouhi thought that while she was in the Los Angeles area it would be great to meet Asbed and Vrej. Between numerous phone calls, emails and texts it was decided that the only way they could all meet was if Takouhi was able to fly to Las Vegas after her meetings in LA. She hadn't been there for a very long time. What would people say about a girl meeting guys in Vegas? What belief systems would that trigger she wondered? Tribal BS or otherwise? But how was that different than her traveling alone and meeting them by chance in Armenia? She had traveled with them before all the way on the other side of the world and was comfortable with them. She decided to go for it. If she only knew where that flight would truly take her. The details were organized with the two boys and the plan was that they would meet Takouhi at the Las Vegas airport.

Plans turned into reality as if someone had pressed the fast forward button on the remote control. It was Friday night, she had completed her business obligations in Los Angeles, and was en route to Las Vegas. As she arrived at the airport in Las Vegas she turned on her cell phone as soon as the plane's doors opened and contacted Vrej to tell him she had arrived. He and Asbed were not in Vegas quite yet; they had last minute business to attend to. They were both to arrive Saturday morning. She was going to leave Saturday at noon so this meant she would only see them in the morning.

"So what exactly am I going to do by myself tonight here in Vegas?" she asked Vrej on the phone sounded a bit perturbed.

"Don't worry, it's all taken care of. Just go to pick up your baggage and there will be two men waiting for you" said Vrej.

"What do you mean? I'm not just going to go up to two strangers in Vegas and say hi how are you doing?" Oh my God she heard her father's foreign accent again! "You did what?" She was walking away from the plane's gate and she noticed that people were looking at her. She was speaking too loud; she needed to calm down, so she sat down in the first set of chairs at no particular gate.

"No, you don't understand. One of them is Arka, Asbed's brother, and the other one is a good friend of ours. They are great guys," the calmer he sounded the greater she fidgeted in her seat. "You can trust them."

"How will I know who they are?" Takouhi had envisioned a smooth landing, meeting her friends and maybe a nice dinner. She was being challenged and not handling it well. She was leaning forward in her seat with her right hand holding her cell phone and the left hand tugging at her hair, as if she was pulling it out of its roots. Of all the languages in the world that she did not know how to speak, she spoke volumes to the travelers around her with her body language.

"Well, you can't miss them. Trust me. One looks like a pirate in that he is wearing a patch on his eye. The other one looks like a biker and is probably wearing a leather vest and biker boots!"

"Fine!" Without saying goodbye she hung up on Vrej.

She put the phone down and leaned back in her chair for a moment and started shaking her head in disbelief at her own actions. 'I am acting like a little brat who didn't get exactly what she wanted. He's trying to make it work and I'm resisting. Why?' She closed her eyes and took in as much air as a balloon can take in just before it bursts. Yes, they may have been waiting for her but she needed to change her state fast. 'If everything happens for a reason' she thought, 'then I have to be open to the reason. I won't learn anything if I close myself off.' The balloon slowly lost its pressure. She exhaled, stood up and continued to walk towards the baggage claim area. She phoned Vrej again and with the sweetest cavity causing tone asked, "Will you stay on the line with me until I find them?"

Sure enough, there they were just as Vrej had described them. Once the targets were in sight she moved towards them leaving a trail of fire behind her. With that momentum she handed the cell phone to the guy with the patch without even introducing herself. He took the cell phone and juggled it for a moment as if she had given him something straight out of the oven. Once he had a firm grip on the phone he put it to his ear and realized it was Vrej on the other line. He gave the phone back to her.

"So you're Takouhi" the first thing she noticed was how much he looked like Asbed.

"And you must be Arka and you are Heros" she said "Nice to meet you guys. I hope I'm not ruining your evening in Las Vegas by having to babysit me," she said feeling her face turning beet red. Or was it the Las Vegas heat?

"No we just got here ourselves and are about to go check in so we can all go together," said Arka.

Takouhi was speaking very fast and changing the topics before the boys had a chance to catch up to her. If she was a car she would not only be speeding but she would be quickly changing lanes as if someone was chasing her. In the taxi ride she was telling them all about how she met Asbed and Vrej in London and the great trip they had had in Armenia. And how they went to Lake Sevan, and how they had a barbeque in Aparan. She sounded like a machine gun. They arrived at the hotel and it was decided that once they checked in and freshened up they would meet in the lobby in one hour. Only when she stepped into the elevator did she stop talking. She looked in the mirror on the elevator walls and started smiling at herself. She crossed her eyes, rolled her eyes and puffed up her cheeks to make fun of herself. Oh how she must have sounded she thought. She wouldn't have blamed them if they didn't want to spend the rest of the evening with her. 'Damage control and status report' Takouhi thought 'Damage: Talking too fast, Status: When coming across the same scenario, *breathe*!'

An hour later they all met downstairs at the lobby. Heros decided that he was going to play poker. Arka asked Takouhi if she wanted to go grab a tea.' It was a good sign that he wanted to have tea with her she thought. She didn't mind, as she wasn't much of a poker player. They told Heros they'd be back in a few minutes and went looking for a coffee shop. As they walked side-by-side Takouhi noticed that every second step Arka took made him bump into her. It reminded her of ships bumping into the fenders, as they were about to dock. She also noticed that as they walked together people would give them a wide berth to pass. It appeared as if they were parting the Red Sea.

They seated themselves at the coffee shop that looked like it hadn't been updated since the sixties with the orange shaggy carpet.

"I met your family from your dad's side in Aparan," *breath in, breath out.*

"Really? That's cool. I haven't seen them since we left in the nineties." Takouhi took a good look at the man sitting across from her. Dark wavy hair, black patch over the right eye, the other brown eye sparkling so much that she could see her own reflection. He looked like one of those handsome European soccer players.

"So I hear you finished law school. Do you enjoy being a lawyer? I wanted to be a lawyer once," she was speeding and changing lanes again.

"Yeah, it was alright. But it wasn't what I really wanted to do. I did political science and economics. At one point I wanted to be a diplomat," during the entire conversation his one eye was directly fixated on her.

"How amazing! I studied political science too. I wanted to be a lawyer and work for UNICEF, but I knew I wouldn't be able to make ends meet with that. Then I too thought being a diplomat was the path to take. But then I got married and realized I wasn't so good at diplomacy!" Takouhi was back! With the mutual laughter she was comfortably able to sit back in her seat.

"So you were married once?" Arka leaned forward and put his hands together, like a detective in an interrogation room.

"Yeah it didn't work out. So much for that belief system that only your tribe will understand you," Takouhi looked away hoping the detective was not an astute profiler.

"I don't know if it means that they will understand you. I think it means that marriage is difficult to begin with and having the same background just makes it a bit easier. Especially with our closeness and commitment to family" he said.

"Is that why you're married to an Armenian?" Takouhi turned to look directly at him again.

It was evident to Takouhi that Arka was not expecting that question as his eye grew wide. He smiled and leaned back in his chair. He was silent for a few moments but looking directly at her as if he was processing how Takouhi would know that information. He wasn't wearing a wedding ring.

"My brother told you? Yeah I married an Armenian because the most beautiful woman in the world, Monica Belluci, wouldn't have me!" Now it was Takouhi's turn to be taken off guard. Touché! Their laughter was drowning out the elevator music that was Barry Manilow. Slowly the coffee shop was disappearing around them.

"I can see your point about marriage and family ties being easier when both people have the same background, but that's not a given. I married an Armenian and it would have been my dream to have a mother-in-law to be my best friend but instead I felt coolness. My grandmother once explained to me that I would experience that coolness if I married a non-Armenian but I experienced it with an Armenian. Go figure." She was hyperventilating, "I do realize that all that is just a belief system and that whether you marry within your culture or outside, the warmth that you and I speak of isn't guaranteed. It's a personality thing, not a cultural thing. I have Armenian friends who are married to Armenians. Some of them get along so well with their in-laws and others treat them as out-laws." She brought her fingers to her lips in the form of a gun and blew away the invisible smoke after having fired. He dropped the cookie he had treated himself to and started laughing at her gesture.

They composed themselves and took a deep breath. For a few moments they just smiled and looked directly at each other. It was the same feeling she had had with Asbed when she had said goodbye to him in London. It was an understanding. She wasn't able to explain it with words.

"Why do you have a notebook and pen with you?" he asked.

The correct answer was out of habit and that perhaps having pen and paper in hand gave her a sense of security of sorts.

"I always carry a journal with me and my pen. I love nice pens, paper, and watches," pointing to all three items on her person as if she was one of the ladies pointing out gift-show gifts!

"Let me see your pen," he said.

The pen was handed to him in the palm of both hands as if it were a fragile newborn baby.

"It is gorgeous" he said, "I bet you write amazing stuff with it."

"Don't know about amazing but I write as often as I can. I especially love writing quotes from my favourite philosophers"

"Oh yeah, name me one!" his sarcastic tone reminded her of her brother when he was testing if she really knew what she was talking about.

"I'll give you a hint 'Ask not that events happen as you will but..."

Before she knew it they both finished the remainder of the quote together and said out loud "Epictetus."

There was a weird pause. They were both stunned at what had just happened. He was looking directly at her and she was looking directly at his one eye. It wasn't a romantic attraction but an amazing connection. The planets had aligned themselves beautifully and the universe was talking loud and clear. There was no shyness and no looking away from each other. Something bigger than them happened at that moment.

"Is your favourite colour..." and before he could finish they both said "blue."

How could so many slot machines be working without her hearing them?

"And your favourite colour for cars is..." and together they said "white."

What happened to the elevator music? She had heard nothing but blue and white.

"And your favourite watch is..." this time they both said something different and started laughing.

"I guess your taste and budget is way above mine seeing that you're the fancy shmancy lawyer," Takouhi came back to the restaurant as she noticed that their laughter had gotten the attention of the nearby tables.

She was completely comfortable with him. If they were being watched, people would have assumed they had known each other for a long time.

"Tell me about the patch" there was a child like innocence about her curiosity.

"I have cancer!" he said expecting some sort of reaction from her.

"Oh yeah, I was told you did, but I thought that they operated and it was gone," her tone was as certain as if someone had asked her does the sun rise in the east.

"You know what's weird? You're the first one that has looked at this the way I do: as if it's not a big deal."

"I don't know how you're going to take this but I'm a firm believer in that although you may not be able to control things that happen to you, you can control the way in which you react to it."

"I totally agree. I look at life so differently now."

"So what's the status of your condition?"

"Well they can't operate because it's in the brain stem so I am going through different kinds of treatments. I wear the patch because without it, I have double vision. I can switch the patch from eye to eye. When one eye gets tired I switch it to the other. That is the only physical aspect at the moment that clearly shows I have an illness. Of course the other physical aspect is that I keep losing my balance so I stumble sometimes. You must have noticed that already," he looked at her with a smirk to see how attuned she had been with him.

"Yeah I did but it wasn't that obvious to me if it was you or I was just walking too close," she said and rolled her eyes in sarcasm.

"You know what I miss the most though Takouhi?" he said and his entire facial expression changed. Whereas a few moments before she had seen him use many of his facial muscles but now his face was blank. For once he couldn't look at her.

"What's that?" as his physiology changed so did hers because they were in complete rapport. Her body's energy level depleted in seconds as did the bank accounts of those playing slot machines next door. Whatever he was about to say it was big.

"I miss playing soccer. I loved it. You have no idea how much I loved it. To me it was the only time when the entire world disappeared. It was my meditation time. It was *me* time!" he had made a fist with his right hand and banged it on the table. Takouhi couldn't believe how this person who had been a complete stranger to her five hours ago was now confiding in her and sharing his tears. She reached out and put her left hand on his right hand without hesitation.

"Hey, don't worry. You'll play again." She wiped a tear from her face with her left hand.

"I hope you're right. No, I mean I know you're right! I will! It's what I love to do with passion." His face lit up as he remembered how running on the field and mastering the soccer ball felt. She could only sit there and imagine how he must have looked running down the field completely immersed in his game. How he must have been so completely focused that he probably didn't hear anyone cheering him on.

Arka and Takouhi didn't realize that they had been speaking for over two hours. It had seemed like five minutes. They made their way to Heros's poker table and found that he was no longer playing and was looking for them. He wondered where they had been and they apologized that they had lost track of time. Takouhi realized right away that Heros was the man in charge and was looking out for Arka. She could see him as Arka's bodyguard. His friendship and loyalty towards Arka was admirable, genuine, and heartfelt. As it had been a very long day they all decided to turn in early and regroup with the rest of the gang in the morning.

The next morning with the aid of technology and back and forth texting it was decided that her new friends and the two flying in would all meet for breakfast. It was full house. Asbed, Vrej, Heros, Arka and Takouhi were all having crepes in the famous French motif hotel. It was the first time Asbed and Vrej had seen Takouhi since saying goodbye at the gate in London. The hugs they gave each other heated the coffee on the nearby tables. One of the first things Asbed said in front of everybody as soon as they were seated around the round table had to do with the gift that he had already thanked her for so many times. His mother had loved the gift so much so that she had taken his cup from him and put it on her desk at work. She sat back and listened as the two boys who had just arrived shared stories about business with the two she had met the night before. The fact that they spoke so openly about their business without thinking there was a stranger in the midst made her feel as if she was part of the gang. In fact she thought of the term kuro, Armenian slang for sister. She had become the adopted sister from the north.

"So you must feel really good about yourself to be sitting with us, huh?" She heard Vrej say in a short matter of fact tone.

"Well I met you and Asbed in Armenia so I know what you're about. And having spoken to Arka for hours last night and what I've seen from Heros I'd say you all are very nice people. So if that's what you mean then yes, I do feel good by sitting with positive like-minded people," she knew there was more to what he was saying. There was another blimp on the radar.

"No! What I mean is that you're sitting with an engineer, a lawyer, and a banker so that makes your stock go up."

Oh boy oh boy… Takouhi had to replace her sweet crepe and take a bite out of his arrogance sandwich. She took a deep breath…

"So," and she put her utensils down ever so slowly and looked directly in his eyes. Takouhi had learned a thing or two from her father's powerful ability to use eyes to communicate "if I understand you correctly, your premise is that simply by hanging out with people who have had education in a specific field my value goes up as they deem me worthy of their audience? Is that correct?" She looked away from him and cut into her Nutella crepe very slowly and calmly. Vrej's body tensed up and he sat upright in his chair. His hands were frozen with the fork that was holding a piece of crepe he had wanted to eat. Arka and Asbed looked at each other and smiled, knowing Vrej had made a big mistake. Heros looked at Vrej and shook his head in disbelief of his comment. Takouhi stood her ground and didn't require protection from her new found brothers. Sitting there around the round table it looked like they were Camelot's Knights. She finished chewing, put her utensils down and again looked directly at him.

"Remember the conversation we had in Lake Sevan about belief systems? Let me share with you another one so we are extremely clear and on the same page. What you just said to me was a direct result of our tribal beliefs. I'm sure it applies to all cultures but I'm going to focus on ours. Success and intelligence are not equated with university degrees, the house you own, the car you drive, the watch you wear, and whether or not your husband or wife is a doctor or lawyer. There is nothing wrong with a university education, in fact that is everything right and that's what you should aspire for yourself and for your children. But a university degree doesn't make you better than anyone. All it means is that you have learned things about a certain topic. Does this make you a spiritual person? Does it make you a humanitarian, noble, compassionate and giving? Does it make you understanding and open to other cultures and ideas? It's not impossible I suppose but in the context in which you are asking this question I can see that it does not."

She grabbed her cup of coffee and took a sip. Nobody wanted to interrupt her. For a split moment she looked at Asbed who casually tilted his head towards Vrej as if to tell Takouhi 'let him have it.'

"The dilemma is that within our communities many of us are equating success, sophistication, and class with money and not with the way in which we treat others. The theory is that with higher education there is higher income therefore there is a higher class of individual. It all depends on how you define class. If you define class by a tax bracket then yes this theory applies however, if you apply class by kindness, grace, compassion, love, tolerance, humanity then that education doesn't necessarily mean you have class. Don't get me wrong it doesn't mean that you can't be educated and be all of what I just said. All I'm saying is that I know many doctors and lawyers who can not hold a conversation about anything other than their trade as they only know their trade. They know nothing about how to be with others and give to others. And there are those among us who have not had the opportunity to have formal education and yet they are enlightened for they seized every opportunity to learn and take responsibility for their lives."

Takouhi's crepe was getting cold. She took another bite. None of them were talking but at least they were eating. Not Vrej.

"Vrej don't misunderstand me it's not to say that fancy cars and homes are bad either. They are things we attain in order to live lives that inspire us and propel us forward. However, if we use it to compare ourselves in order to validate our self-worth due to our insecurities and allow these material things to define us then we are in trouble. They don't define us they are just things we like. And yet I see this all the time. A gentleman wearing a fancy watch and making sure the world sees it by putting his hand on the table. If he took that watch off, is he no longer who he thinks he is? If so, then he is leading a shallow life. So to answer your question, I will say yes not so much that my stock has gone up but rather that I have met open minded and positive people and it doesn't matter to me if they are engineers, lawyers, or bankers. If I couldn't have a conversation with all of you right now then I would not be here."

Takouhi looked over to Asbed, Arka, and Heros and received a winking ovation and the biggest Nutella covered smiles. Vrej looked like a deer caught in the headlights that were Takouhi's eyes. The poor guy didn't have a chance. Takouhi didn't feel satisfaction or get a thrill for making Vrej stand out like that in front of his friends yet on the other hand if she was their adopted sister she had the right to speak her mind. Vrej and Takouhi had been so close with all their conversations and she really did appreciate all the times they had spent together in Armenia. It was unfortunate that he showed his true colours with such an ugly question. She really thought he was at that stage where he was questioning tribal beliefs and transforming them constructively but maybe coming back to his turf and being surrounded by his immediate tribe it had reinforced the old BS in him. At Lake Sevan she had thought she had reached him and maybe she had on the topic of relationships but clearly he still had a long road to journey. Of all the Nutella crepes Takouhi had eaten in her life that particular one would be the most memorable.

After that breakfast it was time for her to leave. However, this time leaving the gang was not as traumatic as leaving them in London. The highlight of Vegas was the conversation with Arka. Vrej's destructive comments that morning would never overshadow that two-hour talk. Her gut told her it wasn't over. There was something more that Arka needed to hear from her.

# 6

# THE BEST OF INTENTIONS

Dive! Dive! Dive! Like the sirens of a submarine Takouhi returned and dove deeply in the adventures of her bubble blowers. In spite of her overwhelming obligations, she could not get Arka out of her mind. She knew that something amazing had happened and there was a reason why she had met him without any previous planning. There was no such thing as coincidences as she truly did believe everything happened for a reason. She knew eventually this reason would be self-evident. She kept reviewing the conversation over and over in her head. If she could bottle his confidence what would it smell like she wondered. His resolve and certainty inspired her such that when she was overwhelmed at work she would ask herself 'and what would Arka do or say in this situation.' She wanted to reach out to him. She focused on Arka and his challenging road ahead so much that one night in spite of having just come home from work at 11:00 p.m., she awoke at 3:00 a.m. grabbed her laptop from her home office table and jumped back into her warm bed. This was one of those rare occasions that her pen would have slowed her down and not been able to keep up with her. She needed to match the speed of her fingers to the speed of her thoughts. She curled up in her blankets and began to type.

*Dear Arka,*

*First of all, I want to say it was a pleasure to meet you and chat with you over tea on Friday night. Even though other plans had previously been made for that night, it turned out exactly as it should have been. I met an awesome human being.*

*Please understand that the following is not an 'I feel bad for you because you have a tumor letter.' I want to share with you some stories that will inspire you because I know you have a long and bumpy road ahead of you. In order to get from here where the bumps are to there where the road is smooth again you have to make some adjustments. You may be asking yourself "Takouhi, why is it that you think you're in a position to give me advise?" Well as I told you in our conversation in Vegas, my father had cancer exactly 10 years ago—in his ear. For the first time in my life I saw my father, my rock of Gibraltar, break down and cry. His life changed, and so did my mother's, my brother's and mine. In a similar way, your life has changed and so has the lives of so many people around you. You know what mom did when he told her initially? She said "So? Everyone has cancer like it's a cold or in fashion. You're not going anywhere unfortunately," and we all started laughing at her sarcasm. The mood changed, our spirits lifted and all of a sudden the world was not coming to an end.*

*What I'm telling you is this. Yes it sucks but you have to get through it. While you can't control what happened, you can control your reaction towards it. Just as important as any type of chemo, radiation, or medication so are your thoughts. How we think affects the body. I grind my teeth for example. The question is why am I grinding my teeth? The answer; I'm stressed out. And why am I stressed out? Evidently I have not been able to process and react to situations in my life in a way that is healthy and benefits me. However, because I am aware of this fact I am working on it on a daily basis. One of the main things that really stuck with me during our conversation was your comment that you hold your feelings and thoughts inside. Luckily, up until recently, you had your soccer to release some of that pressure but apparently and obviously there's a lot of pressure there that wasn't released. Did you keep your thoughts inside so you wouldn't disappoint or hurt anyone's feelings or expectations? Or felt that if you shared your feelings it would be a sign of weakness? Those are pretty strong beliefs. Only you know the answers why you kept and still keep stuff to yourself… but… the time is here and now that you have to be selfish 110%. You're not the selfish kind. I see that clear as day… but let me put it in perspective for you. Why is it that when you're sitting on a plane and they tell you in case of emergency when the oxygen masks come down, first put one on yourself and then put it on your child. It sounds selfish doesn't it? But thinking you are being unselfish and immediately take care of the child first, by the time it's your turn you will pass out. So in the short term although you saved your child, in the long term you're not around to help the child grow and develop. So ultimately you have hurt the child. It's time for you to be selfish.*

*Remove all negative thoughts in your head, cut yourself off from people who look at you with pity, and surround yourself with people who inspire you and will take you to another level of possibilities. Do not feel sorry for yourself. As difficult as this situation is to comprehend, remember, there are people in situations worse than yours. You don't believe me? Take a visit to the pediatric burn unit in any of your local hospitals and that's only one example. I'll share one of my own experiences about cutting negative people. I had a very close and long-term girlfriend who, one day, decided that she was going to be a "real" friend to me and tell me how things "really are." She said, "Chances are your dad isn't going to make it." My friendship with her ended that day. I removed myself from her sphere of influence. I didn't want to be around someone who was going to influence my thoughts in a negative way and in turn have me look at my father in that way. We do pass along thoughts and emotions from person to person whether they're negative or positive. If we don't get rid of the negative comments and thoughts, we end up damaging ourselves with long-term consequences. The latest thing is for people to detoxify their bodies with organic food, yet nobody is putting value on detoxifying our beliefs and thought processes. Mumbo jumbo philosophy is what my dad may have said in the past with his old BS but even he is revisiting and transforming his beliefs. You haven't met my father but believe me when I tell you if he can do it so can you! During my sheep days I wouldn't even dare write a letter like this, as I would be too concerned with thinking I have overstepped invisible boundaries. But now, all I know is that my intention is to help so why not? Your thoughts and the way you look at the world determine how the body functions and heals itself. Going to the gym to work on the body but walking around with old belief systems and internalizing guilt or frustration (as examples) is like ordering a diet soft drink with your burger. You accomplish nothing.*

*Remember how we compared ourselves to what our parents went through to get us here, and how this makes it impossible for us to complain about anything as nothing can compare to their hardship? Yet we have challenges that they can't imagine or relate to. We think that if we don't uphold the old beliefs that we are letting our parents down. That in lieu of all their sacrifices the least we can do is to uphold tradition. They did so much for us thus we must return the goodness. Yet it is our duty to take the lessons from their lives and improve upon the old beliefs in the journey that's our life. It would be a shame to limit ourselves in this new world with old beliefs. Ask yourself, would your parents think it smart to buy a new computer in 2006 and upload 1990 technology? We've carried guilt for years and it has gotten heavier year after year. That's like walking around with heavy suitcases everyday. Your body wouldn't handle it so how could your brain? So in summary, be selfish! Do whatever it takes to beat this! Remove yourself from negative people whether they're family, friends, or whomever. Watch what you eat but more importantly be aware of your thoughts. Whatever you focus on expands. If you focus on the negative it's what you're going to get. It is just like riding a motorcycle. Look to where you're headed. If you look at the curb you're going to go towards the curb. If you look at the road ahead you're going to go there. Look at the road ahead Arka jan, because it's there it's waiting for you to make awesome memories with all your loved ones.*

*I know you already know all this. You're intelligent, sensitive, and spiritual and I don't profess for a moment that I can even imagine half of the thoughts that are running through your head. This is my way of reaching out to you. Sometimes we may know things inside but we need someone to kind of stir us a little. It sure helps when it's on paper so you can refer back to it from time to time if you need to. We may know many things but sometimes we forget.*

*This letter was written with the best of intentions. If I've disrespected you in any way I do apologize. No disrespect was intended at all. (And I didn't mean to be rude at the airport either when I just handed you the phone without introducing myself. Really!) You have a great group of friends who love you. Tap into them for all kinds of support. Your wife is also the closest ally you have. Tap into her love for you. I look forward to meeting her in the near future. They all need you as much as you need them. To me that is a win-win situation. Now you've got a sister on the 49$^{th}$ parallel, for life! A long life! Perhaps to the point where you'll say, "I'm sick and tired of your frigging philosophies and sayings! Be quiet already!" You can call me anytime you want to chat. You already have my number. If you're into emailing and want to drop me a hello feel free to do so. I'm an email and text junkie. Hey at least I admit it..*

*Can't wait to see you again and again and again,*

*Takouhi*

It took her two hours to write the letter. It was almost 5:30 in the morning and still dark outside. She read and reread the letter for another hour and half. 'Was there anything else she could have added?' she thought. Was she being audacious by writing him this letter? But, what if it was exactly the thing that he needed to hear. She comforted her insecurities by remembering his smile when they had realized they had so many things in common. Surely he would appreciate a letter like this, she knew she would if someone had taken the time to write it for her. Her thoughts overwhelmed her like the sudden rains that overwhelmed the city's drainage systems. She pushed her laptop away and hid under the warm covers of the bed as if to hide. But the thoughts followed her there. Within moments the alarm clock sounded. It was now 7:00 a.m. She jumped out of bed in an effort to outrun her thoughts. No such luck, they followed her into the shower, back to the bedroom, the kitchen, and to the car. She turned her car on and as per her usual routine allowed the engine to warm up. She turned on the radio and like a gift from the universe heard "I did it Myyyyyyyy Waayyyyy." She sat back in her seat and looked out of her sun-roof. 'Very funny' she said to the sky above 'very funny!'

In spite of the timing of 'ol blue eye's advice, in the coming days Takouhi found that she was still second guessing herself and could not send the letter. There was a tug of war between beliefs old and new. Although she had nothing but good will in mind she thought what if his wife wouldn't appreciate it? She thought about the limiting belief systems that may overshadow this intention. One of them was that his wife may not appreciate another woman that she didn't know write him a letter. To complicate things she thought if the wife was not an open-minded person she would wonder how in the world Takouhi ended up in Las Vegas speaking to her husband for over two hours. That was a possible version that Takouhi took into account when deciding if she should send the letter. However, there was another version. A more empowering one that she hoped his wife would identify with. Takouhi put herself in her shoes for a moment. If she had a husband who had a serious illness like Arka, wouldn't she want all the external support that she could get to make him get better? If Arka's wife truly loved her husband she wouldn't care who was reaching out to him and how they met. She would befriend an external positive source as opposed to repel it. And anyway, there was nothing in the letter that showed any ill intent. It wasn't that the letter contained earth shattering information or anything of the sort. Takouhi was well aware that everything she had written was already out there. She had made it personal for Arka to relate to through her own experiences. The value in the letter wasn't necessarily in the content. It was the idea that someone out there who he had just met thought so highly of him that she had taken the time to reach out. The spiritual connection outweighed any kind of belief system whether tribal or other that may have applied in this case. 'You're not a sheep' she kept saying to herself 'Do it or you'll regret it. It doesn't matter what people say. Your intention is pure and good.' Yet she continued to hesitate until the night she dreamt of her grandmother.

She dreamt that her grandmother and her uncle, who happened to have the same name as Arka, where standing in a field of golden wheat. In the background were beautiful willow trees with their long branches dancing in the graceful summer wind. She noticed the afternoon sun reflect off the flowing river. It was as if she was a helicopter viewing all this from above. It occurred to her that what she was seeing was a scene from her recent trip to Armenia. She knew that river well. It was the Aras River she had just seen in August. Her attention focused back on her grandmother. She looked like she was in her fifties the way Takouhi remembered her. Her uncle looked young as well, in his early thirties. When she focused on them she realized that they were simply smiling and nodding their heads in approval. But she didn't understand completely what that meant until she saw that her grandmother had both palms of her hands open and in them was a beautiful little red ladybug. Takouhi had always had a fondness for ladybugs and Grandma knew that. She must have been crying in her sleep because when she awoke she felt tired, her eyes were puffy and her cheeks felt salty like the beaches of the Dead Sea. The next day she sent the letter via priority post.

Many days passed, she didn't receive any kind of response. The Christmas season was starting. The longer she didn't hear back from him the closer she came to forgetting about her recent dream. She began to think that maybe she did offend him in some way. She started looking for advice from outside sources to see if there was anything she may have missed. It was mentioned to her by one of her Armenian friends born and raised in Armenia that the men there are full of pride and they don't want help from anyone. What if that was true? Then as opposed to giving him sugar she had handed him poison. No he wasn't like that, was he? She felt like a swan, on the outside allowing others to view her as gliding effortlessly on the water but under the water she was paddling like mad. Why didn't she get a response? Another night of these ramblings in her mind was no longer an option. The mental anguish she was subjecting herself to was becoming too great. She decided to take matters into her own hands and sent him an email.

*Dear Arka,*

*I hope you're having a great holiday season surrounded by all your loving family and friends.*

*I have a quick question. I am assuming by now that you have received the letter that I have sent you. I haven't heard anything from you and I recently noticed that my spam filter had been automatically deleting everything that it didn't recognize without allowing me to see it. (I've changed the filtering system since then). The only reason I bring this up is that if you've tried to contact me there's a good chance I didn't see it. And if you haven't and in some way I have upset or offended you please know that it was not my intention at all to upset you. I wanted to inspire you, remind you what a wonderful person you are and that you mean so much to so many people. I have to get that off my chest. I did not want to start the New Year with uncertainty. I wish you all the best the New Year has to offer.*

*Your sister, Takouhi*

Within minutes of pressing send, turning her attention away from the computer and coming back to it, there was an email from Arka in her inbox.

*Hi Takouhi,*

*I did respond to your very kind letter as soon as I received it weeks prior. Thank you very much for your kind wishes. I wish you a Happy New Year and all the best. You are a very caring person. I wish you a very joyous year full of happiness and success.*

*Thank you,*

*Arka*

It had almost been three weeks since she had written the letter until his response. All the belief systems that had challenged her regarding this matter suddenly disappeared. What had been real in one moment did not exist in the next. She was right to keep moving forward and challenge herself and her BS. Based on her reactions during those three weeks she realized she had a lot of work to do in order to become stronger but the important lesson was that she hadn't given up. She had followed through. It wasn't the thank you that she had needed. It was knowing whether he could relate to the letter. That night she knew that for the time being, the train of thought that was called BS had pulled into the station allowing for a good night sleep. Encouraged by the fact that he had responded she thought in the coming days she would focus on what would be the best way to strengthen Arka's immediate team members from inside out. Takouhi had Asbed and Arka's wife on her radar.

# 7

# TIES THAT BOND

In mid-January, Takouhi opened her email on a Wednesday morning to find an email in her inbox from Vrej. He and Asbed had decided on a last minute trip to Vancouver to go snowboarding in Whistler and Blackcomb. They were to arrive the following Friday evening. Takouhi did not need coffee that morning to wake up. Her excitement was not just due to the fact that she hadn't seen them in three months but also that Vrej coming to Vancouver meant he had no hard feelings over their last conversation in Las Vegas. In a six-month period, they had traveled and kept in touch as if they had grown up together. As for the other two brothers she had met only three months prior, she had only heard from Arka by way of his email confirming he had received her letter in mid December. She had no contact with Heros. Takouhi had wished him a Happy New Year but hadn't heard back. She hadn't really expected to hear from him though. Takouhi was moved by the concern he had shown that night in Las Vegas where he had been looking for Arka with the same panic in his eyes as a father after losing his child in a crowd. She had felt guilty that what was meant to be a two-minute tea break had turned into a two hour conversation that had resulted in joy for her but sheer panic for Heros. And although she respected his obvious loyalty towards Arka by way of his actions she couldn't see herself having an in-depth conversation with him. Not because he wasn't capable but because his intricate multi faceted security system was up and nobody knew the password. Heros was exactly what his name meant in Armenian. He was a hero, a soldier and a bodyguard. Takouhi focused her attention back to Arka. She decided to send an email Wednesday evening to Asbed to see if there was any chance of Arka joining them. She suggested to Asbed that the fresh crisp Vancouver winter air would be incredibly beneficial for his brother's health. Asbed's response in the same evening was that he had asked Arka but was advised that it wasn't a good time. Takouhi assumed it was due to him not feeling well enough to travel and didn't insist.

The two days since receiving the email passed by as if someone had simply pressed a button and skipped to the next chapter on the DVD. It was Friday night and she was anxiously awaiting the call to say that they had arrived. Although it was customary for her to want to greet newcomers to Vancouver at the airport, they had insisted in their email correspondence that they would rent a car and meet with her once they checked into their hotel. By the time they called her it was close to 11:00 p.m. They had walked to the closest restaurant by their hotel and were already ordering food. When Asbed called he simply said,

"We're here at Brown's Restaurant, do you want a tossed salad, or a Greek salad?"

She walked in to find a round table of characters. To her surprise Heros was there as well. The stranger next to Heros was in fact his brother. The hugs they gave each other could have taught hot chocolate a thing or two about warming the soul. Once again it was Takouhi around the round table with the Knights. She started driving fast and changing lanes again but composed herself quickly when she saw Heros roll his eyes. The boys were all avid skiers. The conversations were mostly about skiing and the mountains they were going to conquer the next morning. The mountains were in her backyard but Takouhi hadn't gone skiing for over twelve years. She was reminded of the conversation she had had with the boys in Armenia where as a tourist she had seen more of Armenia than they had whilst they were living there. In spite of having a mini cast on her recently broken thumb by way of a car door slamming shut on it, and despite the fact that her ski skills were rusty, she decided that she wasn't going to give up the opportunity of being witness to their impressions of the beauty of the mountainside. So what if she would make a fool out of herself? She was all for it! The troops were tired and called it a night. She recommended that they head out towards Whistler at 5:30 a.m. to avoid traffic and get a head start on the mountain. Takouhi had decided that she would drive up by herself mid morning around 9:00 a.m. after finishing up some work details that could not wait until Monday. It was a win-win situation as far as she saw it. She would get her job done and at the same time she would reduce the opportunities for embarrassment while skiing.

The next morning Takouhi was at work at 6:00 a.m. She couldn't sleep knowing her friends were in town and wanted to get to them as quickly as possible. She managed her obligations at work and was on her way to Whistler by 8:00 a.m. It was an extraordinarily beautiful winter day. The visitors had brought the sunshine from Los Angeles with them. The sky looked as crisp as the ocean below as she drove on the Sea to Sky Highway. There was nobody on the road but her. Her tax dollars at work. The road was all hers. She loved the twists and turns on that Highway. She remembered the times during the summer months when she used to take her motorcycle and drive to Whistler and back before anybody was awake and on the roads. It was her road, her journey, her thoughts, and the universe. Reminiscing in the time capsule that was her car, before she knew it she was in Whistler.

It was 9:30 a.m. and Takouhi was ahead of schedule. The night before they had decided to meet at the ticketing booth at the base of Blackcomb at 10:30. She took her time putting on her gear and slowly made her way towards the meeting spot. No matter how cool she may have wanted to look, her ancient ski gear dated her. In the meantime she was desperately trying to look fear in the eyes by convincing herself that skiing again after a twelve-year break would be as easy as learning to drive the motorcycle. After all, what was the worst that could happen? Oh yeah, she did drop the motorcycle once! Finally she saw them come to the booth one by one. Two were on ski's the other two on snowboards. She was ready, no turning back now. She sat on the ski lift with Asbed and Vrej. The other two were behind them. Six months ago the three of them were in a taxi directly in the heat of the summer sun fighting over the iPod on their way to Aparan and now they were going to the top of the hill under the same sun but half frozen. She kept repeating to herself that things happen for a reason and in doing so reinforcing that belief within her system like a retaining wall. Takouhi managed to get herself off the lift and ever so slowly make her way down the hill. She couldn't help but notice the style in which the boys were skiing. Asbed and Vrej had a competitive streak between them and were racing with each other. Knowing that she was challenged by way of thumb and ability to ski both boys would always stop at some point to make sure her thumb was still attached to the rest of her body. As she was heading down the mountain, she noticed how Asbed looked at his surrounding. She remembered how he had looked toward the valley in Aparan and compared it to that moment. He would turn his attention from tree to tree as if he had engaged in some kind of conversation with them. He was waving his hands around and pointing at different things on the mountain. She finally came close enough to hear him repeatedly say 'Wow!" as he proceeded to take in deep breaths. He hadn't moved a muscle in Aparan while enjoying the view, but in Whistler he was fully animated. Again, her role had become that of an observer. She was on the mountain taking in the fresh air, which was exactly what she needed after her hectic work schedule. The irony was that she was doing this with people she had met on the other side of the world. Were they sent to her so she could learn to play and relax? Or was she sent to them because something was coming around the corner?

That evening they followed each other back to Vancouver. She hadn't realized that they had only come up for one day of skiing. They were leaving the next morning. It was decided that they would regroup after changing and freshening up and meet at a local restaurant for a late dinner.

"Where are you?" she heard as she reluctantly picked up her phone knowing she would hear frustration on the other side.

"I'm sorry I'm coming! I got paged and had to come into the office to put a job together! I'm not even on call but… anyway... it's a long story but I am on my way."

"You do realize it is 10:30 p.m. on a Saturday night?" The tone of his voice made her think how lucky he was that she wasn't his girlfriend as she would have reached through the phone and God help him.

Just before she left the office she decided to send Arka a quick email. Initially she wanted to report on Asbed's rude tone over the phone like a sister tattle telling on her brother but she changed her course.

*You missed out Dear Arka. The fresh mountain air would have confused your lungs but it would have been great to see you! Hope you're feeling great and that you are surrounded by as much love and camaraderie as I was this weekend! Thank you for lending your friends and family to me. It made a world of difference!*

*All the best, Takouhi*

She made it to the restaurant and the marionette that was Takouhi dropped on the chair as if the puppeteer had dropped her strings. She avoided Asbed's eyes, as she wasn't in the mood for a lecture. During dinner the questions and comments were flowing about Vancouver. What is the population of Vancouver? What is the standard of living like? How safe is it and what is the medical system like? She was representing Vancouver and she was fine with that as she loved her city. The questions were typical of tourists and she was happy to oblige them. Although she was physically exhausted from all the day's activities she was craving some in depth conversation. Initially she had avoided Asbed when she had arrived but her mood had changed as she had focused on her city. Now she wanted to speak to Asbed about Arka. It seemed unlikely that she was going to have that opportunity she thought as the sands designated to the hourglass of this trip were running out.

"What are you thinking about?" she heard Asbed's voice. In spite of their being five people around the table Takouhi instinctively knew that he was speaking to her. She just smiled for a few moments to herself and finally did look up to see that yes he had been asking her the question. He had curious eyes that had shine and sparkle to them. His curiosity was much like how she would imagine a little boy to be when they had just received a new toy, wondered how it worked and proceeded to dismantle it. She didn't get a chance to respond. Just as she had finished that thought the boys decided it was time to head back to the hotel as they all had an early flight to catch the next morning. Takouhi decided to show them a shorter route to get back to the hotel as their GPS must have been in bed with the gas stations. It was decided that the easiest way was for them to follow her in her car. In doing so Asbed ended up in Takouhi's car while the other three followed in the rental car.

"So I haven't had the opportunity to really talk to you this weekend and oddly enough you asked me what I was thinking just as I was thinking it" said Takouhi.

"What do you mean? We've all been talking."

"Duh, I realize that. I guess I wanted to ask you about Arka. How is he doing?"

"Oh like that you mean? He's fine I suppose." He shrugged his shoulder and looked outside the window at the stores on Robson Street.

"Do you ever talk to him about it? Do you ever ask him how he's feeling?" trying to bring his attention back to the cockpit.

"No, not really" he said sounding short and to the point, "but I can tell you this."

"What's that?"

"My brother is an amazing person. He has gone through so much in his life and come out of some really sticky situations. If anybody can figure this out it's him." Wow, he has a positive belief system and isn't thinking poor us. She nodded her head and simply hummed. Arka was also lucky to have a brother like you she thought. At the same time his abruptness had indicated to her that she wasn't going to get far talking about Arka that night.

Suddenly he changed the category as if he was playing the game show Jeopardy. Takouhi for $500 I'll take relationships please!

"You know what I want?"

"In what category? Relationships? Job?"

"Relationships! I want a woman who has a huge heart, is super giving and generous," the words flowed out of him with such elegance as if he had been practicing how to say it in front of a mirror for hours.

"So what's the problem?" she was chuckling and suddenly the winter cold was no longer an issue, or was it because her heated seats were working?

"There's no problem. That's what I want? Do you think it's possible?" he looked at her as if she was the designated foreman by the jury and she had the answer in the envelope in her hand.

"How does that saying go? If you can dream it, you can achieve it if you truly believe it!"

"Don't know if it exists. Maybe it's just a dream. No such thing as love anyway!"

Didn't she have this conversation with Vrej six months ago? Both boys had the same BS about love.

"You know it seems that you and your friend have the same BS?"

"What do you mean? Which friend? And why are you so rude all of a sudden?" He had been short with her when she was late, he had been abrupt with her when she had asked about Arka, now he twisted his body to face her, put his arm on the dashboard and was fully engaged.

"Vrej! I had a conversation with him about love in Lake Sevan! And BS stands for belief systems silly."

"Oops. Sorry" and started laughing "You spoke to Vrej about the existence of love? Really? Where was I?"

"You were there physically but somewhere completely different mentally!" She knew where he was. He was with Arka.

"What do you mean?" his tone matched his relaxed posture as he sat back into his seat.

Takouhi realized that what she had just said wasn't true. In fact, her entire conversation about relationships and love had taken place by the beach of Lake Sevan as she was walking with Vrej. Asbed was nowhere near. She was referring to other times where she had caught him mentally drift off whether it was in the church in Yerevan or the little hut in Aparan. Luckily they reached the hotel and there was no time for further clarifications. She jumped out of the car and hugged the tourists. The ice on the roads melted in a five kilometer radius. Distancing herself from them was becoming easier and easier as it was becoming evident that goodbye was simply a see you later. There was nothing dramatic about it anymore. By the time she got home it was already past midnight. But she was curious and couldn't resist checking her email. There in her inbox was a reply from Arka!

# 8

# BRAT TO BRAT TRANSMISSION

Takouhi stared at her inbox and hesitated to open the email. She kept playing and tugging at her hair too frozen to proceed. She finally clicked the button and with her shock all tiredness disappeared. 'Mail Delivery Failure.' What? Upon closer inspection she realized that in her haste to leave the office and join the boys in the restaurant as opposed to typing in yahoo.com at the end of his email address she had typed yahoo.ca! Canada! It was in her blood! She took it as a sign and didn't pursue the matter any further. It wasn't the right time she thought!

It had been awhile since she had heard from Arka. Almost two months to be exact. Having just spoken to Asbed she knew he was well but she wanted first hand info. She thought there should be no reason to hesitate contacting him again since they had an amazing conversation in Vegas resulting in the letter. Her intention was to make sure that he was in a positive state of mind, that his pistons were firing and he was using premium fuel to navigate through the day.

It was February. Takouhi sent him an email the day after Valentines. It included an attachment that spoke of loving constantly, not just on Valentines Day. She thought he would enjoy it.

*Hi Arka,*

*Just checking on you and making sure you know that a sister up north is thinking of you on a daily basis and sending you nothing but strength and support through the emails. Positive energy transcends any distance or technology.*

*This is an excellent read. It's not a sappy Valentines or anti valentines message. It has some profound thought most of which I know you already know. However, human nature is such that sometimes we get locked into auto pilot mode and go through our days in a haze. I know you will enjoy it so take a few minutes and disappear in the pages.*

*Ciao for now, Takouhi*

This time she made sure she typed yahoo.com. Yet she wasn't expecting a response. Especially since he had been non communicative for so long. But within the hour she received an email response.

*Hi Sis,*

*Thank you for not forgetting me, I appreciate it. I hope you are doing well and everything is okay. I'm doing okay, off course been better, but will get better. I have a sister full of support and encouragement, how could I possibly not get better.*

*Thank you,*

*Arka*

Something had happened between his last communication with her way back in December and now. She sensed it but couldn't put her finger on it. At the same time she wasn't going to doubt it and she went with it and the emails flowed.

## BRAT TO BRAT TRANSMISSION

*Dear Arka,*
*Promise me, if you ever get into one of your down and out moods (as we all do all the time) just send me a quick email. You don't even have to write anything. In the subject line just write bad mood or pick me up and I'll come right back at you with something. There's radiation and then there's Takouhidiation! Come on, you got to laugh at that one!*
*But seriously, please don't thank me for anything. I am your sister in great times and in challenging times. And how can I forget about you? The other day I was just relaxing on the couch after having had taken a shower and my hair was wrapped up in a towel on my head... (not a pretty sight.. trust me!).. Anyway, the towel crept down and covered one of my eyes. Hmmm, I thought, so this is how Arka sees now. So I got up and I walked around the house with one eye covered. What a complete paradigm shift. You are amazing and strong. All I'm thinking is how many people you are influencing right now by your strength and I'm thinking how many people you're going to influence with your positive stories of perseverance when you beat this. I can't wait!*
*Calvin Coolidge wrote: "Press on. Nothing can take the place of persistence. Talent will not; the world is full of unsuccessful people with talent. Genius will not; unrewarded genius is almost a proverb. Education alone will not; the world is full of educated derelicts. Persistence and determination alone are omnipotent."*
*I'm going to talk out of school here. Did you know that your brother Asbed adores you? Not just because you're his brother but because of things he's seen you do and overcome in the past. Now I don't know details because unfortunately I haven't had the chance to have one on*

*one time with Asbed that much. However, as the adopted sister I'm telling you he is another major source of positive energy coming towards you. Feel it, use it, and recharge yourself. That's what we're here for in good and bad times.*

*Okay back to work. Yes it's Sunday and I'm at work. It's the only way I get real work done without everyone barging into my office. Friday I could have killed both my assistants. My office door was open and I could hear both of them sharing Pillsbury dough recipes. I wanted to go Rambo on them and yell 'I'll show you Pillsbury!'...*

*Are you laughing? Good!*

*Ciao for now, Takouhi*

*PS Looks like I may be coming to your area in March. I can't wait to see you and the rest of the gang again.*

Takouhi would usually write her emails prior to work commencing or on her breaks as she had to remain extremely focused during work hours. There were so many details that she had to take care of especially in dealing with worldwide operations. Missing a detail would have disastrous effects down the line. At times her co-workers would give her the nickname that was similar to the boss of the modern version of the British spy. On paper what her divers, or bubble blowers as she called them, did seemed glamorous in flying all over the world to the rescue of ships but in reality everybody worked their butts off. She lived vicariously through their adventures even if her life was anything but glamorous in that office. At the end of the day as she was packing to go home she checked her personal email and there in her inbox was Arka's response.

*Hi Sis,*

*I am always glad to hear form you. You are a very unique and caring sis that lights up the spirits. Keep up your good spirit, never lose that character of yours. I don't even think it's possible even if you tried.*

*I am in Mexico for treatments now, but I will definitely see you when you get in town. Take care of yourself sis and see you soon.*

*Brat Arka*

It was Sunday night and she didn't want to look at the computer at work anymore Takouhi drove home with Arka sitting next to her. He may as well have been as she had started speaking to him. There was so much that she wanted to tell him. She wanted to share stories with him that would inspire him to keep moving forward and not give up. Sharing personal stories was done in such a way so he could visualize someone having gone through difficulties and coming out on the other end. It was her way of training his mind to see beyond his situation towards all the positive possibilities.

She had just met him a few months ago, so why was he taking up so much room in her mind? Was she feeling sorry for him in spite of saying and writing that she wasn't? No! That was an easy answer. She would never behave towards a person in a manner that she wouldn't appreciate herself. There was a spiritual connection with him that she couldn't explain. She identified with him. Having so much in common made her constantly think 'What would I wish for another human being to do for me if I were in the same situation, without my asking?' She realized that she would never ask or want to impose on anyone. If someone did something for another person it meant more if it was natural and by choice rather than with coercion or guilt. Arka was exactly the same way. He would never ask her or anybody to be there for him. She instinctually and organically wanted to. It was the right thing to do. If she had tools that would help change his flat tire as he was pulled over on the curb of the road of life, then it was her obligation as a person to do so. Takouhi could not just drive by and let the man be stranded on the side of the road not when she had some tools in her trunk. If she knew somebody liked something she would find a way to make sure they got it. She wasn't trying to win friends nor would she advertise her actions. In fact, she loved doing things for people in the background without them even knowing it. One of her favourite secret agent actions was when pulling up to a drive thru window at Tim Horton's coffee shop she would advise the cashier that she wanted to pay for the person that was two cars behind her. At first the cashier had thought it must have been because it was someone Takouhi knew. But when Takouhi did that often, and the cars behind her were different each and everytime, eventually the cashiers picked up on what she was up to. No explanations required. It brought a smile to their face which was matched with Takouhi's smile in rapport and the person who got a free bagel and coffee, well... something told her they had a productive day! It was the way in which she showed how she valued people. It was the way in which she showed she had rapport with them. That was her natural state whether in her family, at work, with friends, strangers and now with Arka.

Her plan was to go home take a hot shower and go to sleep. After all, Monday was just a sleep away. The pager went off as soon as she walked into the house at 9:00 p.m. Another deep-sea vessel had a propeller emergency in Mexico, which meant she had to organize crews and equipment. Funny, isn't that where Arka said he was? This time she sat behind the desk of her home office and began with the calls. By the time she finished calling the divers, the ship owners, and the airlines, it was 2:00 a.m. She was tired but felt inspired to write to Arka again.

*Dear Arka,*

*What's this? You signed off as brat? That's my nickname! Seriously, I've been given that nickname as I love to joke around and have fun with people in a positive way that is. From now on these are going to be considered B2B transmissions! Brat to Brat! Seriously I can't believe you're in Mexico as I just put a dive team together to go to Acapulco. Apparently a cruise ship has touched bottom! We think the captain was checking out the topless women on the beach and lost control.*

*How amazing it must be to receive treatments in Mexico. My father went all the way to Germany four years ago to get his third, yes third, back operation for an experimental treatment that wasn't offered in Canada. It worked!*

*I was thinking about what you wrote in regards to not losing my spirit. In May of 2001 I took off on a road trip by myself. I was completely frustrated with the people around me. I felt stuck between extremely traditional BS and protective upbringing and the so-called modern world. I had left a very dysfunctional marriage and felt very betrayed by my own tribe aka Armenians. I felt let down, I was depressed, I was sickened by the community and their backwards thinking about certain things. I felt that I was a bird in a cage and my spirit was just crushed, no creativity, no voice, no love for life. I was 50 lbs overweight. Migraines like you wouldn't believe! In fact at one point I was being sent from doctor to doctor with them thinking I had what you have. I left and I didn't tell a soul where I was going. Even I didn't know where I was going. My parents were freaking out as they had lost all control over me. I was cutting of the tribal umbilical cord. I needed to find me again. I had forgotten what I believed because I was told for so many years what I should believe and what I should be...I got on the ferry and drove to Victoria. I parked the car and went for a long walk by the water. There was an old Native Indian man drawing some sketches in a booth by the water. I was nervous walking around by myself and travelling by myself because as much as I always wanted to go and discover things on my own I was never allowed to do so. I kept to myself and didn't engage in conversation with anyone. Then the old man said, "Daughter can you come here for a minute?" He asked (and I kid you not) "Daughter, why are you so troubled? Don't you know who you are?" He continued "Don't you see you have the spirit in you? You are Pocahontas! That is the name for the playful and mischievous one," he said. I looked at him and asked, "How do you know this sir?" "You have the spirit of the wolf, you are a loyal leader to your tribe but they can not put a collar on you and control you for that is what is killing your spirit." Then he reached into his bag and took out this beautiful native choker made of red garnet, white engraved bone, and leather. "Pocahontas I give this to you so you remember that you control your destiny. Nobody can put a collar on you but you." Can you imagine how I felt? Tears were streaming down my cheeks. He wouldn't take any money from me at all. He said it would ruin the spirit in which he was giving the gift. The universe brought me to the old man, I decide how I process his words and determine my destiny. And that's what I've been trying to tell you...It's up to you and your thoughts. Don't engage in trivial everyday thinking as in bills, family issues and childish disagreements. Focus on the now! Cherish everything you have. Time is not to be wished away. In every moment there is a lesson. Do everything and anything you want now as much as you can. You're not walking a lonely road. We are all walking with you. Fate brought me to gate 22 where Asbed was sitting which set a chain of events in motion ultimately bringing a sister to a brother but now you decide how you process your sister's words in determining your next steps.*

*After I left the kind old man I found a place by the water and wrote this poem...*

Thought of as a princess in a protected world
Was a joy to be with yet they could not hold.
Left her tribe to find her way
Jaded and confused she ran away.
On her journey she did find
Those who were evil yet most were kind
She stood strong and tall and faced them all
For they weren't allowed to see her fall.
There were times where she could have caved
For the road less travelled was not paved
Although her heart was torn and tattered
Finding herself was all that mattered.
As she looked out to the ocean blue
At the bald eagles that soared and flew
Nature spoke to her from the morning dew
"Live a life of shero! Be authentic and true."

*Do something for me during your treatment these few weeks. Imagine the doctor's amazement after you have fully recovered from this little blimp on the radar. Picture the doctor saying 'it's a miracle again and again... and truly feel what that feels like! Make your body shiver with the energy you give yourself! Don't see yourself in light of your weaknesses, remember your strengths and push forward.*

*Your sis*

She would have to be in the office in four hours, but she felt energized, like she could run around the sea wall in Stanley Park twice. The energy she received internally feeling that potentially she may have made a difference for him propelled her more than any ships propeller could, no matter what the size. In the morning as per usual she sat behind her desk and right before the work started spinning around her she retrieved this email.

*Hi Sis,*

*This story was the most amazing story I heard not because of Pocahontas but because of the incredibly divine intervention you had during the most, perhaps, vulnerable time in your life to guide you in the directions you needed to find yourself. Yes, I do believe in destiny...for what it's worth, it makes us who we are. I hope you are doing well, take good care of yourself Pocahontas,*

*Ciao, be cool*

*Tvoi brat Arka*

Something amazing was happening. If she felt upset or overwhelmed with work all she had to do was think of Arka and her paradigm would shift. Arka put Takouhi's life in perspective. If she thought she was having a bad day she would think to herself 'Arka would give anything to be in your shoes right now. Get over yourself and move forward!' How could she complain of having any problems when he was the one in a hospital bed? And in spite of all that he was still emailing her. He was a fighter and she was in full battle armor with him.

A few days passed. Then she wrote him again.

*Dear Arka,*

*I've shut it down early tonight. I actually left the office at 5:00 p.m., can you believe it? And I'm so tired that I don't feel like doing anything except for talking to you. Today is a very hard day for me. In fact the next three days will be. Grandma died on the 23rd of this month last year. Three days from now. Last year today, she spoke for the last time to my brother and me. In fact right about now at 8:00 p.m.! We went to the hospital to see her. When she saw us, she said Mernem Boyeed; I'd die for you. Moments later she slipped into a coma and I watched her take her last breath. Have you ever witnessed that? It's the most amazing thing to see the spirit leave the body. It really is as beautiful as a birth. My point isn't to speak to you about her passing rather; I want to tell you about her. What a strong woman who loved to love. She loved to help, she loved to encourage and for whatever reason, she loved having her pictures taken.*

*I saw her pretty much everyday, my work is close to my parents' house and they all lived together under one roof. My parents had the upstairs two floors while my grandparents had their own private apartment downstairs. But the doors were always open and they always ate together. During the weekdays the routine was that at lunchtime I would go have Armenian coffee with my mom and grandmother and have my fortune or as I call it my daily hope-a-scope read. I called it the hope-a-scope because both her and my mother had this uncanny ability of reading me and my mood without knowing the details of what I was going through. They were extremely connected with me. And as such they would always give me encouragement and advice by way of pretending that they were reading my fortune. They acted as if it was the lines and shapes left by the coffee on the walls of the cup that were giving me advice. They were just the messengers, the translators if you will. Maybe they wanted some distance, just in case their advice would lead to something tough, I would blame the cup and not them. No matter what their intention, my beliefs transformed the tradition of fortune telling to hope-a-scope, where I listened to a pep talk or felt like I had my own personal cheerleaders for five minutes and then being sent back into the world! Seeing that I love cars so much I saw it as a racecar that pulls in for a pit stop, gets refueled, checked, and pushed back out into the race.*

*You know what I miss about her the most? Sunday afternoons were our special time together at her house for Encouragement 101 as I saw it. That day was different in that my brother and I would go to the grandparents' apartment from the outside door and not from the door upstairs at my parents.' We were seeing them exclusively. Grandmother would blitz the table with food as grandmas do and just talk about stuff. But at the end she would always say: "be humble and let others learn from you." She meant, lead by example and don't get lost in the crowds. Of course there were always other types of BS that she had shared that had frustrated me throughout the years but on my journey I was slowly realizing that one person does not have all the answers. I took from principles of family, closeness, giving, sharing, integrity, honesty, and leadership. I adjusted, or rather, I am still adjusting and transforming some of the more tribal and trivial BS of he said, she said and what will they say genre. She had so many sayings and she would recite poetry in a heartbeat. God knows how much I miss her.*

*In Aparan I was so envious of Asbed. I saw him sit with your grandmother and listen to her. I missed my grandmother so much at that moment that I wanted to capture the significance of my vision for him. I took as many pictures as I could from a distance. Then in Vegas you were mentioning how your grandma who lives in Los Angeles picks up the phone, calls you, says hello and goodbye and puts the phone down. An action by her that takes insignificant time yet makes a significant impact. So much so that you shared it with me! Grandmothers are another excellent source of inspiration and healing. By the stories you have shared about her it's clear to me that she loves you unconditionally. While she's around use it. Hang out with her. Sit next to her. Let her put her hand on you and feel the warmth. Did you see the picture of Asbed in Aparan with your grandmother? I'll attach it so you can see what I mean.*

*When I wrote the first letter to you (which feels like ages now but was only four months ago) I was torn. I'll be honest with you. I didn't know if I should send it, didn't know if I would upset you, didn't know if I would upset your wife or Asbed for that matter because I thought they might think who is this stranger giving advise. But in reality I was more concerned about upsetting you in any which way because that wasn't my intention in the least bit. So I spoke to grandma that night before I slept and I asked her for guidance. Not only did I dream of her that night but she was standing next to her oldest son who had also passed away recently. There was a beautiful ladybug on grandmother's hand. They didn't say a word to me. They just stood there and smiled. The ladybug is significant to me because anytime I look for guidance, a ladybug shows up in the unlikeliest of places. It has always been a sign that the power that is, is responding. So I sent you the letter the next day!*

A day later she received his response.

*Hello Takouhi,*

*So who are you? Whichever one it may be...Takouhi, Brat, Sis, Sistra, Pocahontas or the cyberspace cheerleader they all mean the girl with the big and caring, loving and sharing, compassionate and giving kind heart. Never let go of that cause that's what makes you who you are!*

*Brat, Arka*

*PS: I am sure your grandma is not missing any moment of your life and her guidance and ever-present soul is always with you.*

In the days to follow Takouhi spent as much time as she could on sending Arka emails of encouragement and stories that he could relate to during the trying times.

*Arka,*

*Did I ever show you this? I sent the actual magazine to Asbed for Christmas but not sure if he showed it to you or not. It's a short humorous story meant to inspire. I was pretty proud of it because it was published in my friend's magazine. I hope it puts a smile on your face.*

*Brat!*

*FROM DIAPERS TO DIVA*

"Many moons ago, when I was at the inquisitive age of four, I remember wanting to ride the carousel at an amusement park in Germany. My biggest dilemma at the time was whether I should choose the car, the plane, or the bike to ride. (Ride the horse on the carousel? What's that? Horsepower? Well, now you've got my attention!) So what do you think I chose? Many dilemmas have come and gone since those innocent days i.e. who do I marry: Mr. X or Mr. Y? (Hindsight speaking: You should have waited for Mr. Z!!)

But alas to a crucial dilemma… Ducati, BMW, Yamaha, Suzuki. The list is endless. So many bikes, so little time! I finally decided on the Ducati. Poor Baby, her first bike was a Ducati. How do you go on living? Yeah, yeah I know… but I saw her and I had to have her. Hey, what's another monthly payment right? The truth is at the time I didn't know the difference between the Ducati, Suzuki or Yamaha. My monster just looked the part. I didn't just want a cruiser or a crotch rocket as they call them. The monster was a bit of both.

Thus was born the Diva... DucatiDiva as I like to call her. I was going through many trials and tribulations. I don't know what I would have done had I not had my Monstro!!! My Diva became my best friend. We had countless number of solo soul-searching trips outside the city. She led me to the banks of the Fraser River where I laid back took out my scratch pad and doodled away. And there was Anderson Lake where she patiently waited as I grabbed a power snooze on a picnic table and woke up to half hour of stretching exercises… (I would have never imagined what my derriere would go through but it was worth it!) She led me to fellow Ducatisti… the big brothers who acknowledged her and treated her with respect. Of course we shmoozed with other bikes as well… this Diva is not a snob!!! It's amazing the number of interesting people you meet when you're on the road on a motorcycle. Don't misunderstand me… it's not to say that interesting people don't drive cars and trucks, but how many times do you see people in cars high fiving each other or passing each other with a cool peace sign. I'm yet to see a GMC driver giving the peace sign to a FORD driver… if anything it's usually the middle finger!! Where's the love people, where's the love!

So there you have it. I chose to ride the bike on the carousel that beautiful sunny day in Germany and many moons later I figured I'd do it again because I wanted to re-create that happiness I had back then. I succeeded! If there's one thing I learned during those two years is that you shouldn't measure yourself by what others think. Do what you want, whether it is going motorcycling, rock climbing, or starting your own business. There is truth and happiness out there and there is a meaning to life. The kicker is that there isn't one truth that applies to all. Everyone's individual truth is exactly that… individual! Life is meant to be fun and as long as you're not hurting anyone what's holding you back? If there is something that puts a smile on your face and brings you inner peace then go for it. You only live once… or do you???

Wow all this from two summers of the Ducati Diva. Imagine what a lifetime of riding will do??? Hmmmm…."

Takouhi didn't receive many emails from Arka and she assumed it was because he was undergoing heavy treatment. Yet it didn't stop her from reaching out. She thought even if he was too tired to respond he may have the opportunity to read.

*Dear Arka,*

*Think through this one with me brother...Do you ever talk to it? I mean the visitor that is in your body or specifically in your head. When you sit still and have moments to yourself with no wife, no Asbed, no mom, no dad, no in-laws, or outlaws. When it's just you and the universe, do you ever go inside your head and speak to the visitor and say: "Thank you for coming into my life and teaching me not to take things for granted. Thank you for making me slow down and appreciate all that is good and beautiful. Thank you for making me not drive like a maniac and get out of the car and scream and yell at people. Thank you for teaching others through me how precious life is." And when you're done thanking it tell it that its time is done. Tell it that the time has come for it to go. Confidently tell the visitor you have learned your lessons and so have all the people around you. You don't realize what a powerful force you are right now... I, Takouhi, believe in you, Arka! Be still, say thank you and let's move on!!!*

She received an email from Arka.

*Sistra,*

*I can't wait to see you again in March.*

*Tvoi Brat,*

*Arka*

Her mission was clear. The countdown began for March.

# 9

# CALIFORNIAN BOMBSHELLS

"Of course I'm going to drive the car down to LA. What a better place to drive a hard top convertible?" Takouhi's employer was trying to convince her to take a flight as he felt it was dangerous for her to drive solo especially in an eye catching car. But she wasn't listening. Going away in March was the perfect eye in the storm in terms of Takouhi's work schedule. At the end of February she would finalize the company's year-end paperwork and take care of all taxes. After that, the operations were left in the hands of her team for a week. To appease her employer, Takouhi asked Charents, her biological brother, to join her on the road trip. Sometimes she wondered if her employer really cared about her well being, or if he was worried that if something happened to her his company might be in trouble? After working with him for almost 17 years, she was still trying to figure that out.

Although she had been in the Los Angeles area last year for two days prior to flying to Vegas, this time it was different. Last year she was there for business. She did what she had to do and left without seeing any of her family. Takouhi had a huge family in the LA area. On her last count she had over thirty cousins. In fact, when she married, way back in '97, the family had decided that it would be best to hold the wedding in LA. She had not seen her family for over six years. It occurred to her that the last time she was there in 2001 was because of a cousin's wedding. That was a very difficult time for her as she was just going through divorce and all the family and tribal BS was coming at her from all directions. She had felt like a punching bag. She was confused and could not respond constructively to the comments that were coming at her. She chose to withdraw as opposed to challenge and fight. She simply wasn't sure what she was fighting for. Takouhi had been in the middle of organizing her belief systems. Keeping the ones that worked and took her towards values that were her core and tossing the ones that didn't apply. How could she argue for arguments' sake? It wasn't about her ego at all. In fact the more they spoke the more belief systems she put in her bag to organize later. Silly comments that were made by people who had nothing better to do but try to bring her down as opposed to help her up. They may or may not have meant to do it. It was probably their own belief system programming that they had never questioned. And there was something to be said when a group of them got together to reinforce their similar beliefs. Tyranny of the masses. It was part of who they were. It struck her that some of them had moved country to country thinking that by moving, they would eliminate the problems that they were experiencing with family and tribal members back home. What they didn't realize is that you can move anywhere in the world that you want but your belief systems come with you and thus you will create the exact same environment that wasn't working for you where you used to live. Change your belief system and change your life! Change your belief system without moving and the place that you have been living for generations becomes a new place you never knew existed. She did value the power of the tribe, of any tribe for that matter. Imagine if you could utilize that power for good to help build you up as opposed to tear you down. It made her think of the power of the mind and terrorism around the world. How people could be so manipulated with BS to do evil to other human beings of any culture and race. Now imagine if you could tap into that for the greater good. Admittedly she was leery of going back after six years but her main focus was seeing and talking with Arka and meeting his wife.

Takouhi's cousin's engagement was a great opportunity to go see the family in Los Angeles and her abers, slang in Armenian for brother. She had a tendency to place all her male friends under the umbrella of aber. Having had a challenging experience with marriage and the terrifying experience with the last man she dated, she had become very cautious with matters of the heart. She was aware that there was a fear in her and she too had somewhat of a security system. Perhaps not as intricate as the one she had noticed on Heros, but it was still there. She would remind herself that the past does not the future make. In doing so she worked on her belief system by way of observing others and reading books on empowerment and growth. By observing those around her who had healthy, compassionate, and giving relationships It was clear to her that just because she had two experiences that would blow away any Tarantino screenplay with its bizarre characters and behaviours, that it wasn't going to deter her resolve in finding her piece of the puzzle. Of course she did take full responsibility for her involvement in those two relationships knowing she had made the choice to be there given what she knew and believed in at the time. When she was ready it would happen. She was as certain about it as knowing how her bubble blowers would react if they didn't get paid on payday! Within the depths of her soul was a blueprint of a relationship that she had envisioned with a man that she would have her last first kiss with. A man with whom she could be her true self without reservations and choose to laugh, play, cry, give, and most importantly, to be still with. For the time being she was happy hanging around with her abers.

Takouhi and Charents left Vancouver on route to Los Angeles March 9, 2007. They had an amazing road trip together. Takouhi absolutely loved her brother. He was her best friend. They would always play fight, tease each other, criticize each other and you name it but it was all done in fun. They talked every day.

"What do you want?" she could see his frowning forehead while nodding his head upwards.

"Nothing! I just called to say hi." Luckily he couldn't see her devilish grin.

"Okay, what else?" Charents would always try to sound as aloof as possible to push her over the edge.

"Nothing, that's all I got!" trying to match his tone but it wasn't working.

"Okay, good talk!" and you could hear the laughter on both sides as they put the phone down.

Takouhi may have had many childhood male friends, many adopted brothers from work and now her new found entourage but Charents was above all of them. When they were younger she would sit on him and beat him up as they were playing. Nowadays prior to doling out a punch she would have to make sure she had planned the route of escape in advance. If she was caught she would helplessly pull out the 'How can you punch a girl' card to which he would reply 'a girl wouldn't have punched in the first place' and they would start laughing as they knew they were just using all these belief systems of what a girl and a boy do for fun. They were making fun of something that was held true for so many people of so many generations and tribes in the past and perhaps in the present. He knew in order to start a play fight after dinner time at their parents place all he had to do was make comments like 'ok we've eaten, now do your womanly duties and clear the table like the good daughter that you are!' That was a sign for Takouhi that it was time to play. Being the brat she was each and every time she would do something different. Once she cleared the table except for his stuff. Other times she would just respond "I've been a good daughter for so many years it's your turn to show what a good son you are" and that would make him go for a spin. What they were doing was showing their parents the belief systems that they had been raised with. They were putting on a comedy skit. In fact they had always performed plays when they were younger. Now it was an adult version of BS 101 in lively and funny conversations.

One day the topic of homosexuality came up as they were sitting around watching the news after Sunday dinner. The news was covering a story on Gay marriage rights. Takouhi and Charents had never had occasion to discuss the topic. It hadn't come across their path within their family or friends for them to think about it or formulate their own BS. But they both knew that the tribe had certain beliefs and they wanted to test their father. Charents decided to play a game with their father.

"Dad, I think I'm gay!" Takouhi's eyes popped open so much that she felt her eyelids were barely holding her eyeballs in place. 'Oh my God! Charents is going to give dad a heart attack she thought!

"I don't care; it's your butt not mine," sounded the eloquent foreign accent as he casually walked by them in the hallway. Surely, he must have had a bratty smile and a twinkle in his eye as he walked on by.

Takouhi and Charents stood motionless in the middle of the hallway staring at each other with their mouths wide open. They couldn't believe how quickly and naturally he came back with that answer. They had no idea he was going to react like that. In fact they assumed the opposite that he would get huffy and puffy and start saying anything negative that he could think of. Brother and sister started laughing uncontrollably with tears rolling down their eyes. They hadn't considered that it might not matter to their father. Now it could have been that he was so sure that his son was not gay that he came up with that quick and witty response. But Takouhi wondered if her father really felt that way and somewhere along the line he had challenged his own tribal beliefs.

It took them 24 hours to reach their destination. They had taken turns driving and were exhausted. Although they had traveled together they both had their own agenda for the week ahead. They decided to do something crazy that was never done in all the times they had visited family in Los Angeles. For the first time they were going to check into a hotel and not play house with family. What that meant was in the past they were going from house to house visiting everyone and out of respect they had to stay at family's houses overnight. It wasn't that they were unappreciative of the love and hospitality. It was just that each and every time they would leave LA somebody would be upset because they had not had an opportunity to visit or stay with them. The other aspect was that if you stayed with family they would interrogate you with the five Ws just like reporters, who, what, when, where, and why. They always felt that they were under interrogation. It wasn't that they had an issue with answering questions as they realized that they had been away for so long and family wanted to catch up. At least that was the positive spin that Takouhi would like to put on it. What made it difficult was when they had to go from house to house and be asked the same questions and respond to the same answers over and over again. Takouhi knew after being in hiatus for six years that was going to be six years times five Ws times at God knows how many houses! She never really liked calculus and this was one equation she really didn't have much time for this time. She was mission oriented on this trip and did not have the resources to be at different fronts. There was no time for the Blitzkrieg method. She knew that she would see at least one chunk of the family at the engagement party and that was good enough for this trip. It wasn't an obligation as she had decided to be there by choice. She loved them so much that she had decided to be part of the celebration but she also knew that her energies were needed elsewhere. Takouhi called the boys as soon as they had settled at the hotel. It was decided that they would pick her up the next day and take her for lunch.

The next day from her room window she saw that the boys were pulling into the hotel's driveway. She swore that the elevator in the hotel was purposely slow out of spite, just to tease her. When the doorman didn't open the door fast enough, Takouhi became one with the glass. Luckily her strong Armenian forehead, like the finest sapphire glass found on a luxury Swiss watch, was intact. She ran from the hotel door straight into the car door. If in the past she was driving fast and changing lanes by way of speech due to her nervousness now she was simply a John Deer Bulldozer destroying everything in her path in order to get to her destination. She opened the car door and jumped in the backseat. She sat back for a moment and put her left hand on her forehead as she just felt the pain. She opened her eyes to see the two seated in the front and the one to her left staring at her. They all had the same expression with large eyes and wide-open mouths. She closed her eyes and she knew that the colour of her face now matched the colour of her burgundy boots and started to laugh. They all turned around and started laughing uncontrollably. She was with her abers again! Vrej was driving, Arka was in the front, and Asbed and Takouhi had the backseat. She tried to give them all a kiss on both cheeks, the customary greeting for her tribe, but it didn't happen as her forehead was hurting and the car started to move. It was surreal to her again as a few months back the three of them were in the back of a car in the valleys of Armenia, then they were on a ski life in Whistler and here they were smack in the middle of Glendale. They decided to drive to the neighbouring city of Pasadena to a very nice Italian restaurant. Just as they parked the car Asbed turned to Takouhi and said.

"This is for you."

"What's this?" Asbed handed her a large envelope that he had on his lap.

"I wanted to get you something unique like your gift to me" he sounded so unsure of himself like a man about to propose to a woman not sure of the answer.

She pulled out a hand drawn black and white picture of a kettle on very fine paper.

"Did you draw this?" she asking holding the picture as if it were the Dead Sea Scrolls.

"Yeah, I wanted to put it in a frame but Vrej said you're leaving tomorrow!"

"I am? No, I'm leaving in six days."

"Oh then here I'll take it back and give it back to you properly."

He took the picture away from her, jumped out of the car, and went to the trunk to gently place the picture down. If she didn't know better, she'd say he was driving fast and changing lanes too.

As she stepped out of the car Arka quickly approached her and said, "Thanks for the customary kiss in the car but I want to give you a hug for being such an amazing sister." Takouhi was not accustomed to her male comrades showing such affection, once again her boots and her face matched in colour. It was the first time she was seeing Arka since Vegas and since having written the letter and all the emails that had come back and forth in that period. Takouhi had forgotten about them. It was her style. She would write and send it off but never think about what she had done until someone reminded her.

The four of them sat down at the restaurant and they started with small talk. She wouldn't have it. She went right to Arka and asked him to speak about the treatments in Mexico. In her emails she hadn't asked details but she wanted to know. He wasn't expecting her to be so forward. He sat back in his seat, his body tensed up and shook his head for moment as if to regroup. It reminded Takouhi of the moment in Vegas where she had mentioned his wife and there had been silence as he was trying to figure out how she knew that he was married. Asbed and Vrej had been looking directly at her leaning forward in their seats as if she had done something wrong and upset him. It occurred to her that she was getting straight to the nucleus of the atom. She was solution focused. Takouhi needed to know what's on the table, what do we have to work with and what do we need to get to fix this. When he did answer with a giant smile that she had grown accustomed to seeing in Vegas the other two boys sat back in their seats and tilted their heads back as if a crisis had been averted. In her eyes, whatever had taken place in Mexico was successful. He seemed energetic and the limp wasn't there anymore. One thing was bugging her however. She wondered where his wife was. She was really looking forward to meeting her. The lunch was short as they, including Takouhi, had family obligations. That evening Takouhi received a call from Vrej.

"So what did you think of Arka today? He looks good huh?"

"Yeah I was amazed! That's some treatment he must have had in Mexico!"

"I had no idea that you had been keeping in touch with him during the last few months via email. And he mentioned something to me about a letter?"

"It's not a big deal. The letter and emails have been my way of encouraging him that he can beat this thing. I had such a great conversation with him in Vegas and I truly feel that he is a wonderful person so whatever I can do I will do!"

"You have no idea how perfect your timing has been with all this," Takouhi heard such a huge sigh on the other end of the phone that it made her sit up from the comfortable lounge chair she was curled up on.

"Are you speaking about how we met in Armenia and that we're all friends?" but she knew that wasn't it.

"Well yeah, I guess that's part of it but I am referring to the timing of you reaching out to him with your letter and emails."

"Well I figured that being in a hospital and getting treatment is not a fun place so you would need a special boost. Even though I'm sure his wife and family were there as support but I figured the more positivity the better" she wanted to sit back in the lounge chair but her gut wouldn't let her.

"But that's what I'm talking about the timing of it all"

"Vrej now you're speaking in riddles. Just get it off your chest already. Say it! You never seem to be at a loss for words so why now. Just tell me what it is you really want to say!" now she was pacing the room.

"She left him!"

"Who left whom?" she caught her reflection in the hotel room vanity mirror.

"Arka's wife left him before he went for his treatments in Mexico!" he said it slowly word by word so it would register for her.

"*What?*"

'So that's what I look like when I am shocked' she thought to herself. Looking in the mirror she saw her jaw dropped and she could see all the way to her tonsils. Her body leaned forward like a tower that was being brought down with dynamite and she barely grabbed the chair in front of her otherwise she would have hit the floor. Takouhi clenched the chair and stood motionless. She was in a state of shock. There was silence over the phone.

"Hello? Hello? Are you there?"

"Yeah," she barely mumbled and was trying hard to swallow back tears.

"Listen, don't tell him I told you. Let him tell you himself" he said "Asbed and I think she had someone on the side but Arka says she's not the type" Takouhi was sure that NASA's satellites would have been able to pick up on his sarcasm frequency.

"You mean all this time I was sending him email he was alone?" Takouhi slowly made her way back to the lounge chair but crouched forward as if someone had just hit her in the stomach.

"Well he wasn't alone, we were with him and his mother stayed with him," he said.

"No, what I mean by alone is that his wife wasn't with him?"

"That's what I'm trying to tell you. Your timing couldn't have been more perfect!"

Vrej did the rest of the talking. All Takouhi could muster was aha, sure, yeah, and okay. Her mental data bank had received an electrical short similar to the blank blue screen she was accustomed to seeing at work when her computer crashed. The BSOD is what the computer tech had called it The 'Blue Screen Of Death' she wondered if she were to look in the mirror right now she would be smurfette!

They made arrangements that they were all going to meet again the next day and she finally put the phone down. Takouhi threw the phone on the bed in disgust. Who would leave someone in that state? Takouhi realized that she didn't know Arka that well. And having been married in the past she realized that one should not pass judgment on another because sometimes you can't force the wrong pieces of the puzzle to fit together. That being said, the humanity aspect should have kicked in, regardless. As a human being, his wife should have helped him in whichever way possible. As soon as she finished that thought she countered her belief system with what if she knew she wasn't strong enough and she would actually hurt him by being in his sphere of influence. Takouhi was thinking if the wife was a negative person then maybe she had realized that for his greater good it was better for her to leave. But one thing really threw all these thoughts out the window and that was if she had left because she had an affair while her husband was struggling with this then, well, she was the ugliest person, who she never wanted to meet in person. She tossed and turned that night. "God please don't let me find out she's had an affair! God please don't let me find out she's had an affair," she kept repeating.

Meeting the next day was difficult. She had info that she wasn't supposed to have and she was to pretend that she didn't know. This time there was a group of them again with a few new personalities. They all made small talk and chatted about where she was from and how they as in Asbed, Vrej and her had met and what an interesting story that was. They all started to scatter and the only three that remained were Arka, Vrej and Takouhi. Vrej and Arka dropped her at her hotel again.

"So what's everyone's schedule for the next five days? Will I see you guys again?"

"Well, I'm busy at the bank. I also have a business trip to go to so I'm not sure," replied Vrej.

"What about you Arka jan? What are your plans this week?"

He grabbed his cell phone organizer and said: "Well let's see. I'm available Monday, Tuesday, Wednesday, Thursday, and Friday!" and they all started laughing.

"Okay, I think my brother doesn't need my car for the next few days. So if time permits I will call you and we can meet somewhere!"

"Are you okay with driving? I can't drive with this patch on my eye!"

"No problem. I'll pick you up if you want," she blew them a kiss and got out of the car. She decided to walk up twelve flights of stairs, as she still had not been able to process the energy cells that were anger. She hadn't slept as a result of the tossing and turning but felt she had energy enough to do some kickboxing. She walked around for two hours. When she couldn't muster up any energy and exhausted all her fuel cells, she made it back to the hotel room. After a hot shower and hitting the pillow in her bed with the same force as a crash test dummy hits the airbag, all she remembered thinking before drifting off into a deep dreamless sleep was, 'Arka, tomorrow we're going to have a serious conversation!'

# 10

# SIR MARCUS AND JOURNAL

Prior to driving down to LA, Takouhi had wondered what else she could do to positively influence Arka. She truly believed that anchoring a positive idea in something that can be touched and seen makes a great difference. She had a little teddy bear that she loved. She asked her mom to put a little leather patch on its eye so it would look like Arka. Her mom wasn't sure what she was up to or if this person Arka would appreciate the gesture. What if he was offended? Takouhi had already crossed that bridge. The chance was far greater that she would do good than harm. The risk would be worth it. She had also picked up a few inspirational books that she wanted to give to Arka as well as a journal. Takouhi loved journals so she thought maybe Arka would appreciate it too. Her initial plans had included his wife. Takouhi had envisioned that at some point they would have gathered together and she would have shared with both of them these tools that she had gathered for him and explain how each and every item may have helped lessen the adversity during the difficult times. Knowing what she knew now thanks to Vrej about Arka's wife, she could not deny the power of the forces that were bringing all this together.

The night before she had fallen asleep with the thought 'Arka, tomorrow we're going to have a serious conversation!' and now the moment was about to present itself. Arka had called Takouhi and they had planned how and when she was to meet him. She was given telephone instructions on where to pick him up. She was in Glendale and had to drive towards Van Nuys. In all the times she had visited the LA area, she had only gone to Glendale and Pasadena. Van Nuys was new territory for her. Takouhi had no idea where she was picking him up from. She arrived at her destination and sent a text message indicating that she was downstairs. She observed the gate of the apartment complex open and out came the soccer player. His style could be described as European chic. He had a nice pair of jeans with a white shirt, a black velvet sport jacket, and blue suede shoes. He walked normally. The only reminder of the cancer was the patch on his eye. He was smiling as he approached and sat in the car.

He had decided that they were going to go to this very cozy coffee house in the Burbank area. In all the small talk that was taking place on route to the coffee house, Takouhi did not mention his wife. They arrived at the coffee house and she went to reserve a seat as it was very crowded. It was a popular place; whoever wanted to be seen went there. He brought their teas and one dessert to share between them. Arka's condition did not allow for him to have sweets but he suggested that it was a special occasion and he couldn't resist the carrot cake. Within moments of sitting down the floodgates opened just as they had in Vegas five months prior.

"So guess what?" he said with a smile.

"What?" she had to pretend that she didn't know what was coming.

"I'm divorced!" he said.

"What do you mean?" she said knowing quite well that she didn't sound surprised, as she should have.

"Yeah, she left before I went to Mexico!" he said.

"Why? What happened? Didn't you guys get along?" she asked.

"She tried to use excuses for leaving. Believe it or not, she even brought you in the picture," he said.

"Me?" Takouhi dropped the fork with the carrot cake. Now that was a genuine surprised reaction, as Takouhi didn't see that one coming.

"Yeah! She found out that there was a girl in Vegas with the group of us, and then you sent me the letter so she was trying to use it as an excuse to leave. But then when she read the letter and realized what it was about and that you had even mentioned "her love for me" in it she knew she couldn't make you the escape goat!" he said laughing.

Takouhi went back for a minute to all the thoughts she had had prior to sending that letter. She referred back to all the energy she had put in making sure that the wife would not have felt threatened by her letter. However, she did also refer back to her thoughts of what the wife may have thought about her being in Vegas with a group of guys. To Takouhi that was the norm. She was always traveling with her abers. In fact she had been in Vegas in April last year with her Vancouver abers prior to going to Armenia in August. When she was in her teens her father would only let her go out if there was a group of abers with her as her bodyguards. These boys were children of her father's friends. They knew that Takouhi was off limits. It had been very frustrating for her growing up with the abers. They would go clubbing and the boys would go gallivanting doing their own thing. Takouhi would be dancing the night away usually by herself. As soon as a non-Armenian boy approached her, the tribal members would appear out of nowhere. It would happen so fast that it would make her head spin. She didn't know if it was tribal protectionism taking place or if they were scared of the wrath of her father!

"So what happened once she took me off the hit list?" she asked.

"Well she said that she was depressed and that this wasn't what she had signed up for," he said without expression as he wanted to see how Takouhi would react.

"Hmm" she was nodding and savoring her carrot cake.

"That's all you have to say?" he asked surprised.

"Well, are you the same person that had a great conversation with me in Vegas five months ago? Are you the same person that was quoting the same philosophers as I was?" she calmly picked up her tea and took a sip. He could only see her big brown eyes peering at him from behind her cup.

"Yeah but what does that have to do with anything?" he asked and leaned back in his chair.

"There are two schools of thought here." She put her cup down, leaned forward and folded her arms on the table. "I can either say what a 'you know what' she is or I can say everything happens for a reason. Which one will move you forward and beyond the negative in your opinion?" she leaned back in her chair mirroring his physical posture and continued "The tribal trap and BS that does not serve us is the first thought. I am sure most people around you are now picking sides. They are calling her names and putting her down and by doing so they think they are making you feel better. And I ask you? Does it make you feel better?"

"You're right, that's what they're doing and it's not making me feel better so I keep telling them to stop when they're talking about her around me."

"Tell me why you tell them not to bad mouth her in front of you" she asked with a smile because she already knew what he was going to say.

"Well because it's not serving me right now. I don't have the energy to give to that situation. I tried my best to reach her. We even went to New York at Christmas time because I wanted to cheer her up. But it didn't work. I guess she didn't believe that I was going to get better and she wanted to have kids. My sickness didn't fit in with her plan. As cold as it sounds she was honest in that it wasn't what she had planned for. I guess it wasn't about love it was about her vision of how life should be. It was fine when I had the potential for making money and being a lawyer because as you know in our tribe for whatever reason they see that as some kind of status! So she was the wife of a lawyer!" he stopped and looked at the ground took a deep breath and looked at the woman who couldn't get enough of the carrot cake "That's another thing I don't understand. What is the big deal about being a lawyer? All of a sudden people are treating me in a weird way. It's just my job."

Takouhi couldn't believe what she was hearing. Sitting across the table from her was exactly what she had described in her monologue to Vrej in Vegas. The crazy thing was that yes Arka was a lawyer but he was also compassionate, caring, spiritual, open minded and so much more, which made him an incredible human being.

"You know what makes this even crazier Takouhi?"

"What's that?

"I told her she can have whatever she wanted because material things don't matter to me in the least bit," he said, "and she took everything. She even took expensive cognac that was given to us at our wedding. But I laughed when I saw what she didn't take."

"What was that?" at this point Takouhi was really curious to what he was going to say and leaned into the table so she wouldn't miss it.

"She didn't take any books. You know what that meant? It meant that had I had kids with her they would never have opened a book to read anything. They would just be out shopping like their mom and covering themselves with brand-name clothes to make themselves feel important!" he said with a bratty smile.

"Did saying that make you feel better Arka?" she said laughing.

"Yeah, a little!" he said as he joined her laughter.

Takouhi thought what a great moment to give him the journal.

"Arka do you write in journals?" she asked.

"Not usually. I am always concerned that someone may find something I wrote and read it."

"What's wrong with that?" she admitted to herself that it was something that had crossed her mind as well. However, the creativity and imagination that resulted from her writing directly influenced her state of mind and allowed her to view the world from different paradigms. That in itself far outweighed any criticism anyone could have given her.

"They are my private thoughts. I know you wouldn't know it by the way you and I have talked about so many things in the short times we have spent together but I'm a very private person."

"Yeah but surely the benefit you get from writing down your feelings must outweigh the negative connotation you have given it" Takouhi was trying to present a very lawyer like argument.

"What do you mean by that?" Arka was intrigued by her approach as he pulled his chair a bit closer to the table.

"When you write in a journal you release a lot of tension. And when you re-read what you have written it actually helps you put things in perspective. I always keep journals. Not necessarily day-to-day but when a thought comes to mind I want to write it down. It helps me keep my belief systems in check. I love looking back at journals I have written even five years ago or two years ago. It reminds me of the fact that belief systems are constantly evolving as we are evolving. What I held to be necessarily true back then and made decisions based on doesn't apply today. My values are the same but the BS is different. " She brought her chair in close as well and mirrored him. Was he buying what she was selling?

"Aren't you concerned that someone may read them and get into your head? What if you're criticized or judged for it," he asked.

"He who hath no sins let them cast the first stone. What I mean by that is who is going to tell me my thoughts are wrong when a) they apply to me and b) I mean no harm it's for my evolution and enlightenment. Is there anyone on this planet that can say their way is the only way?" she leaned back in her chair and her mischievous eyes rolled to the right.

"Now if I were to write in my journal step by step ways in which I want to kill someone that's a different story" and they both started laughing.

"With that in mind" she continued "this is for you!" and she reached into her bag and pulled out a beautiful journal with an antique old world map cover. He didn't say anything. He just sat there motionless looking at the journal that she had placed in front of him on the table. Why was it that every time they were together having coffee there was nobody else around them? Wasn't this coffee shop full a moment ago?

"You don't like it?"

"No I love it!" he said and looked up and smiled.

"Will you try to write in it even if you think someone will read it?"

"I'll try but I can't promise you anything."

"It's not about me. You don't have to promise me anything. It's for you and your thoughts. Write about your belief systems. Think of things that are motivating factors for you right now. Think of the life you want to live as opposed to worrying about our cultural and tribal norms. Focus on where you want to go, not where you were. Remember what I wrote to you in my letter in regards to focus and the motorcycle analogy. Whatever you focus on you will give energy to it so focus on a positive outcome and put all your energy towards that. Think about all the emails and conversations we have had thus far and write about what you think is BS. And by BS I mean Belief Systems not the other connotation!" and they both started laughing again!

After a few more sips of tea they decided it was time to end the evening. As they walked towards the car she went to the trunk and took out the bear.

"This is for you" she said and gave the teddy bear with a patch on one eye to Arka.

"What's this?" he said startled and lost his balance.

"Well, you've heard of a voodoo doll right?" she said with a smirk on her face.

"Yeah" his hand was covering his mouth and he was moving around as if he was dancing.

"Well, think of this as a 'Can Do' doll!' she said with a smile.

"Are you serious? Did you buy the bear with the patch or did you made it?" He was still dancing.

"The idea to put a patch on the eye was mine but my mom made the actual patch" she said "I figured he would be a great friend to have to remind you that you will overcome everything and anything that comes your way! And you know what I've named him?"

"What's that?" he said just glowing with smiles.

"His name is Sir Marcus Aurelius" she laughed as she animated the bear and placed it on Arka's shoulders.

"You're nuts!" he said laughing "But I tell you what. Why don't you take him with you as you are going to be driving back home by yourself. Let him keep you company!"

Takouhi was a bit confused. He seemed to have liked the bear but didn't want to take it home with him. She didn't argue. Marcus went back in the car.

On their way home Arka received a call from Asbed. He was checking on him to see where he was and what he's doing. When Asbed found out that Arka was with Takouhi he told him to pass the phone to her.

"What are your plans for tomorrow?" Asbed seemed rushed

"Where are you?" she could barely hear him.

"I'm going to Vegas but I'll be back tomorrow. The three of us we'll go out ok?"

"Sure. Either call me or Arka and we'll organize it!"

The way everything was continually falling into place effortlessly reminded her of how the beautifully engineered parts on her sports car came together in unison and created something bigger than the individual parts. She needed to have a conversation with Asbed and tomorrow was less than 24 hours away.

# 11

# RELATIONSHIP BS

The following afternoon, Arka and Asbed picked up their kuro from the hotel and they went out for the day. Asbed was driving with Arka in the front passenger seat. As she looked at the interaction between the two brothers she was reminded of her relationship with Charents. She felt right at home in the car as if she was watching a scene from her house in Vancouver. The way in which they spoke to each other with humour and laughter made her miss her brother, even though he was somewhere in the same city. At one point they pulled over at a corner store and Arka got out of the car pulled out a bunch of lottery tickets and decided he was going to go inside to check them and collect his millions. Asbed and Takouhi waited for him in the car.

"I can't believe she left him" Takouhi leaned forward from the backseat as if to speak in his ear.

"Why can't you believe that? This is LA," he didn't move a muscle. She was so close that if he had turned to the right his nose would have hit her chin.

"It's not right no matter how much I try to encourage him to look beyond it. Mind you, he doesn't need much encouragement because he is focused on himself, which is great but..." she sighed and threw herself back into the backseat.

"But what?"

"I just can't figure out what kind of a person would leave someone in this situation. I can't figure it out. I say to myself everything happens for a reason and he's better off this way, but the cruelty and lack of humanity just hurts me as an outsider let alone him."

"You know divorce is hard to begin with when you're healthy but when you are faced with what he's got, I just can't imagine how he really feels inside. He seems to have things under control but I wish I knew how he is translating the world around him with his thoughts and belief systems."

"Well, within our circle of friends some of which you have already met, we think that he actually may have a chance to heal himself now without having to deal with the BS of her and her family. And just to clarify, I don't mean BS as in belief systems you keep talking about," he turned around from the front seat to look directly at her, winked and they started laughing. Arka returned to the car with new tickets and new hopes.

Shortly thereafter, the three family members went to a coffee house. Her two abers had brought her to Burbank. What she loved about southern California was the abundance of sunshine and the ability to sit outside most of the year. Their winter was Vancouver's summer. They found a table underneath a palm tree and sat down. She could tell that Arka was not feeling well by the way in which he grabbed the chair to sit down. He put his entire weight on his arm to support himself as if he was going to fall. He was pale and seemed tired. He finally leaned back in his chair, tilted his head towards the California sky and closed his eyes as Asbed and Takouhi carried on with the conversation.

"So you have an Iranian girlfriend" Takouhi looked directly to Asbed with a smirk on her face.

Asbed's coffee cup stopped in mid air before reaching his lips. He put the cup back on the table, looked to the ground.

"Yeah, I do!"

"Hum" she leaned back in her chair nodding her head like a wise elder who had been enlightened having discovered the meaning to life!

"Who told you?" He looked to her from the corner of one eye without raising his head from the ground. The grin on his face was equal to a bumper sticker that read 'Busted! How did you find out?'

"Nobody did, I just figured it out," she said with a smile. "Something about you listening to Iranian pop songs in the car. Armenians from Armenia don't usually listen to Iranian music. Generally speaking of course. However if you were an Armenian from Iran then I wouldn't have even thought twice about it. And also I've heard you have conversations with others about how in the past Armenian Kings married Iranian Queens or vice versa as if you wanted to justify it somehow."

"Does it matter?" He lifted his head, looked directly at her and was ready to present his case.

"Depends on who you ask."

"What do you mean?"

"Well, depending on who you ask you are going to get a different response or reaction based on the belief system that they hold as their truth."

"What belief systems apply to this case?" he asked.

"You're kidding me right? Well, let me tell you what the majority of our tribe may say about you dating a non-Armenian. First they will say that you're going outside the tribe thus turning your back on your own kind. Then they will say your religions are completely different. You have a Christian upbringing and your girlfriend is Muslim."

"So what that I am going outside my tribe? Look at you two." Asbed's arms became animated as he pointed to both Takouhi and Arka. The energy waves carrying the passion in his voice must have been absorbed by Arka's system refueling him to be able to pop his eyes wide open.

"You both married Armenians and look where it got you."

"Yes, I can see how you would use that to prove your case." Takouhi replied.

"Not to mention the fact that how are we Christian or in her case Muslim when we don't even practice it or go to church." Takouhi worried that the passion in Asbed's voice might turn on the security alarms on nearby parked cars.

"Listen, you are getting defensive. I am not telling you how it is. I am sharing with you what the potential BS out there is. But to counter your points one might give you the following argument. In regards to practicing our religions I understand what you're saying but realize even if you don't go to church or mosque two people are merging from two different worlds and with it their own BS. Remember Armenia's church and state were once as one. Laws and customs were based on religion. The do's and dont's of society were based on the Bible whether you stepped foot in church or not whether you realized it or not. The same applies with the Muslim world. Their laws and traditions are based on the Koran. There's no right or wrong I'm just sharing with you a possible response."

"It's not impossible to be with someone of another religion" said Arka leaning forward and joining in the conversation.

"I never said it was" Takouhi replied and looked towards Arka noticing that he didn't look pale anymore. 'The Californian sun is doing it's magic' she thought.

"I think what Takouhi is trying to say is marriage is difficult and there can be many challenges so if you come with the background of the same BS then it may be easier," Arka was acting as translator for Takouhi to Asbed.

"Exactly! That being said you are right that my marriage failed and so did Arka's. But that is not to say that there is no Armenian out there that will complement our piece of the puzzle. Or for that matter anyone from any other race or religion. The reason our marriages didn't work out wasn't due to us marrying within our tribe. It was due to us not being compatible with the person we had chosen. There is nothing wrong with you dating whomever it is you're dating right now. You just have to make sure that you are both on the same page and united about the main things in life. There is no reason you cannot have children that will benefit from your culture's history and hers. The most important thing is to know each other well, admire each other, love each other, respect each other, and be a team. We are saying focus on what brings and keeps people together, which is love. Tribal dogma will always try to separate and keep us apart. So the bottom-line, my dear Asbed, it's not about your girlfriend's religious or cultural background it's about the values and principles you have in common. Spirituality isn't just about churches, mosques or temples. Spirituality ties into humanity and the ability to respect every human being on this planet—including the person you are building a home with."

"So to make a long story short," interrupted Arka "Do whatever you want to do. Just make sure you are focused on whether you and the girl are compatible and don't focus on the tribal he said she said. You don't need to justify anything to anyone. Just make sure you can sleep in the bed you're making!"

"Whenever we get together we have these in-depth conversations!" said Takouhi as they all laughed. She leaned back in her chair and took a sip of her cold coffee. The two brothers had the most amazing genuine smiles. They should have made money advertising for toothpaste commercials.

"So tell me what you want in a relationship Takouhi," asked Asbed.

"Oh man, now you've done it!" said Arka laughing.

"I want a man who knows what he wants and what he wants is me!" and they all started laughing.

"Seeing that you asked," she said showing her own toothpaste commercial smile "let me tell you a thing or two about relationships. As you know I have many brothers at work and after hours. There have been many times I have been their advisor regarding relationships. Of course this is a double edged sword in that I give insight that works and inspires them but before doing so I end up being the representative of all women by hearing things like 'Why are you women like this?" They all started laughing.

"Some of my brothers have been known to play the field. They managed to have a few relationships going at the same time. I used to tell them that the reason they had two at a time or that in spite of being in one they were still wondering if relationships were right for them… it wasn't because they weren't meant to be in a relationship it was because they hadn't found their hearts' home yet. And yes, of course things change when you're in a relationship but in the right one you welcome the change.

"Ah you're being naïve, some guys just cheat!" replied Arka.

"That may be but I'm not talking about them!" Takouhi replied.

"Anyway, cheating doesn't mean you don't like the person you're with," Asbed jumped in with his in-depth analysis.

"Oh no, don't get me started!" Takouhi shook her head and rolled her eyes at Asbed with dismay.

"You mean more than you already have" Arka was trying to lighten the mood with his comment. It worked as they started to laugh.

"It's a guy thing versus a girl thing" said Arka "When guys cheat it's because they can't help it; it's their biological need but when a girl cheats it's emotional. It's because the person they are with isn't giving them the attention they need."

"Oh my God! Is this really your belief system? So it's okay that guys cheat even if they are in relationships because it doesn't mean anything? Or is this just an excuse for a guy to use to gallivant through town? I don't need to know if either of you truly believe this BS or have acted on it but let me tell you this. First of all, I know many women who just as easily cheat as men cheat. Not because they are lacking emotional attention but for the thrill of it just like men. Second of all, if you are in a relationship and think it's no big deal that you are swimming in the pool then you are not only hurting the person you are with but also you are ultimately shortchanging and hurting yourself. You are missing out on the true essence of what a real relationship is. We are meant to be in relationships. As individuals we are supposed to be strong, self-reliant, independent yet when we join someone who shares our values and has similar goals, we become stronger and can reach greater results faster than if we were by ourselves. A healthy relationship pushes us beyond ourselves. Now keep in mind, this only works with the right piece of the puzzle. You can't become bigger or better than what you are if you're with a person that is not compatible with you. Nobody teaches this to us in school... there aren't classes on compassion, humility, spirituality, how to love, how to give, how to compromise…and it's not an easy subject to talk about with brothers, sisters, mothers, or fathers. I don't have all the answers but I know what I want. Since you asked I'm sharing it with you to help you figure it out. And yet something tells me you already know this. Decide exactly who it is you want." She stopped for a moment, took a deep breath and looked at the two boys who were leaning forward in their chairs and listening to her every word as if she was giving them the combination to the Federal Reserve's Vault. She continued, "What I mean is decide the top five characteristics you want in your partner. Things that will make your heart melt each and every time you see her. Asbed remember what you said to me in January when you were in Vancouver about the qualities you wanted in a woman? I believe you said you wanted someone who's got a big heart. Add to the list as much as you can. Do you want someone who is strong and independent? Do you want someone who lights up the room when she walks in, that no matter who she is speaking to in a gathering you look at her with awe? The list is yours to fill. Decide what you want and I guarantee you she will come to you assuming of course she's not already with you as in your case Asbed. One of my favourite authors Stephen Covey says "Begin with the end in mind" in this context I believe what that means is that if you don't envision exactly what it is that you want you are going to be jumping from branch to branch and are going to be at the mercy of one woman to another. Eventually you will become disillusioned in terms of what a relationship is. Once you have decided who will stand beside you, it is in your best interest to give it your all, without any reservations. If you can do this with a woman no matter what tribe you are from then you are a lucky man. But many of us don't bother getting to the heart of the matter and discussing what values and principles we hold in common in order to build a future together. Love isn't just about looking into each other's eyes and sex. Love is about intimacy of thoughts, values, principles and beliefs between two people where nobody can intervene. Love is looking down the road in the same direction of the 'High' way. The higher way!"

"You mean it's the 'high' way and no longer Myyyy Waayyyyy?" Asbed sang and winked at Takouhi instantly transporting her to the scene of the Taxi on route to Aparan in August where they were arguing which Frank Sinatra song was best. She could not stop laughing. Arka's laughter was not as loud as the other two in that he didn't know the history behind Asbed's remark but their laughter was contagious.

"This perfect relationship does not exist Takouhi, you are way out there! You're being naive" Asbed said, "there is nobody I know that is in a happy relationship. People get married or are in relationships because they figure it's time and that's what their respective cultures tells them to do."

"How is knowing what you want, envisioning it and bringing it to life being naïve. Or are you better off not trying and just settling as opposed to thinking you're going to try and then fail. Remember if you do not go after what you want then you have failed. You may not have seen a perfect relationship because you are possibly in a circle of friends that shares the same belief systems that it doesn't exist. How do you expect a different result when you have circled yourself with people with the same BS? How do you expect different results when you continue acting the same way day after day?"

"So why aren't you in this perfect relationship?" Arka asked.

"It's not what I want right now. He is out there and I will meet him. Everything in the right time, place, and sequence."

"Wow, we went from tribal BS to relationship BS. Should we now discuss and solve the problems of the Middle East?" asked Asbed. They were silent for a moment, looked at each other and simultaneously said, "Don't get me started!"

It was time to go home. She wondered if someone was listening in on their conversation, and if so, what they would have thought.

She had one more evening before leaving for Vancouver. The drive back was going to be a lonely one as Charents had to fly back earlier than anticipated due to business obligations back in Vancouver. Vrej, Asbed, and the rest of the gang were busy. Arka was to be her tourist guide. She picked him up from the apartment complex as before and they decided to head to the beach where he knew of a great Italian restaurant. They headed to Marina Del Rey. She had heard of that location but had never gone there. It was a beautiful place and full of tourists. That was what she loved being surrounded by the ocean, the waves, and people from all walks of life. They went to the Italian restaurant he had mentioned. It was a very casual atmosphere known for its large outside patio overlooking the beach. The patrons were all wearing flip-flops and shorts. The restaurant was renowned for serving an endless supply of garlic bread in the shape of little golf balls. They ate so many prior to their main course being served that they couldn't finish their meals. Together they coined the phrase 'puffs' for the garlic bread.

"Thank God we're sitting in an outside patio otherwise we'd all smell like we're wearing Chanel No. 14.5 L'eau du Puff!"

Arka almost choked on his puff as he started to laugh.

The conversation they had had the day before with Asbed regarding relationships must have been ringing in Arka's head as he decided to bring up the topic again.

"You know you were right about what you said yesterday."

"Which part the tribal BS or relationship BS?" she asked as she munched on her puff.

"The part about guys and girls cheating and stuff" he said and continued "I admit that when I was married my eyes roamed. And I did believe in the BS of it being a guy thing not an emotional thing. I guess what I'm saying is that had I actually followed through with it I could have somehow justified it." He put his puff down and Takouhi wasn't sure if it was because he was stuffed or was getting emotional.

"So what did you do?" her eyes were so focused on him that a sniper's red dot appeared between his eyes.

"I couldn't do it. In fact I made sure I put myself in a position that I wouldn't be tempted. I thought it wouldn't be fair to the woman I married and wanted to build a future with. There was something bigger than the accepted norm and I was realizing it," he said.

"Why do you sound sad as you're telling me this? You should be extremely proud of yourself for not crossing the line, challenging old beliefs and replacing them with new beliefs."

"But you don't understand Takouhi!" he said, "I just found out that she cheated on me and that's why she left. And that she's pregnant!"

Now it was Takouhi's turn to almost choke on her puff.

"So what I'm saying is that you were right. Girls cheat too and it doesn't have to be emotional. Yesterday I said that girls leave if the person they are with isn't giving them attention but in spite of my present condition I was trying everything in my power to make sure she was taken care of emotionally. But she did what she did anyway. So in hind sight I should have cheated huh?" Takouhi could have sworn that his eye was glistening but she didn't have a chance to confirm her observation as he quickly got up and walked away towards the restroom.

Takouhi put her utensils down, took a deep breath and leaned back in her chair. She looked towards the sky and thought 'Seriously, what is the lesson here? It would be too easy for me to call his ex-wife names. What should I be doing here? Or should I stop overanalyzing everything and track her down?' She looked back down to find that he had returned to his seat. His hair was a little wet around the edges, he had poured water over his face to calm himself down, yet he couldn't disguise the redness in the one eye without the patch.

"You know I'm glad you didn't cheat. You did everything right! I know it's difficult to comprehend right now as the wounds are very fresh but maybe all this happened for you to realize what type of woman you were going to be spending your life with. Maybe all this as painful as it is, is happening for you to see other people's true colours. My dear, it's about Karma. Don't worry about her. No need to get angry or upset or anything like that. The universe takes care of all of us. We are all here to learn certain lessons. Don't spend time judging her. Your energy should be put to better use!" she wasn't sure if she was talking to him and giving him advice or trying to convince herself.

Their drive home from Marina Del Rey towards Van Nuys was very quiet. Although Takouhi's spiritual side truly believed in the majesty of the universe and how everything does happen for a reason there was a duel inside her. The spiritual side said there's a bigger picture, there's a plan and everything happens for a reason. The human side couldn't shake the feelings of betrayal and disgust. And she thought if she feels like this then how does this person sitting to her right feel when he's already anguished about a great illness. They arrived in front of the apartment building and they both got out of the car. The hug he gave her melted the lipstick in her purse. She wished him well and they both agreed that they would keep in touch via email and text. She said she would arrange to come to visit him again soon. She watched as he slowly walked away with his head towards the ground and disappeared through the door of the apartment complex. She stood there leaning against her car and looking at the surroundings. It was very quiet and she could hear the crickets chirping. She looked up to the stars and began to converse as if she was in the boardroom and they were the shareholders

'And there you have it ladies and gentleman. We just witnessed the ramifications of mistreating another human being. We just witnessed what happens to a human soul once crushed. Don't you think it's time to show the possibilities of the opposite? Don't you think it's time to prepare and prevent as opposed to repair or repent? Lead by example huh? Ok, let's do it! I'm up for it."

# 12

## SHERO TAKES FORM

Takouhi drove back, filled with thoughts. In fact she was so caught up with her thoughts and reviewing all the events that had come to pass during the week that her drive north seemed to take only an hour. She was still processing all that happened during that week in Los Angeles. She thought about all the conversations she had about different belief systems. What was the underlying theme that came up for her? What was it that she valued? Although it was customary for her to do so on road trips, for the first time in a long time she didn't want to listen to music or personal growth CDs of any kind. There was too much going on in her mind. She was formulating thoughts. There was a lot of work going on. She kept referring back to *shero*. This term had stayed with her since she had heard it for the first time in the 90s. It was referred to by someone as a female hero. She liked the name but not the concept. She felt it was more than just a female concept. As she reviewed all the conversations during her drive back it finally dawned on her that of all the amazing principles in this world there were five that resonated with her the most; spirituality, humanity, enlightenment, responsibility, and opportunity. In fact every conversation she had had whether it was in Armenia all the way to 24 hours prior had some element of the five principles in it. That's it! That's *shero*. Now it made sense to her!

During work hours, Takouhi blocked out everything, but in the late afternoon, she would go to her emails. Her only way to reach Arka was through email. Both of them were not good in conversing over the phone as they felt on the spot. Conversations on the phone were very basic as "Hi, how are you? How is the weather?" Emails were where Takouhi would try to get her ideas across to him. Everything she did from the time she arrived back in Vancouver was put in context of shero principles. She was testing her belief system. When she sent an email she wanted to make sure that it had substance and it fit in with this concept. Long gone were the sheep days. If she had felt she had left them eight years ago, imagine how she felt now when she felt empowered by being able to speak her mind and express her BS without the worry or concern of tribal judgment and ramifications. It wasn't that she was against the tribe or all the beliefs. The questioning and transformation wasn't going to be black and white. There were certain things that were remarkable about her tribe that never had a chance to reach its constructive potential whilst in the shadow of overpowering unsubstantiated man made ancient beliefs. She simply believed living shero principles were a call to propel her and others to a higher standard of living that went beyond identifying personal value and worth with a tax bracket. A way of living that brought people together as opposed to repel them from each other. Shero principles were a way of finding balance between who a person was and finding out the beauty and lessons within and of others. If life was defined by opportunities, Takouhi did not want it to be defined by the ones she had missed. She wrote an email yet again.

*Hello again my dear brother,*

*As I was thinking and driving (no not drinking and driving), I thought about your mother and mine. They are great aren't they? I can only imagine how much your mother loves you and what you mean to her being her first born, just like I'm my mom's first. But it's not even about being the first as I know my mom adores my brother as well and I'm sure your mom adores Asbed too. I've heard you say how you love and respect your mom not just because she's your mom but as a woman, and I've heard Asbed say the same thing. I've even heard Vrej say how much he loves your mom (and we all know he doesn't express himself like that often). All of you have said the same thing, so it sounds to me like you've got a powerful source on your side. You are exactly where you need to be right now with your mom. Remember if you're hurting she is hurting double, that's what most moms do. A month ago without realizing it the closest person to you physically (your ex) was draining the positive energy from you. Now your mom is going to replenish it just with her presence, her smile, her gesture, a touch. And let's not forget about your grandmother either. You have two amazing sources as far as I can see!*

*I wrote this poem a few years ago for mother's day and sent it to my favourite mothers. Share it with her if you think she might appreciate it and it may put a smile on her face. I look forward to meeting her one day.*

**A Mother's Love**

A mother's love is very pure
For only she can endure
The pain and troubles thrown her way

As her children find their way
Unconditional love without a doubt
Even if sometimes they scream and shout
We know deep in our hearts they want the best
For their children that won't give them any rest
And if at times we the kids seem ungrateful
Make faces behind your back and seem spiteful
Don't worry it's just a phase
Bad memories time will erase
So here we are on Mother's day
With a love that grows stronger day by day
Love you dearly this is true
We would be nothing without you!

Takouhi was hoping that this email would help him see the opportunity that had presented itself: receiving unconditional love. The mother would be able to give Arka way more unconditional love than anybody around him presently. Takouhi's mind was racing in terms of how she could reach him to help him with this period in his life. In the middle of the night she would wake when ideas came to her and would sit behind the computer with her emails. She would write one email after another and save them in drafts so she could send them to him throughout the days. Takouhi did not want to send too many in one day as she wanted to give him time to absorb and think about the ideas. She was digging into the reservoir of knowledge on her bookshelf and the notes she had written in her personal journals throughout the years. The quote book she had started years ago with quotes that had inspired her found its way into emails to Arka in the hopes it would inspire him. She had truly adopted him as her brother and wanted to do as much as possible for him. It was simply a knowing that she was doing the right thing. She didn't need anybody's approval. She had nothing to prove to anyone. Sometimes he would respond but most of the time he didn't. It didn't bother her, she knew he was reading. For every 20 emails she would send, she might receive one in response. It didn't matter. If only one email inspired him to keep looking forward during those moments when he felt down and out, then that was good enough for her. She was not attached to whether there was recognition or appreciation to the emails. It was of no consequence to her. The bigger picture was more important.

*Hi Arka*

*How are you? Where are you?*

*It's Saturday and I needed to review some financial papers for my parents and do some shredding of unnecessary old stuff. As I was reviewing the papers, I came across a cheque that my father had written to my mother July 21, 1992. On the envelope it says Happy Birthday, from your loving husband. I opened it up it was a cheque for $500 made out to my mom but the cute part was that in the memo field it said Love, Your husband P.S. Do Not Spend! I was in tears when I saw this, part laughter but mostly because it was so sweet. In 1992, times were tough in terms of money. The point was that he did this for her and of course she didn't cash it but it was so cute. That cheque was priceless. That to me is the salt and pepper of life. That is what stopping to smell the roses means. That's why we shouldn't tell ourselves that we'll be happy when I have this or that. We should make an effort to be happy on a day-to-day basis and appreciate all the people in our lives. Everything does happen for a reason. I love the fact that you know this and the fact that you appreciate things. I keep* *the cheque in my organizer now and I've been looking at it since I found it. When I get cranky I look at it and it puts things in perspective for me. Thought I'd share!*

*Your Kuro*

*PS: Do you want to do coffee May 19 – 21? I have a long weekend and I hear that the carrot cake around your neck of the woods is yummy!!*

This time she got a response right away. She knew why. He had a date to look forward to.

*Hello Sis,*

*I'm doing good will be better for sure...after all, I have your unconditional support. Carrot cake sounds like a plan ...I am up for it...*

*See you soon*

*Your bro*

Takouhi was under a lot of pressure at work as her boss had left for a few months and she was in charge. In spite of all that was going on around her, she wanted Arka to have something to look forward to. Little did she realize the ramifications of the conversations and actions a la shero that were soon to take place in her travels to Los Angeles in May.

# 13

## THE ULTIMATE GIFT

Spiritually she needed this break from the "real' world. She needed time out even if it meant getting on a plane and having time to reflect. She was hoping that she could make a difference for her friend by getting him out of his routine and having something to look forward too. In fact, it was a win-win situation. He was helping her as much as she was helping him. She wondered what new things she would learn.

There was a huge storm brewing at her work place and she knew the opportunities to leave would be as limited as the ways in which her father could style his receding hair line. All the ducks were eloquently placed in a row and she had organized her schedule such that she was only going to miss one day of work. Her one workday was equivalent to two work days for the normal working world. In spite of the mentally and physically taxing workdays, she never questioned working herself to exhaustion. All she saw was the great learning she had attained and the opportunities for personal growth. Money was important but being part of something bigger was more rewarding.

She worked the full Thursday and managed to get an afternoon flight to Los Angeles. Everything went as smoothly as a well organized assembly line. It usually did as she was focused and had envisioned each detail prior to commencement. Arrived at the airport, went straight to the rental car, to the hotel and checked in and last but not least the phone call to Arka that she had arrived. She picked him up from his parents' house. As was his customary way, he would be waiting for her at the bottom of the apartment complex. As he approached the car she noticed he was a bit off on his walk. His balance was not like in March. As he walked towards the car he was listing towards starboard like a ship but would regain his balance right away. She had rented a sports car for the fun of it. Since they both liked cars, she figured why not make it fun for him as well. As per tradition, they headed to Studio City to their favourite carrot cake joint. And the conversations began again.

"Arka jan have you written in the journal that I bought for you?" She knew that would make him squirm. Takouhi was pushing his buttons for fun knowing he was very private and didn't write too much, especially compared to her.

"Yeah I actually did!" He said with a huge smirk on his face as he leaned his body forward with a huge smile. Takouhi was surprised and fell back in her chair.

"No way, you're just saying that because you knew I would ask!"

"You want proof?" The brightness of his smile could have helped a distressed ship to port.

"Whatever, now I know you're kidding because you don't have the book on you and I don't have the means to go look in your house" She spoke in a rational lawyeresque mode.

He was quiet for a moment and then looked at her with a sparkling yet serious eye, "If I am telling you that I have written in my journal that you gave me, then please believe me. But I will tell you this, I only wrote a few pages."

She was inquisitive and her curiosity made her lean forward to match his posture.

"How did it make you feel when you wrote in your journal Arka?"

"Just as you had said it would. It actually made me feel lighter. The moment felt right. I just grabbed it and started writing. I couldn't believe how fast it was coming through me. It just flowed. And when I was done and I re-read what I had written, I was surprised. I wondered where it had come from and how long it had built up inside of me."

"May I ask what you wrote about?"

"You know I already told you that I'm a very private person. The fact that I have even written is amazing. Especially if you recall the conversation we had last time about someone else reading my journal and how that would make me feel."

Takouhi knew not to push the subject any further but she was so curious, especially as to how it was written. She would love to compare writing styles. There were times when she would write it was all about the little things in life, but her best writings were thoughts and ideas. These thoughts were usually universal, to do with humanity and spirituality. Whether it was something triggered by a news article, a book, watching the news or the political satire of Stewart and Colbert and the way in which they translated the world around them with humour. Takouhi wondered had Arka written about his past, his present condition, or about universal ideas and truths. Was there anger in his writing or was he at peace with himself and others around him?

"I can't believe you have taken off work to come here to be with me!"

"Why can't you believe it? You know how hard I'm working. I need a break and you need a break so it's a win-win situation."

"Yeah but you could go anywhere and just relax for a few days. Why are you coming here? Weren't you just here two months ago?"

"Is this the part where you want me to spell it out for you? Okay fine, I'll say it. I'm madly in love with you, you are the love of my life and I cannot live without you! And I have a thing for guys with a patch on their eye!" She stuck her tongue out at him and started laughing. He joined her laughter to the point where they were both swimming laps in their tears.

"Ok smartass, that's not what I meant! Really Takouhi why are you here? How did you get here?"

"I took a plane."

"Stop it! Answer my question"

"You are wearing all those crosses around your neck. Does that mean you're a spiritual person?"

"At this moment I am taking all the help I can get to get better."

"You see I believe that the power that is, the light which is good, which is the universe, has brought me to you. Keep in mind; it's not just about you it's also about me. We are meant to be in each others' lives for a reason. We may not know why at this moment but you have to admit how interesting the events that have come to pass up to this point have been. The pieces of the puzzle have come together effortlessly to bring us here today, on May 17."

"Takouhi jan, I'm not sure about all that stuff but I can tell you this." All of a sudden there were tears rolling down his eyes even the one that was covered with a patch. "Others talk about being there for you, but not many people actually get on a plane and come down to physically spend their time with you. Let alone all the way from Canada! Do you have any idea what this means to me?"

Takouhi had never bitten her lip so hard so she would prevent herself from crying. She didn't expect that, nor had she asked for it. Like an eagle, her spirit was soaring through the sky.

The next day Takouhi spent the morning taking care of business from her hotel room. Arka had medical appointments, so she worked a bit. At 6 o'clock, she drove to pick him up. Takouhi had mentioned to him that in all the times that she had visited LA, she had never had an opportunity to visit the sites.

"You've never been on the walk of fame?" asked Arka surprised.

"Why are you so surprised? I've told you about how many cousins I have, and you saw in March I was only able to get away because my brother and I were staying in a hotel."

"Don't they know that you're here now?"

"Nope, it's all about you! I'm staying in a hotel on purpose. If I stayed with them I'd have to play house and then have to explain you to them."

"What? You're embarrassed to talk about me?"

"What do you mean embarrassed? Where did that come from?"

By this time they had arrived at the restaurant and had been seated. Takouhi noticed how others were looking at him. Some looked away in discomfort while others stared with 101 questions they would ask if they were given the opportunity. It was the reaction of little children that they both enjoyed. They usually found a child's innocent unprocessed and unfiltered remarks the most amusing when they simply asked 'Are you a pirate?'

"I'm not letting this go. What do you mean? That I'm embarrassed by you?"

"Look at me! I can't even eat food without slurping. I know people are staring at me and wondering what is going on and maybe what you're doing with me?"

"Ok maybe they are but who cares what they think? The ones that have a human and compassionate side will get it. The ones that don't today hopefully will some day. But they are not our concern at the moment. As for me being embarrassed of you that doesn't compute with me. If I were embarrassed wouldn't I rather have gone somewhere else to take a few days off? My staying at a hotel has to do with you but in a different way. It's not embarrassment. It's me wanting to be there for you and protect you from their BS."

"Oh here we go" and they both started laughing.

"That's right! Belief systems darling!" and the laughter continued to the point where even Takouhi was slurping her food. They started cracking up because now they were both trying to imitate each other to see who could look more hideous. Takouhi didn't like to lose! They finally composed themselves and she continued.

"Belief systems in that they would ask me who you are. Then they would try to fit you into a category that makes sense to them. Are you my boyfriend? My lover?

My best friend? If I were to go on further and tell them about your condition then I would hear further BS and opinions about your chances, what's going to happen, what the heck am I doing spending time with you and the list goes on."

"What are you doing?"

"I'm slurping my food with my aber!"

"Carry on then!"

Takouhi looked up and he had such a look of contentment on his face. Even though she could only see one eye as the other was under a patch, the one that was uncovered was shining.

"Arka, don't get me wrong. I love my family and friends and everyone here. But what I do not need most of the time is the negativity that is seen as 'real.' I want to focus on all the things that can be, positivity and growth. In a situation like this with you, I have already seen glimpses of negativity any time I have shared information about you. That is not going to help me help you. What you need is vitamin P… vitamin Positivity."

"Ok Guru, are you done?"

"Done with what?"

"This vitamin P business! Be careful not to overdose me!" Takouhi's only wish at that moment was that their surrounding tables could be infected with their laughter.

Arka decided he was feeling well enough that they should go see the Hollywood walk of fame. They were so close that it was an opportunity he didn't want her to miss out on. Takouhi walked ahead of Arka as the signatures and footmarks fascinated her. She remarked how tiny some of them were and compared it to her feet.

"Not everyone has mammoth sized feet like you do," she heard Arka explain from close by.

"What do you mean? If my feet were smaller I'd fall down they'd be no balance."

"Whatever!" he said realizing that she was going to let him push her buttons.

"I'm a perfect 10!" just to make sure he understood she put the palm of her hands in front of his face.

"How do you figure that?"

"Well, Shoe size 10, dress size 10."

"IQ 10" He had taken her joke and added to it. But they understood each other well and couldn't stop laughing. She carried on looking at the other names on the walk but was always aware of his presence and was watching over him. This time she heard a different voice.

"Excuse me sir, I hope you won't take offence in me saying so but" said a strange man.

"Yes, what is it?" replied Arka with a startled face. His body tensed up.

"You're a very lucky man sir, your wife is beautiful" said the stranger.

"She is isn't she? Thank you for saying so!" Arka replied with a smile. As the stranger walked away he asked her "So did you hear what the man just said?"

"Yes, I did. Funny how the universe gives back huh?" she started laughing.

"Ok now I want to hear how you're twisting this in the positive."

"Twisting? Who is twisting? Facts are facts! You were trying to put me down by saying I had large feet and a complete stranger looked at me as if I was perfect! The universe was speaking to you factually and the fact is that I am hot!"

"Oh and might I add ever so humble!" Arka placed his hand on his chest and bowed down to the humble Queen with humour filled sarcasm.

As she was driving towards Van Nuys to drop him home after the eventful evening she reflected back on their conversations that night.

"Arka it is funny how we have such a great sense of rapport huh?"

"Yeah, but where were you when I needed you five years ago?"

"What do you mean?"

"I needed my kuro on my side to help me defeat the bullies playing in the sandbox" He looked out the window with a big sigh. Arka's tone was unclear to Takouhi. She couldn't determine if he was being serious or joking.

As she pulled up to the apartment complex Takouhi broke the silence.

"I can't go back in time but I can be fully present now to defeat this bully!"

Arka simply smiled, kissed her on the cheek, and listed away towards the safety of his pier.

Saturday was the day where she knew she had him for most of the day. He had no plans. The only thing that would lessen their time together was if he wasn't feeling well or was too tired. She picked him up as usual from the front of the apartment and off they went. Today's agenda: Marina Del Rey. Arka had decided that it would be a great day to go to the beach. They walked along the beach until they found a bench by the canal where sailboats would come back and forth between the Pacific Ocean and their berths in the Marina. The bench was underneath a tree that reminded her of a willow. In spite of the slight overcast, it was still a nice and warm breezy day. From the bench they could even see the planes taking off and landing.

Their conversations went all over the map. They spoke about personal triumphs and disappointments. But they also spoke about global events and politics. It was really curious that they both had shared the same undergraduate degree. Of course his was always going to be better than hers in his opinion. Only because he was a USC Alumni! Every time he would say that she would cringe so he did that on purpose.

"Don't you know what it means to be a USC Alumni? It's such a big deal. In fact you are pretty much guaranteed a status of sorts if you have it. Have you not noticed it on license plates that say USC alumni?" Arka would try to present his case

"I don't understand the status that you speak of? Did you go to university to learn and get enlightened or to tell the world you hung out at a particular university?"

"You don't get it! People get off on things like that here! It's about who drives what and where you've been and who you know!"

"Is that what all people are like here?" Takouhi said in a facetious tone.

"Oh you know what I mean! Even my ex-wife who hadn't stepped foot in that university wanted one for her cars license plate so people would think she had gone there!"

"Now that's pretentious! But all people do not your ex-wife make my dear! From what you have told me about her, she is definitely one of God's special creations!" she rolled her eyes and continued.

"I went to a university in Vancouver. It was a great experience for me. But the thought of advertising it on my license plate doesn't make sense to me. Don't get me wrong I understand camaraderie and a sense of accomplishment but to have it on my car so others will think I am special or that it gives me status? What am I telling the world that that's it, that's my biggest accomplishment? It doesn't make sense to me. I went to school for me. Not that so and so will say she went to that school thus she is smart and thus she has class. I've had this conversation before haven't I? Remember how I shared my views with Vrej in Vegas? In our communities, or as you've heard me say tribes, there seems to be a preconceived notion that whoever goes to university has class or is enlightened. Although that maybe possible, it's not an automatic given. In most cases you go to school and you are trained in the field of your choice. Does that make you a spiritual person, a humanitarian, enlightened in the ways of the world and other cultures? Do you necessarily learn about taking responsibility for yourself and your actions? Do you learn how to see the opportunity in everything not just when things are going well but when things are not?"

"Good lord! What university did you go to? Did they teach you that?"

"No it's not that they teach you that or not. I'm just speaking about the fact that just because we go to university we are not coming out with class as is assumed. We come out with a greater ability to make a better living for ourselves. That does not constitute class. Maybe a different tax bracket. Do you see where I'm going with this?"

"Yes I do. I see your point. But that's how all our communities operate. He's a nice guy and a catch because he's a doctor. She's a nice girl and a catch because she's a lawyer."

"I'm not saying that they're not nice people. Maybe some are. But to automatically assume that they are compassionate human beings who know how to treat others in a kind way is a huge presumption on our part. How many lawyers do you know who are in it just for the money? Or doctors for that matter. How many times have you heard about the atrocious bedside manner of a doctor? How many times have you heard about ambulance chasing lawyers? Within our tribes when we say the typical doctor or lawyer criteria it's to do with what they can buy with that not necessarily the good they can potentially do for others. Unfortunately we have been wrapped up in the do re me society. What's in it for me!"

"My ex was like that!"

"What do you mean?"

"I'm convinced that I was the best suitable candidate with the proper credentials and shingles! After all I did finish USC and Law School. She was a lawyer's wife, so lots of status in the community."

"Pretty sad to hear that my dear. But you just proved my point. What do you think her status is now with the community that she left you when you are in this condition? The same community that brought her status up now brings it down. She was a sheep following the BS. The problem with tribal BS is that it can work against you as easily as it can work for you. But if you live a life with principles like spirituality, humanity, enlightenment, responsibility, and opportunity then you hold your own compass. These values will never work against you. Especially if you own who you are!"

"She said she was depressed!"

Takouhi noticed that he was started to focus on the negative. She needed to turn the ship around fast.

"Ok let me tell you something about her leaving! Whoo hooo!!!" She jumped off the bench and started doing jumping jacks.

"Are you crazy???" Arka started laughing, "how is this funny?"

"Glad you asked! Without her leaving I wouldn't be able to sit here with you and get this incredible tour of all the sites that you have so graciously been accompanying me too. Not only are you giving me a tour but also you are a unique tour guide with one patch. Aren't I selfish? It's all about me!"

"You know it!" Their laughter was so loud it caught the attention of the people walking by who were used to the loudness of their silence.

They started walking to the main road in Marina Del Rey. Takouhi loved some of the houses and the beach. She visualized what it would be like to live there. Maybe someday she would if she wanted it. They decided they would go to the same Italian restaurant they had visited for the first time in March. She was craving the "puffs.' It was warmer on the patio in May causing the smell of the garlic bread to linger in the open air like the morning mist in Vancouver's harbour. As they were gorging down the puffs Takouhi took out her favourite pen and notebook and started to write down some thoughts.

"What's going through your head again?" he asked with curiosity.

"I just thought of some things I want to remember to write about later."

"Like what?"

"Well the entire concept of class and what it means to our tribe. And how it has always really bothered me that it sometimes is a given rather than earned title. I have always wondered if there is a way in which it can be measured or attained by values and core beliefs leading into action."

"Interesting concept. How would you propose one would go about measuring that or determining whether someone has class if not by the shingle on their wall?

"I'll let you know when the Lego pieces of my mind present their case."

"I will tell you one thing though! I do love your pen. I told you I loved it back in Vegas didn't I? I can tell you like that high-end pen. Did you buy it because people will know what pen you are using and thus think you have class? What makes it so special for you? Or is it special?" He was throwing it right back at her but she was ready. He on the other hand was not ready for her response.

"Yes you're right. It's a high-end pen. And yes it cost me a lot of money. But the people I work with have no clue of the value of the pen nor if or what it represents. So the materialistic class aspect of the argument is thrown out the window. It holds tremendous value for me for many different reasons. For one thing, it's blue and the texture is made to look like water. For many others, and me blue is the colour of spirituality. It calms and soothes me, just like the ocean. The end of the pen is made to look like a diver's helmet. How fitting in that that is the industry that I am working in and whether I like the people I work with or not, the entire diving industry fascinates me. The ability to go underwater fascinates me. I appreciate all the technology and resources that have gone into enabling us to see things we would ordinarily never see. And then there is the signature of the author of one of my favourite books *20,000 Leagues Under the Sea,* by Jules Verne. What an imagination the man had for his time. So you see my dear, this pen is of tremendous value to me. Do I have class because I am using it? Maybe. But I am the same person without it. The pen is what I like; it doesn't define who I am! Anything else?"

"Cheque please!" Arka lifted his hand as if to motion for the waiter.

They both knew how to push each other's buttons. Takouhi wondered how life would have been like had she met him five years ago just as he had mentioned the night before. Yet she also realized she wouldn't be who she was today without having gone through the experiences that she had had. And chances were that Arka would not be able to appreciate these conversations way back then either. She believed that everything happens for a reason. All the pieces of the puzzle had fallen in such a way to bring these two together in Marina Del Rey on that Saturday afternoon. Where it would take them who knew. The key was to enjoy the moment. There was nothing more precious than that. The only thing they were guaranteed was that moment. Who knew if tomorrow would come or not?

"But seriously I do love your pen, it's very classy and makes a statement," the hook.

"So does this mean that you don't have class because you don't have one?" the line.

"Well, I've seen one in the pen store, it's exquisite, black carbon fiber on silver accents. It's not as fantastic as yours but it's still a piece of art. Check it out if you get a chance. I've wanted to buy it but now that I'm not working there's no point. Anyway, I out-class you! You have the pen but I have the law degree!" and the sinker.

Spending time with him was such a pleasure for Takouhi. They understood each other. The conversation flowed about so many topics under the sun. Never did she hear him say why me? She was proud of him. Takouhi saw life as a journey not a destination. She wasn't a sheep. What she meant when she thought sheep was a follower. Someone who didn't question things and just followed the tyranny of the masses. The more she questioned belief systems, the more she shed her sheepish clothes. One of her most disliked sayings as she had grown up was "everyone else is doing it." She needed to know why. Why is everyone doing it especially where in most cases it doesn't serve them? If everyone was doing it and it made them happy then it would have made sense to her. But people were doing hurtful things within her tribe just because it had been done like that for generations. It didn't make sense. Scared to stand up and change. Scared of the unknown. Scared of the possibility of failure or being wrong. Safer to be a sheep. Takouhi wasn't concerned whether her tribe would approve or disapprove of her life. She was her own boss in her life. She wasn't looking for their approval and maintaining her status in the community. She was looking for further growth and enlightenment. Life is evolution. If you don't grow, you die. That is as true to companies as it is to personal growth. How could she do wrong if she lived a shero way of life? Takouhi wasn't looking to be measured by tribal definitions of success. On her journey through life she wanted to make sure that her biography would have at least one great chapter, one extraordinary chapter, followed by a chapter that was beyond extraordinary and it would simply scream shero on all its pages.

How could she not experience this friendship and this spirit sitting across from her? Why did it need to have a label to justify its existence? No wonder people thought her friendship with Arka didn't make sense. The tribe was too busy thinking what a waste of time. Takouhi was thinking it was time well spent. It made her think of the toy that toddlers were given to play with. Where you put the square in the square hole and the triangle in the triangle. Youngsters were trained to fit and conform. It made sense to teach the young some structure, but as adults we also needed to learn life isn't just black and white and things fitting perfectly in a mould. She always felt that everyone had so much more to offer to themselves and the world. Yet limited themselves with fear and negative BS that they probably didn't make but was passed down to them from generation to generation. If only they didn't spend so much time thinking about what others thought about them and their actions. If only that time was spent on improving themselves with shero principles.

The final day had come. She was leaving that afternoon to return to her bubble blowers. Takouhi checked out of the hotel. She had a few errands to run prior to picking up Arka for their last lunch. She took care of her errands and drove to the apartment yet again to pick him up. They decided to go somewhere close as time had become a precious commodity and she didn't want to get stuck in traffic on her way to LAX. That being said, they got stuck in traffic on route to the restaurant.

"What did you do this morning? How come you were late picking me up?"

"By the time I packed and checked out and then I had to go to the mall to grab something."

"For your mom?"

"No, for me, me, me!" She started to giggle.

"What did you get?"

"I went to the pen store to get a refill for my pen as we don't have it in Canada."

"Oh you did? Did you get a chance to look at the pen I was telling you about? The one I said I wanted to buy but didn't."

"Oh, I knew there was something that I wanted to see! I forgot!"

"I can't believe you! After all that conversation we had about the pen and noticing things and selfishness!"

"Gee are you calling me a hypocrite?"

"Yeah if you're giant size 10 shoes fit!"

"I guess you're right. I can't believe I forgot. The least I could have done was ask to look at it huh?"

"Yeah, the least you could have done! How crazy is this! Selfish, selfish, selfish! She needed a refill and that's all that mattered!"

There was awkward silence in the car for five minutes. The traffic on 405 was at a standstill.

"You're right. I can't believe I didn't remember especially after all the talk yesterday."

"Okay, let it go. Get over it. I forgive you but I'm not surprised. Nothing surprises me anymore."

"Is that so?"

"Yup!"

"Are you sure about that?"

"I know you had good intentions Takouhi, but we can't help it. We're just human! We're naturally selfish!"

The awkward silence continued until she couldn't take it any longer. Takouhi reached into her carry on that was on the back seat and pulled out a pen box with a bow on it and put it on his lap.

"What about now?" she said with a smile.

He didn't know what to do. He didn't know what to say. All he could do was just stare at her with his one beautiful brown eye. His one eye became as round as a watermelon. He was speechless. Arka took off his seatbelt as if he wanted to get out of the car. Takouhi thinking she had been in control this entire time was taken aback.

"What are you doing? Put your seatbelt back on!"

"You let me go on and on and hurt you and you said nothing."

"You weren't hurting me. You were playing. I know who I am and I know who I am not. If you call me selfish does that mean I'm selfish? I don't think so! I was having fun actually. Seeing the paradigm shift was amazing!"

"You're nuts. I can't believe you bought me the pen! I can't believe you did this!" He said as a tear welled up in his eye.

"It's the least I could do. After all if you're going to hang out with me I have to make sure you have class!"

His humility tears turned into tears of laughter. They understood each other and that's all that mattered.

It was a little gift; simply a pen but the gesture incorporated all shero principles. 'In life what we can potentially do is limitless and yet we limit ourselves based on the belief systems and principles we tap into' she had thought. The sheep period for Takouhi had become something one might have read in a dusty history book. Sherovision illuminated the road ahead making it very clear what she needed to do next.

# 14

# SHERO IN ACTION

As she was flying back she was reflecting on her last few days. Nothing was more precious than those few moments on the freeway when she had given him his gift. She remembered the morning when she had decided to go get it. It was out of her way but she had a mission. She arrived at the pen store and headed straight for his pen visualizing what he would look like writing in his journal with it. What it would mean to him to have it. Then she saw the price tag and cringed. Yikes! But the opportunity to make someone happy, someone who had a challenge far greater than the challenge of paying off her credit card, far outweighed a price tag. Okay, so she would have to work a few extra hours. And this was where the magic had happened. The universe rewarded her good intentions. Positivity makes all things possible. When she had purchased the pen and was on route to pick up Arka, she saw a text on her cell phone. It was her employer trying to make it up to her for her extra efforts in the only way he knew how. The text read, "Buy yourself something pretty on me." She made it work. She connected her boss with Arka. He just paid for something that would make Arka happy. Her employer was a good man with a good heart and constantly worked towards personal evolution. That was one of the things she admired about him. It wasn't naïveté on her part. The hope of him seeing the bigger picture one day was what kept her going. So she did buy herself something pretty. It was a beautiful memory that had a material price tag but was priceless. And yes, she knew she had worked very hard to have been given that opportunity to buy something for herself. Her boss was a smart man and didn't give things away for nothing. Everything was calculated. Although she would try to explain that moment with words in her journals nothing could take away the vision of his face receiving that gift in her minds eye. Nothing!

When she returned back to the helm in Vancouver the emails continued. As usual they were more from Takouhi to Arka as opposed to the other way around. That was okay. She needed to make sure that he received his daily dose of vitamin P.

> *May 23/07*
>
> *Thank you for all the great places you took me to in the last few days. I truly had a wonderful time. Did I mention how proud I am of you? You inspire me big time! So yes, you're probably right when you say that all acts are selfish ones. I came to see you not just to give you a little change in your routine but also because hanging out with you energizes me... there's nothing more satisfying than hanging out with someone who is so like minded and everything flows and it's easy going and you can just be without any pretense or anything... and most importantly, destiny finally brought me to the garlic puffs!*
>
> *May 24/07*
>
> *Wanted to share something with you before I forget and get caught up in work...*

*"Always follow your dreams and believe in yourself - for someone as special as you has the ability to create a world of exciting tomorrows!"*

*Let these lines be your life's path and steps. My mother gave me a card on my university graduation that had this written in it. I carry it with me always. Thought it would make a difference for you as well.*

*May 24/07*

*Okay don't think of this as another email. Think of this as me sitting next to you and chatting with you throughout the day like we did when we were sitting on the bench by the water at Marina Del Rey. You know what would be great? The ultimate thing actually? No matter where we are or what we're doing, say in 40 years, we'll go back and sit on that bench again and you'll watch me freeze again in the shade. I'll wear the same jeans that you didn't like so much. In fact, let's do it every year and see at what point I will burst out of the jeans!*

Takouhi couldn't believe it she actually got a response back from him.

*Dear Takouhi,*

*What a great idea!*

*I think the bench idea is very exciting but if I were you I wouldn't keep my hopes high about having to wear the same jeans. I think that's overly optimistic, but having to wear them for couple more months that may work out by some miracle. But don't ever stop dreaming that those jeans will fit you beyond couple of months.*

It was working. As long as he was writing something humorous then it meant that he was in a positive state of mind. She never doubted that he was reading all her emails.

*May 24/07*

*Two things before I shut it down for the night. Firstly, I want you to write one thing in your journal. Write down the letters of your name and put a characteristic to it that describes you now, like A for Authentic, R for Regal, K for Kind, A for Aspiring. I guess you can see how I see you huh?*

*Secondly, here's another poem fresh off the press just for you!*

Do you have days
When your heart is heavy
When it feels that the angst
Will break the dam and the levy
When you have so much to say
But are tongue tied
Troubled nights
Where you cried and cried
But there are moments
That take your breath away
Making up for the sadness
That sometimes leaves you astray
That's why we were told of faith love and hope
So with all lost moments we could somehow cope
We gain the strength to put negativity away
And we Thank God for this magical thing called...
Living in the moment everyday!!!

*PS. Have I redeemed myself with this poem after blitzing you with all the emails? I'm coming down in July! You can run but you can't hide!*

She could not believe it, there was another response in her inbox. Two emails from Arka in one night.

*Sistra,*

*Did you redeem yourself? But did I ever tell of your need for redemption. Redemption is for the one condemned. And you, my sis could not possibly be there. You don't ever have to redeem yourself. Stay artistic, be cool, don't work too hard, live life and everything else will fall in its place and if it doesn't then trust me it shouldn't have been there to begin with...*

*PS Puffs and carrot cake in July... excellent!*

The interesting thing to Takouhi was that the more she would give of herself, the more she felt she got in return. Giving was getting. Was it selfish? She didn't see how if it was done to make another person feel good. She wanted to live by example. She had her own chapters to write in her own book. In order to begin writing shero chapters she had to live it first.

# 15

# ANOTHER DOSE OF SHEROTHERAPY

Once again she was at the airport. The July long weekend had arrived. It was 5:00 a.m. and she could barely keep her eyes open at the airport. It didn't help that there were very few travelers and the quiet in the airport was lullabying her to sleep. She wondered if having coffee administered intravenously would make a difference compared to just drinking it. How many times had she been to LA this year? She was starting to know the customs agents on a first name basis. She was headed down to give and maybe even receive some vitamin P. Every time she travelled she wondered in what condition she would find him in. He had sounded pretty excited about a new business venture.

By the time she checked into the hotel she was so tired that she didn't call Arka right away. Her resources were very low. Her fatigue was affecting her demeanor with people and she couldn't even muster the energy to communicate. She would not be able to pretend to be present, nor was it her style. Better to step back and regroup as opposed to push forward and crash. By the time she awoke it was 3:00 p.m. and there were numerous texts from Arka wondering where she was. She jumped up and called him right away.

Luckily everything worked out. It happened that for the first time ever he was going to be dropped off to save time from her having to pick him up. He called to say he was downstairs at the hotel lobby and she went running. In the elevator she wondered what he would look like this time. He was constantly changing as a result of the chemo. Last time he looked as if he had had a stroke. The muscles on the right side of his face had stopped fighting gravity. And there he was waiting in the lobby. He had shaved his head and had a cute belly thanks to the hormones they were giving him. They had decided prior to her arrival that they would go to the beach to see the fireworks. It was July 4th after all.

She did the driving and he gave the directions. He was her GPS in so many ways. His presence directed her to fine tune herself and her beliefs. They found a place on the crowded beach by Santa Monica Pier. They grabbed the blanket that she had brought from the hotel and sat close to the water awaiting the fireworks.

"So here you are again!"

"Yup!" Takouhi was so tired. She had slept but her mind was exhausted. Her intuition told her that things at work were changing. The reason she was able to take some time off was because her boss was finally back after being away for over two months.

"And you're here because?"

"Arka jan, are we going to have this conversation again?" she snapped at him but caught herself. It wasn't his fault that she was so tired from work and she chose to come to spend time with him. Nobody forced her. "What I mean my dear is that you know I come here because I love the pleasure of your company and if I can get you out of your routine and help you beat this thing then why not?"

"I have to tell you something that is on my mind but I don't know how to say it and I don't want to hurt you if I say it wrong." Arka was looking at the water as if it were Takouhi.

"Arka, I usually tell people who are in those same shoes that they should concern themselves with the points they want to make and not necessarily worry about the persons' reaction. So you can say whatever it is that you want to me but I decide how I translate and react to it. So let me hear what you have to say and you may be pleasantly surprised at my reaction or not. But it's my reaction; you can't control it!"

"Well the thing is this. Since I've met you, you have come here to spend time with me three times so far this year. And I know you have a crazy schedule at work and I truly appreciate you and your friendship. I just want you to be on the same page as I am."

"And what page is that?"

"The friendship page. You know I can't give you more than that"

"I wasn't aware I was asking for it? Have I given you that impression?"

"Well it's just that I know between your crazy career and the full time attention you give me with your texts and emails and physical presence, you don't make time to be in a relationship. Don't you want to have love in your life? Don't you want to have kids? Don't you want to get married?"

"Wow, you do have a lot on your mind! I thought I was mentally exhausted!" and they both started chuckling.

Takouhi took a good look at him and responded.

"You sound so tribal right now. Are you saying I'm wasting my time with you?"

"Well, it depends what your objectives are in life?"

"My objectives are to live a fully engaged life with shero principles. Yes, I do want to be loved. Yes, I would love to have children. Yes, I would love to adore and be adored by someone. But at the same time we all have different paths in life. Not everyone is meant to be a mother or a father. You can't force someone to love you and you can't force yourself to love someone. But to bring it back to your main point which I believe is making sure that I know that you want me as a friend correct?"

"You're beautiful. You're super smart. You are caring and loving. You would make any man proud. I don't even know what your ex was thinking when he let you walk away. I can't believe I'm saying this but I just don't think like that anymore. Five years ago if you had crossed my path I would not be saying this."

"I'm not concerned about five years ago. All I know about is now. Thank you for all those beautiful compliments. If that Italian movie goddess that you love so much heard you speak about me like this she'd get jealous." She looked over at him and he had a big grin on his face. He was visualizing and putting the right side of his brain to work. She knew he was thinking of her in a split second. That was one way in which Takouhi knew how to lighten the mood. She continued "Thank you for thinking so highly of me that you would even make reference to my ex-husband and his loss. The fact is in spite of the hardships of my divorce, it was one of the best blessings I have received. I know I tried my best to reach him. I know I did all I could do for him but at the end of the day when one person is on FM and the other is on AM it doesn't matter how pure your intentions are. We were in each other's lives for those moments. It would have been an amazing partnership had we understood each other but we didn't and we couldn't and we had different paths to take. It was very painful for me. I had to fight many tribal belief systems and was washed away by a tidal wave of angst but I came through it. I wouldn't be the person I am today had I not gone through what I did. Who knows where he is. Who knows what he's doing. I've never wished him ill. If he had known better he would have done better. Maybe he's the same person or maybe he's grown. The fact is that in a very short period of time you have become someone very near and dear to me. It has become my objective to help you get over this and move on. Perhaps I was sent by the powers that be to help you see things in another light. From a human perspective I can see that you have been hit hard twice; the first time with your illness, the second time when your wife left you under these circumstances. I'm not here to judge her actions, especially since I have never met her. I do admit I have opinions that I am not proud of but I will keep those to myself. All I can do is be here for you in whatever capacity you need me to be in order to keep you going. This is just another bump in the road. I don't want a relationship. I'm not your lover, your girlfriend, your fiancé, or your future wife. I don't need a title to be what you need me to be right now. But you are loved with a limitless capacity. I am so wrapped up with work that not many people can reach me and if you recall our conversation with our other brother Asbed back in March, I'm not ready for a relationship. But there are changes on the horizon. I can feel it. In the meantime I am pushing you forward and you are doing the same for me. If you need a label call me your sister, your cheerleader, or your coach. Call me whatever you need to call me to help you feel better about the situation."

"I feel guilty!"

"Why?"

"Because I am fighting this and I know I will get better but I don't want to hold you back from opportunities."

"How are you holding me back from opportunities?"

"Well if you see a handsome, intelligent, charismatic guy you won't even notice because your head will be down as you're texting me!"

"Don't you worry, if I see that guy, I will notice him. I can multi-task after all!" And they both started laughing. It was heartfelt laughter that made Takouhi think that if Arka had been a deep-sea diver he was now decompressing after that conversation.

"I told you it wasn't as bad as you thought. Was this the reaction you were expecting?"

"Takouhi, I don't know what I was expecting to be honest. I was just worried that the more time you spend with me the less you would with someone that can give you everything I can't."

"Don't worry about that my dear, everything happens for a reason. I am exactly where I need to be right now, next to my adopted brother!"

The fireworks started just as they finished their conversation. Almost as if there was a celebration to end what he had thought would be a heavy conversation.

The next day for the first time ever, Arka asked if Takouhi would take him for his chemotherapy session. He warned her that it would take a couple of hours. She was so excited that he was letting her into this part of his world. On route he wanted to stop off at a children's clothing store to pick up some new born baby clothes.

"Is there something I should know about?" Takouhi asked with a mischievous grin.

"Whatever!" and he started laughing.

"What do you need to buy? Do you want me to come in with you?"

"Yeah, please do. I may need your opinion."

They walked into the children's store. There was no shortage of curious looks from the people in the store. The looks came mainly from the customers. Some would pretend not to see them. Others would stare, possibly wondering what was wrong with him. Takouhi wondered what they were really thinking and wished she could somehow hear the BS in their heads.

"What do you think of this one?" Arka managed to pull her back from her mental ramblings.

"It's cute but who are you buying it for?"

"There's this nurse at the oncology centre we are about to go to. She has always been super nice to me over all these months. She's due to have her baby so I wanted to give her something. I know I won't see her again after today because she will be on maternity leave."

Like her favourite ice cream on a hot summer day, Takouhi just melted. 'And you wonder why I come to spend time with you?' she thought. How thoughtful and how engaged he was with the world around him. She had met someone doing the same thing she would have done. Wow, what a mirror he was for her. She was feeling selfish by thinking that she would have done the same but it felt so good to see there was someone with sherovision in her midst as well. In 24 hours she had gone from having a depleted battery to feeling fully charged. He was opening up and showing her his true colours. There was nothing more beautiful she could have asked to see at that moment.

Of all places the oncology centre was a few blocks away from the famous or rather infamous Rodeo Drive. Takouhi had never been in a place committed solely to cancer. When she drove into the buildings parking garage the valet attendants were at hand to take care of their car, one less thing for patients to concern themselves with. They took the elevator from the garage to the third floor. The door of the elevator opened directly into the medical reception centre. The entire floor was dedicated to oncology. The standard soothing colours of white and beige were prevalent in the office. Five receptionists manned the phones and organized the files of the patients walking in. What struck her was how the faces of all five receptionists lit up as they saw Arka walk in. "Hi Arka, how are you feeling today?" He was their star. She guessed he had been there so many times that he had a following. He had the present for the nurse in his hand and explained to them who it was for, which evoked such big smiles from the ladies that Takouhi swore she could see all their cavities. Takouhi had no idea what to expect when she entered there. She wasn't ready to see what she saw. They sat in the reception area and waited for his name to be called. It was July 6, 2007. Within five minutes he was asked to follow a nurse inside to wait for the doctor. Takouhi asked if she could join him and he said no. She didn't realize at the time that she would be sitting there by herself for two hours in the waiting room. He disappeared behind the closed doors. She sat back and took a look around at the people sharing her atmosphere. What she saw humbled her. There was no discrimination. This thing called cancer didn't care. In those two hours she saw a baby come through with a patch on her eye. She saw an African American woman who spoke of her breast cancer. She saw an elderly man speak of his cancer that had spread. Nobody had a problem opening up while sitting there. It was as if the cancer had united them. She thought why this has to happen for people to see life differently and appreciate things. No discrimination. Then the pen and the notebook came out and she wrote:

**No Discrimination**

I don't recognize race.
I don't stay in one place
I don't know about countries
I don't care about political boundaries
I don't understand the languages of the world
I don't focus on your age whether young or old
I don't accept the importance of money
I don't acknowledge colour whether white, black or honey
I don't concern myself with the truth or pretenders
I don't differentiate between the genders
But I do know this...
When I come into your life for a while
I'm definitely not greeted with a smile
Your life changes in a blink of an eye
And most of you focus on the word why
You all come together with the greatest intention
And all of sudden like me there's no discrimination
Together you understand that the greatest antidote
Isn't just medication yet love, faith and hope.
Cancer is my name and I don't know your world
But I am a great teacher so I am told!

It came to her naturally. And she continued to engage with the people around her. They were all so vulnerable but fighters. After all they were there to beat what they had, no matter who they were. By the time Arka came out, most of the people had come and gone from the waiting room having left Takouhi with her thoughts, notebook, and pen. She was never alone. Arka looked pale and tired. All she could do was drive him home. But he wanted to speak some more.

"Thank you for coming with me," he said.

"Are you kidding? It was my pleasure! I was pretty humbled I must admit though. I know you have cancer but seeing it affect so many people in one room is something else. I know my father had it but I never went to the oncology centre with him. Mom did all that. I guess they wanted us to be protected from that environment and look at me now!" she said with a smirk on her face. "But who goes with you when I'm not here? I"

"Well in the very beginning my ex came with me. But then dad would just drop me off and come pick me up in a couple of hours. "

"What about your mom?"

"She is such an amazingly strong woman. She is like me in many ways. Very reserved and holds her feelings to herself. You know I have never seen her cry over this entire ordeal. Actually I did once when she didn't think anyone was watching. I saw her reflection in the mirror in the bedroom downstairs. She was crying but she will never cry in front of me. I love her so much!"

Takouhi wondered if she would one day have the pleasure of meeting this amazingly strong woman. She hoped so. She would love to be able to tell her what her son thought of her because she knew that the son would never be able to tell her to her face what he had just told Takouhi.

They finally made it home through the crazy LA traffic. Takouhi was becoming a savvy LA driver in her opinion whereas Arka thought she was driving like a grandmother. He managed to drag himself out of the car and into the apartment building. She knew that she wouldn't hear from him that night and that was ok.

The next day Takouhi awoke to her cell phone vibrating off the night stand.

"Good morning" she said in a very crackling voice.

"Good morning? Sister it's 2:00 p.m. Where have you been?"

She had not realized how tired she had been. The entire oncology experience had really affected her. She didn't realize how drained she was. In fact she didn't even remember how she parked the car, came to her room, washed up and slept. But slept she did. Wow!

"Good Lord. I'm so sorry. Have you been trying to reach me?"

"Hey, if you wanted to sleep you could have done that in Vancouver."

"Are you kidding? If they knew I was in Vancouver the pager would be going off all the time!"

"Aha, so you are using me as an excuse to come here and sleep!"

"Ok, enough already! What are we doing?"

"Well if you get your giant feet out of bed and come pick me up, we'll go to La Jolla and old San Diego."

"That sounds like fun. See you soon!"

She was at his door at 3:00. Considering where her hotel was, where he lived and the fact that she had to get dressed and put her war paint on as she called it, it was quite an impressive feat! There he was again at the foot of the apartment complex. Off they went on another journey. She had been to San Diego in the past but not Old San Diego. Their first stop was La Jolla a city right on the beaches of the Pacific Ocean. Water splashed against the cliffs of the city on that extremely windy day. The city was comprised of small stores and quaint little restaurants. It was a very cozy environment. Takouhi could tell that Arka was not feeling too energetic but he wanted to make sure they had done something different.

"Let's go eat! Are you hungry? It takes food to support your stature!"

"Ok Arka jan, someone is being a bit cheeky and thinks he can get away with it. I get the size 10 part but take it easy. Unless you are prepared for countermeasures with no holds barred!"

"You mean I can't use the cancer card for you to feel sorry for me!"

"Come again? Ah, nope!"

They found a nice quiet sandwich shop by the cliff overlooking the violent waves of the ocean and sat down to eat.

"Did I ever tell you about the fact that I wanted to have a restaurant?"

"No, really?"

"Yeah, it has always been my dream to open up a nice restaurant and have nice clientele and I would go around the tables and greet people."

"Wow, how do you go from being a lawyer to wanting to open up a restaurant?"

"That year I went to Italy it left such an impression on me. I really enjoy the ambiance of a fine restaurant."

"Well then why don't you do it?"

"I will when I get better."

"Let me get this straight. You want to open a restaurant. You are going to wait until you get better but in the meantime you are thinking about opening up a joint law and real estate firm?"

"Yeah that's right. Why do you sound so surprised?"

"Well I just assumed that seeing that you are in the situation that you are in, you would appreciate how important the present is."

"Are you saying there is no future?"

"No I didn't say that and if I even for one moment believed that then I wouldn't be sitting here now would I? I'm just saying why not take advantage of the opportunity that has been presented to you? Clearly the universe is saying you shouldn't be a lawyer. You don't need that stress. At least it appears clear to me because I am on the outside looking in. So why not do something you will enjoy. And while you're doing what you enjoy it may help you heal because happiness boosts your immune system. Stress works the exact opposite way. It will destroy your immune system and right now your immune system needs all the help you can give it."

"But I have to help them out. It was a good idea. And why not do something together with Asbed and Vrej?"

"Brother, I never said don't do anything with them. They both love you and would do anything for you. Maybe they don't realize that you would rather be doing something else. Maybe they are doing all this for you. Wouldn't it be a shame that you think you're doing it for them, they think they're doing it for you and at the end of the day nobody is doing what they want to be doing."

"Is that possible?"

"Of course it's possible. Haven't you ever asked them?"

"But you don't understand Takouhi. They sacrificed so much for me to go to law school and this was going to be my time to help them. This was my time to pay them back for their efforts, especially my brother Asbed. He has done so much for me."

"Have you ever told him that?"

"He knows!"

"How do you know that he knows if you don't talk to each other?" As soon as Takouhi finished her question she went back in time to that moment in Vancouver where she had asked Asbed if he spoke to Arka about his condition and he responded by saying no. It appeared that there was an unspoken understanding between them. They did not speak about certain topics, thinking there was an understanding. Takouhi never doubted for a minute that the love was there between the two and that it was super strong. But it's tough to help someone without communication. Nobody is a mind reader. You may have the best intention but you will come up short. It will be like wanting to see a beautiful sunset but always heading east. It doesn't make sense.' Takouhi thought that Asbed would not care whether Arka should pay back for Asbed's sacrifices from the past. The only thing Asbed would want more than anything was to have Arka around forever. She knew he would do anything for Arka. If only they would communicate. Maybe that's why she was there.

"Arka why don't you talk to him about it?"

"About what? It's too late, too many people are counting on me!" His short answer stopped her in her tracks.

With that she knew that particular topic had ended. They continued on to Old San Diego. He was proud of his old stomping grounds, and had many stories to tell. He lit up as he reminisced about the past. Takouhi could tell he was in a happy place. She may not have understood all the stories but it made him happy. She was just listening. It was as if he wanted to have someone be a witness to him having had a past. That he wasn't always like this. Takouhi already knew that but she indulged him. She thought if he was happy then his immune system was doing its thing. The evening was beautiful.

On the drive back home Arka was quiet. His eyes were closed. Takouhi realized it must have been a long day for him especially since he had chemo yesterday.

"I see things so differently now." He said silently without opening his eye.

"Nothing matters. Relationships don't matter. People are selfish. You get together with someone and it doesn't work out. Then it hurts for a while. Then you get over it and start again and it becomes a repetitive process. It doesn't mean anything. There's no soul mate, twin soul or whatever else you have talked to me about in the past. People just come together at any given time because the circumstances are right. What true love? Please."

Takouhi realized that she was in the presence of a very hurt soul who was gently opening up.

"Wait a minute. Are you saying that you don't believe in finding your soul mate? Well if that's the case then guess what? You will prove yourself right! It's called the power of the subconscious mind. You are creating your own truth. Your conscious mind says one thing and the subconscious makes it happen. If what you just told me is your vision then guess what? That's exactly what you're going to get over and over again until you change that vision. Pretty simple really. What you conceive you can achieve if you believe right?"

"Are you a part time Guru?"

"You are definitely one of my most hard-headed students!" They laughed all the way home together.

The last day was finally upon them. Takouhi hated packing on the last day. Whether she wanted to admit it or not she had become attached to her aber, his stories and mannerisms. They had started a tradition where she would arrive and they would have carrot cake and on her departure they would go to the Italian restaurant and have garlic puffs! This time Asbed decided to join them. She hadn't seen him during the entire trip. In fact she wanted to but Arka kept saying later. Later had finally arrived. It was nice seeing him. She was still blown away at how much had happened since she had met him in August of 2006. So many friendships had begun since then. Not just fly by night friendships but with real substance and amazing learning experiences. She didn't realize how much she missed him until she saw him again. What was interesting was the way in which Arka acted around Asbed. He was the older and wiser brother, even though they were only one year apart. The last time she had seen Asbed and when all three of them were together was back in March. The difference was that she was now closer with Arka and knew how he felt towards his brother. It hit her all of a sudden. What if he is telling her that he is fighting but looking at his brother as if he will not see him again? To her they were like twins. The thought of one being without the other didn't seem possible. She froze for a moment at the thought. What would Asbed do without Arka? Then her mind wandered to the parents and other family she hadn't met yet. What about his mother? He was so private that he never spoke about any of them in any detail. The only time he had mentioned his mother was that time when they were coming back from the oncology centre. Takouhi had an additional mission. She wanted to make sure the mother would never outlive her son and both brothers would grow old. Maybe it was an impossible task. Maybe it was way over her head. But the only way to find out was to try. She was being a giving human but also realizing that she would be learning valuable lessons helping her further evolve as a being. She remembered reading somewhere that the greatest growth in a human being comes in times of crisis. Well if her past was any regard for that Takouhi did not shy away from crisis and drama.

"Earth calling Takouhi… hello where did you go?" asked Asbed

"Sorry just thinking about work!" replied Takouhi without flinching. Asbed was too clever to buy that. He could tell she didn't reveal the correct version of her thoughts. He had always been very attuned to Takouhi's mannerisms. They both looked at each other for a moment. Although Takouhi had advocated the benefits of verbal communication the day before with Arka, she could appreciate that there were rare occasions such that required no further verbal explanation.

"Eat your puffs before they get cold" she heard Arka's voice

She wondered, 'how many more times will I have the opportunity to eat puffs with you?

# 16

# FREQUENT FLYER

Takouhi came back from her weekend getaway energized. It didn't last long however as she was thrown onto the barnacles at work. Every year the workload would increase as the company grew and grew. The company and jobs increased yet the number of personnel to carry out the jobs remained the same. There was so much pressure that it was inevitable that something was going to give. Like the great San Andreas Fault she knew an earthquake was going to hit and there was going to be a few casualties. You didn't need to be a rocket scientist to figure it out. Her boss was extremely concerned about her but because he had been away for so many months and detached from what was really going on in his business he wasn't able to help her. There was trouble over a large contract and the demands on her were over the top even for her standards. And the worst part of all, her emails to Arka had become as rare as rain in the Sahara Desert. A friend of hers shared an analogy with her. She compared Takouhi's situation with that of a frog and a boiling pot of water. She said if the frog was directly put into a boiling pot of water the frog would immediately jump out for self-preservation. However, if the frog was put into a cold pot of water and slowly the heat was turned up, little by little the frog would start to cook and not realize it. Thus in translation, Takouhi was the cooked frog! Frog legs anyone?

Two weeks prior to her birthday Takouhi received an unexpected package from Arka. He sent her chocolates and cookies with a note that said. "You're working too hard!" She didn't pay attention to the note but when her birthday came along the first week of September she had no issues with jumping on a plane and wanting to spend it with her friends in LA. This was to be the fourth time she was going to LA in 2007. She was making up for six years of her absence since 2001.

After spending a hectic two months away from LA, she picked up Arka and took him to the oncology centre for his chemo treatment. Again, he didn't want her to come inside. She sat in the waiting room with all the others. Once again came out her voice by way of ink.

> *As I sit here at the oncology centre, I am humbled by the person who was sitting to my left a few moments ago before the doctor wanted to see him. He is intelligent, wise, strong, proud and humble. He is a natural born leader that commands respect. Yet he is humble enough to know that he doesn't know it all and thus has an insatiable desire to learn. The more I peel away all the different layers of his character, the greater my fascination and desire to discover more. A Danish philosopher named Kierkegaard once wrote: "Purity of the heart is to want one thing only."*
>
> *If there is one thing I want it is for him not only to continue with his strength and resolve to overcome this but also to practice patience. His body has in a very dramatic way told him to slow down and he needs to listen. We've discussed this before; the cancer came for a reason or perhaps many reasons. Now he has to follow through*

*with the lessons, whether it's for himself or for those around him. I take comfort in knowing that every time I return to Vancouver I leave him in the hands of an amazing group of individuals that love and adore him. There are so many people who would trade places with him in a heartbeat. Personally I want to see him reach all his goals and he will, of this I have no doubt.*

Takouhi put her pen down and decided to text Arka at that moment. She was sure that he had his phone with him on the other side of that door. "Be happy now in spite of the unease in your heart as you face this adversary, for it's your happiness today that will guarantee that you will have a tomorrow." She wanted to make sure that he read that and hoped it reached him at the most opportune moment.

After the chemo treatment they were both tired. Takouhi dropped him off at home and she went to the hotel to crash. It had been a long day. The next day would be her birthday, but it was the last thing on her mind. She was in LA but in bed at 8:30 p.m. It didn't matter. She was hoping that her presence made a difference for him.

She heard her phone vibrate while she was in deep sleep. At first she had no idea where she was and for a second she thought it was work paging her for an emergency call. She turned the light on and looked at her cell phone. It was 12:01 a.m. It was Arka. The text said "Happy Birthday Principessa" She could not have asked for a better birthday present.

When Takouhi awoke the next day she phoned Arka right away so they could plan her birthday. She had this notion that they, including Asbed and Vrej, would all be together. She thought it was funny that last year she spent her birthday in Armenia with Asbed and Vrej. A year later she was in Los Angeles. 'When did she become such a world traveler?' she thought. The day was all about her. That's not what she wanted but that's what her friend had planned. Arka decided that they were going to go shopping. Arka and Takouhi had the same taste in clothes, cars, watches, pens, books. It wasn't hard for them to find ways to get into trouble. The only thing that slowed them down was Arka's lack of energy and his inability to walk for too long. They spent the day shopping and eating. He was having fun and so was she. They decided that it was time to go to her favourite place again the beach. Their bench was waiting for them at Marina Del Rey.

"Do you think I will see your next birthday?" Arka's voice was barely audible. He couldn't even look at her. His eyes were focused towards a large sailboat with beautiful white sails as it floated down the canal towards the majesty of the Pacific Ocean.

"Why are you thinking along those lines?"

"I don't know. Life is a trip. Look at us now sitting at the beach. You didn't exist in my world last year this time and today I feel honoured that you flew all the way down here to spend your day with me."

"Are you kidding? The pleasure is all mine. I have my very own pirate that I get to walk around with. "

"Yeah and it's not even Halloween!" he said and continued "I look hideous huh?"

"If that's what you think okay but the more hideous you look the more beautiful I look in comparison to you!" She was trying to steer the ship around.

"How rude!"

"Well if you can't take it then don't dish it out"

"Hideous is your size 10 feet, you wooly mammoth."

"Wooly Mammoth? Where did that come from?" and she started laughing.

"Well, you're from this tribe aren't you? We're all hairy!"

"That's not true. You should see my mom and grandmother. They have no hair on their body. They are so fair. Our tribe comes in all shapes and sizes but you already know that."

"It's weird isn't it? I've seen Armenians with blue, green, and brown eyes. And I've seen them super dark and super light. Go figure!"

"I know Arka, I always used to use that argument when I was told that I had to marry within my tribe. I used to say look at all the different varieties of us out there are you telling me that our tribe has never mixed with others in the past. Our DNA is so different that there's no way we have stayed in the same pool. A few mommies and daddies left the tent at nights and did unmentionable things."

They both started laughing so hard that the passersby's were wondering what was going on at that bench. Takouhi wondered what they saw as they walked by. Did they simply see a man with a patch and a little belly sitting next to a woman with shiny braces? Or maybe they saw a beautiful friendship.

"But you are a mammoth you know that?"

"Now you're being mean."

"No hear me out. You are rare like Woolley mammoths. I've never met anyone like you. You are rare."

"Hold on a second! Woolley mammoths are not rare! They are extinct!" she started laughing.

"Oh you know what I mean. I know they don't exist anymore." This time his voice was serious and reflective. "I think your nickname should be Lil M."

"Now I know you're playing with me. I know you don't think I'm little and we have established that mammoths are extinct. The only thing that works is the woolly part!"

"As you wish" he said laughing "but Lil M it is!"

"You know what we should do? When you get better we are going to travel the world and learn all the languages."

"That would be awesome! I love that about you, you appreciate all the tribes in the world."

"I appreciate everyone in the world, their language, music, habits, food. I absolutely value the richness of diversity."

"Even the ones that have done you wrong," he asked with puzzlement.

"Well I have to admit some of the stuff I went through was extremely painful whether it was my divorce or the last episode with the man who ended up stalking me. However, I take responsibility for my actions and I know I learned from those episodes in my life. If I didn't learn anything then it would be a shame. Do you want to hear something interesting about my belief system?"

"Are you kidding? Of course!"

"Well in my what I call sheep days where dad's rule was the rule of the land, I did everything as I was told. I questioned it internally but I still followed through. All my father had to do was look at me from across the room with his huge eyes and I was in line with the sheep."

"If his eyes are anything like yours then I can see the cause for intimidation." Arka's chuckling reminded her of Santa Clause at the photo booth in the middle of a mall.

"Very funny! Anyway, in my twenties I started to realize that he had been that way for what he thought at the time was the best thing for me. He was protecting me from the outside world. I guess like so many fathers and daughters he wanted to protect his little princess. Imagine how he must have felt because he was young and came to this new world with his young wife, two little kids and carrying in the suitcase of his mind belief systems from another part of the world. This world was extremely foreign to him. And to top it all off they didn't speak the language. Now he had to deal with raising this little 'know it all' creature."

"Your poor dad. I can just picture you in pigtails running around with a pen and paper like a mini reporter." Takouhi couldn't help but laugh at Arka's comments because it took her back to a time when she had actually done that.

"Yeah, I think they both knew a long time ago that I was not going to be the sheep. I would always question things and reformulate. I drove people nuts constantly asking why? Why is it this way?"

"Well did you find your answer?" Arka was fully engaged with Takouhi and looking directly at her lips waiting to catch every word.

"Unknowingly they held me back when I was younger. But I can't get mad at them for it. That wouldn't be constructive. I focus on the good aspect. I focus on the loving family unit. I focus on all the camping trips, road trips, you name it. My parents were always there for me and my brother in every which way."

"So your strategy is that instead of focusing on what you have missed out on, you're focusing on all that you got?"

"Yes that's exactly right! The irony was that as much as they had tried to protect me from the world in my teens I threw myself into the fire in my 20s and now 30s. I chose to work for a male dominated industry. The sexism, the crudeness, the so-called 'realness' started shaping me. I was an anomaly in that industry. I had lived amongst them but they didn't understand my way of living and BS. We would get into arguments about how things were in my tribe and the guys at work would tell me how crazy these things sounded to them. What I had seen for so many years as real and had made decisions based on was deemed archaic."

"So you're saying the BS was coming to light?"

"Yup, my view of the 'real' world changed incredibly. That was part of the reason I wanted to work and go to university at the same time. At university there was another belief system of how things should be, but then I would go to the reality of the work world in the afternoon and butt heads with these rough and tough divers."

"You know Takouhi, your job fascinates me. There is nobody I know that has an interesting job like yours."

"Well, the interesting part was that I was part of them and yet wasn't. Because my belief system was still ingrained and I was still sheep-like. I felt I had to marry an Armenian and I would look at the handsome divers only from afar. In a world full of choices I had to choose from a little Armenian pool. Is that fair?"

"I guess not, but Takouhi, you just went from a university belief to work belief to a relationship and marriage belief."

"I know I'm just expressing the different levels and layers of BS in my evolution."

"Ok I'm following you please continue," Arka was still focused on Takouhi's face and the way in which she was fully animated with her hands in order to express herself.

"It wasn't fair that I had to choose from a small pool but I didn't focus on that either. When I got married to an Armenian and followed the rules to the tee, I learned more lessons. But the Armenian princess that daddy was trying to protect was learning the lessons in a painful way. And this is where it gets really beautiful."

"As beautiful as my reflection in the mirror?"

"It's all about you isn't it?" and they both started laughing.

"As I was saying" as she looked at Arka in an attempt to appear serious by rolling her eyes, "sometimes if the lessons are not painful then you don't grow as a person. There is no growth in the comfort zone. I was evolving and I didn't even know it. My greatest growth came after the divorce. One of the saddest things I heard tribal members say without even knowing what was going on in my life was "don't hang around her; she will give you divorce ideas," or "she has a good job and money therefore *lezoon yergarela*" (she thinks she has the right to talk back!)."

"Oh that's a good one! I should remember to use that one! But seriously, the people saying these kind of things must have thought that money means power and that's how they controlled their household. The golden rule, the person with the gold rules! That would be something generally a man would say because their kingdom and power was being challenged by a woman."

"I guess I was challenging the status quo. The sad part about it all was that when I was married I never threw the fact that I was making more money in the face of my ex-husband. In fact, knowing well that there's a belief system that most men in our tribe measure their self worth by the amount of dollars they bring home I was very sensitive to it. I would always make sure that he knew he was valued in other ways and that the money would come."

"Takouhi dear that's a tough one even for me. As open minded as I may think I am, I'm not sure how I would handle not bringing home some gold."

"Well, my belief system in terms of relationships was that it was teamwork, not one person dominating over the other. I never wanted to put my man down; if I did, I would be putting myself down. After all, the person you are walking beside is there because you chose him. You represent him; he represents you, hopefully with utmost class and grace."

"That's a pretty cool belief but you definitely would need both people to subscribe to it in order for it to work."

"I just assumed that he was from my tribe and he would understand me since I had bought into that BS" that was such a sore spot for Takouhi which was evident from the tears that were building in her eyes, "of course when the tides turned and he started to bring home some money towards the end, in his mind's eye his personal self worth and stock value went from .10 a share to $100 a share Euro."

"Wow that would have been a great stock to stick with!"

"It's my birthday! Should you be pushing my buttons like this?"

"Oh, relax, I'm not making fun of you. I'm doing what you always do to me when you think I don't notice"

"What's that?"

"Change my paradigm, add humour and change my state, so I don't feel sad!"

Takouhi was impressed by her astute aber.

"So do you think we get along because we are from the same tribe," he asked.

"Well, there is the familiarity. So maybe. But since those days of the Sheep and now focusing on something bigger which you've heard me say shero. It's not about the tribe, it's about the quality of people and their values and belief systems. When you find someone who shares similar values and taps into positive beliefs, who is constantly wanting to evolve and grow as a human being then you make sure that person is somewhere close to your constellation. Hold on to them just enough so you learn from them but not so much that you prevent their progression and evolution."

"Lil M I would hold on to you but there is so much of you to hold on to especially with your size 10 feet!"

"Smartass!"

Of all the birthdays she had had in her adult years this was by far one of the most memorable. The conversations with Arka not only enriched him with information yet it also reaffirmed to Takouhi her evolution. She owned her constructive beliefs. But she couldn't help but think about his initial question.

"Takouhi, do you think I will see your next birthday?"

# 17

## PANDORA'S BOX

Takouhi was concerned. Arka wasn't the same. Since her return to Vancouver she had noticed a real decline in correspondence. In the past he would at least send one or two emails or texts a week. Now there was complete silence. Although her emails continued she wasn't as confident that he was still reading. There were moments that her negative thoughts crept in. Then fear would take over and she would worry about receiving a call from Asbed saying something she would never want to hear. She wondered what was going on with him really. Was he feeling ill more so than before? Or was he simply working hard and focused on his new business venture with his brother? In typical Takouhi fashion she reached out to him in the only way she knew with a letter included in a box of goodies.

*Dear Arka,*

*Another letter? Oh my God! Enough already he says! This time I'm not even going to write a practice copy. I'm just going to write what I feel and cross out mistakes, assuming I make any because we both know that I'm perfect!*

*What's with this package you ask? Well it's a 'just because' package... no special occasion in the classic sense. So what's in Pandora's Box? What is it that once you open your life will never be the same again? What great secrets will be revealed as a result of this box?*
*It's 8:20 p.m. Thursday September 15/07. You should see how beautiful the city lights look tonight. I can't wait until you see Vancouver. I really believe you will love this place. The world will be in awe of it in 2010 at the Olympics but I hope you get to see it before then, as well as then. You will spiritually connect with this environment with its lush green beauty, fresh air and glacial water. I am not doing it justice. You have to see how beautifully city and nature complement each other here.*
*What does all this have to do with the box? Let's see, what do we have? Item one is incense, similar to the ones I gave you already. It is lavender. Very soothing. You said you don't have an incense holder. I know it's kind of girly but it's the nicest one I could find for now. Just place a stick in the holder and light it. Sit back, close your eyes, breath deep, and let your thoughts just drift away. Allow yourself to think about what you really want in life and how you envision getting there. Remembering it's one thing to have a vision yet without the action of getting there the vision remains a dream. Take your time in doing this. When you open your eyes and feel you're up to it write down some notes in the journal I gave you way back when I introduced Sir Marcus to you. I know you don't like to write your thoughts down in case somebody finds it, reads it and judges you. But you grow when you have the courage to be and show who you are to the world. To be your self you also have*

*to show your vulnerabilities. You will be surprised how people will love you more for being real and open and raw. And just because you wrote something a year ago doesn't mean that you can't change your mind and refine your thoughts. Change is inevitable.*

*I light an incense almost every night. In fact, along with my routine I put on my favourite CD in the background Iriknain by Khatchatour Avetissian or play any of a number of songs by my favourite Duduk composer Jivan Gasparian. I know there are tons of CDs out there with Tibetan chants etc that are just as powerful and soothing. It all depends on what works for you and what moves your soul. You only find out by experimenting and sitting still. Sitting still and thinking about being independent of others BS and focus on what you hold true for yourself. This leads me to another poem I wrote during my adventures as the Ducati Diva. I know that you think the motorcycle is dangerous. However, without that period in my life I wouldn't be able to write to you like this today.*

**Independence**

Independence is strength beyond measure
Each moment to oneself one must treasure
For anyone can be with friends and lovers
But only when alone one truly uncovers
The true desires and wants that are inside
That makes you tick and come alive.

*As you are sitting still, think about who you are and what BS you hold true in your life and which ones do not serve you anymore.*

*Item two is a cup, or, as I call it, a self-portrait. I love it so much that I even made one for myself. It's a cartoon picture of a little boy pirate holding a sword with one hand and with the other holding the hand of a little girl dressed like a princess who is also holding a wizard's wand. Did you notice how the patch is even on the right eye just like yours is? I found this picture as I was walking through Victoria a few weeks ago and looked up at a children's shoe store and there we were, you and I on an advertising poster. How can you tell me that's not you with your cute little patch? And as for the girl with the wizard's wand, well, that's me of course wishing she could magically make this tumour in your head disappear. Meanwhile she is holding your hand and walking with you.*

*With a cup comes tea of course. Organic good stuff. Green tea is good for you right now. It has lots of antioxidants that are required for the body more so with your little glitch. A temporary glitch I might add. Yeah Takouhi, two years temporary he says, to which I would reply relax. In the big scheme of things two years is nothing. And we both know it will be going away by your next birthday.*

*My favourite content of the box is the piggy bank. Do you know that I have had it for ages? It's a cute little cartoon dog dressed as a pirate with a patch and it has a little bird sitting on its shoulder. I've always been drawn to patches and pirates. So in some way you are a self-actualized prophecy. Talk about the law of attraction working! This ceramic bank means the world to me and I want you to have it. We can use it to save up for all the language learning trips we plan on going on. A vision without action remains only a dream. We can dream but we're also movers and shakers, right? We'll both contribute as much as we can and each time I come to visit you in Los Angeles I will add to the bank. In fact, if you look inside I already have.*

*Well did you notice the paper quality just changed? Believe it or not I had to change my notepad because the other one finished. I wasn't planning on writing so much but I guess I'm in the zone today. Honestly I am going with the flow here, there is no rewrite going to happen. What you get is a first hand and only draft. I kind of like this. I am being my authentic self. Okay back to the box.*

*Next on the list is the umbrella. Like the song. You know what I'm talking about. I love this Umbrella because I ordered it through UNICEF. The umbrella is covered with hellos in different languages. That is exactly what we should use the ceramic bank for. Travel and languages.*

*And now, we come to my last item, the crème de la crème if you will. It is a little gold cross. This cross has been with me for over 30 years. I have never parted with it. My grandmother gave it to me. I want you to have it. Don't wear it if you don't want to but keep it close to you or in your room somewhere. Grandma would definitely want you to have it. I want Grandma's spirit and energy to be around you and I want her to protect you. I know she will as she has a soft spot for you. Plus, you and her son share the same name. This is my most valuable possession, a part of my soul and a part of a woman who helped shape me. When you have a child in the future, make sure he or she gets it in order to pass the good vibes. If you have twins, well sorry can't help you!*

*So there, a Pandora's box.*

*Love and vitamin P to you always,*

*Takouhi*

*PS. You once asked what I wanted from you. The only thing I want from you is for you to heal yourself. It's not only the cancer I speak of. Let go of past hurt and forgive others and yourself. I won't go anywhere unless you want me to. A friendship is not a burden. It is an opportunity to learn about yourself and heal yourself and others as a result. I take responsibility for being here. I choose to be on this journey with you wherever it takes us. We all have choices in life from the moment we wake up until the moment we sleep. I know you keep saying you don't want me to get hurt. You are helping me grow and evolve as a spirit just by being around you and if I am helping you in any way in return then I am blessed. When you beat this thing I want to work on all the ideas we have like goodwill for humanity. There is nothing you will not be able to do and it will be my honour to share that with you."*

Even that was a long letter for Takouhi's standards, but she had been honest. She said everything she felt needed to be said. Takouhi had sat down and written for two hours without correcting, changing, or adjusting any of her thoughts. Silence lingered in spite of her having sent the box on September 16. However, on September 29, thirteen days after she had sent the package she was deafened with a sonic boom. Apparently that was the day when he received it. All of a sudden she received a sea of texts the most important of which read:

*Takouhi,*

*I just booked tickets to Vancouver for October 18. My brother, his girlfriend and I are coming!*

*Arka*

# 18

# WELCOME TO VANCOUVER

She couldn't believe it. She was sitting on her couch very still, tears flowing down her face. She was frozen with excitement. Not knowing if this was a dream or not. Just a month ago Takouhi and her mother were sitting at the airport waiting for her cousin to arrive. She specifically remembered asking her, "Do you think Arka will ever walk through those arrival gates?" And Takouhi's mother said, "why not?" He didn't have much energy, his body was constantly changing with the chemo and radiation, he had to carry tons of medication on top of everything else and yet he was packing a bag and coming. She was humbled. Did Pandora's Box reach his soul? This was confirmation for her that amazing things happen when people show their spirit and humanity to one another.

She couldn't remember the last time she was so excited to go to the airport. The house was clean, the car was washed, and she was at the airport two hours before he arrived. She knew he was coming, but part of her didn't believe it. She hadn't seen him since her birthday in LA. Then, there he was. Limping and titled to the right but he was there. His hair was growing in again, and it was black and beautiful. He was puffy again, his stomach had grown and his cheeks were puffy and red. She no longer noticed the patch, it had become part of him. With tears in her eyes and her voice cracking she joked, "Wow, this is proof that Canadians will let anyone in," and they both started to laugh as they gave each other big hugs.

When they walked into Takouhi's house it occurred to her that it was the same time of night as she had been writing him that long letter over a month ago. He walked in to see almost the same vision she had been trying to describe to him in her letter of what Vancouver looked like. He went over to the balcony and looked out. She stood leaning against the living room wall and watched him from afar. Her tearful eyes caused a leaky condo situation. 'If the law of attraction is so simple why aren't we all doing this all the time?' she thought. He didn't move from his spot by the balcony door for ten minutes. She wished she could use that princess wand from the image on the cup to hear what he was thinking. Was he saying wow? Was he saying why am I here? Or was he wondering what this will look like from above? Or maybe he wasn't thinking. She didn't want him to see her cry so she quietly went to the bathroom. When she came out, he was on the couch, asleep. He looked pale and clammy. She covered him with a blanket. He must have been so exhausted from his travels. Coming to Vancouver was a big event. She sat behind her home office desk and began to write about the image before her. However, she knew no matter how often she spoke of it in the future she could never pay the tribute it deserved with her descriptions. It would be one of those moments where she anticipated just thinking about and her heart would instantly well up with gratitude and love. If there was any kind of emotion she could wish for people was to feel this at least once in a lifetime. No amount of drugs or alcohol or any other substance could evoke such bliss and love, where all that mattered was the love for that other person. She knew he hadn't just come for himself or to spend time with Asbed. He had sensed how much it would mean to Takouhi for him to come and see Vancouver. In spite of everything he was going through he still came to Vancouver. Takouhi thought that 'that was humanity when you go above and beyond your needs and you just give.' And he gave his time to her.

Asbed and his girlfriend arrived the next day. The four of them spent three days hanging out together. Asbed had already been to Vancouver in January of that year but it had all been about skiing. This time it was all about showing Arka the city. On the second night Arka kept insisting that he wanted to cook for all of them. While Asbed and his girlfriend went sightseeing and shopping, Takouhi took Arka to the grocery store so he could buy all the ingredients for his fancy feast. The experience in the grocery store was like taking her personal pirate on a treasure hunt. They searched for specific spices, special sauces, and special focaccia bread. After they got home, he asked Takouhi to leave him the kitchen and get busy elsewhere. She left Arka and briefly went to work, picked up the happy couple from their sightseeing tour, and took them back home. The three of them walked in and there was steam everywhere. The kitchen was so hot that the windows had fogged up. Takouhi had wondered if Asbed had ever seen Arka cook before. The look on Asbed's face was full of pride as evident with his beautiful smile. Arka had mentioned in their day trip to La Jolla that he wanted to open a restaurant and here he was being the chef at large in the kitchen. It was a self-fulfilled prophecy.

On the second full day of the visit they conquered the town. Takouhi took them to Granville Island and for a drive along British Properties as they were looking at the view of downtown from there. She was showing them all the houses her father had built, the mark he had put on the land if you will. They were drooling at the houses and the view.

"Wow and we think the views on the silly mountains in the valley overlooking the smoggy city are beautiful," Arka said in amazement.

"Can you imagine waking up, wearing your robe sitting on your balcony and eating a bagel with cream cheese and smoked salmon?" replied Asbed.

Takouhi thought, 'How's that for visualization?'

Finally the day came where they had to say goodbye. She couldn't believe it had gone by so fast. She had enjoyed the interaction between the two brothers. She loved walking behind them as they walked side by side. The way they would point out things in the windows of stores, and decide if they liked it or not. Watching their mannerisms when they spoke with their hands as visual aids made her think she was watching mime. She rarely saw them together. What she noticed was there was great rapport but no real conversation. Did that make sense? They were so different in so many ways and yet so connected. They made many statements without saying a word to each other. It was as if she was watching a beautiful play unfold in front of her with the two main characters not really having much dialogue yet she understood what the play was about. Was she the adopted sister because she could tune in to their frequency? It reminded her of something. She imagined if she was sitting on a plane and a movie was playing. If she didn't have her headphones on she would not know what the conversation was about. She would probably try to lip read or guess the actor's movements and motions, but she would have probably missed the core meaning of the movie. In this case, she was looking at the screen and had her invisible headphones to their conversation. So much so that at times they realized she was in tune with what they were up to and all three of them shared a smile.

Asbed and his girlfriend left on an earlier flight thus Takouhi had Arka for a few more hours. Although she was sad to see them go she was excited to have Arka for a few hours by herself. He was tired. He had given all his energy to be with his brother. It seemed as soon as his brother left so did his energy. His paleness returned and he just wanted to be still somewhere. Those few days had been more activity than he had been used to. Perhaps the fresh clean Vancouver air shocked his system. It reminded her of the conversation in September while she was in LA when she had asked him to come and visit. The thought was that the fresh air would do him good. Not just that, but at the time he was well enough that he was jogging and exercising. She had visualized how he could go jogging on the Stanley Park Seawall, which was a moment away. To Takouhi there was nothing more spiritual and healing than being in nature. But he couldn't do it at the time. He kept giving her reasons why he couldn't come.

"I couldn't leave my mom it would not be fair to her!"

"But your mom would want what's best for you and she is more than welcome to come here too."

"But we're also setting up the new office."

"Wouldn't it be better for you to take care of yourself now so you can better serve the office in the long term rather than focusing on the short term set up?"

"Yeah but I would be letting them down. It would be selfish of me."

She finally had snapped and said, "what if you don't take care of yourself, get more stressed out and are not around anymore? Then what?"

He had just looked at her with a grin and said, "then I guess it wouldn't be my problem anymore would it?"

While she was remembering all this she asked herself, 'How different am I?' How many times had she outstretched herself for those she cared about including work? Through Arka's actions or inactions, she was learning more about herself. He was her mirror. She allowed things to unfold around her as they were and was in tune enough to pick up on the lessons as they were presented to her. Why was this happening now and not before? Simply because she wasn't open for it and like Arka, she was focusing on all the reasons she couldn't do something and not focusing on the reasons she could or should. He had no clue the impact he was making on her life.

They went for lunch but were very quiet. As they were driving over the beautiful Lions Gate Bridge on their way to the airport he finally spoke.

"You know Lil M, I know you may not think so but you are one of my closest and dearest friends. I need you to know that."

Takouhi was driving and biting her lip.

"Don't think I don't realize that you have always sent all the emails and texts. Don't think I don't realize how much effort you have put in to reach me. I'm not being like this on purpose."

She couldn't help it she jumped in "Like what? Suffering from EC?"

He looked at her puzzled. "What's EC?

"You have another condition. You are emotionally constipated." Tears of laughter were flowing from his eyes.

"Okay, okay, continue with what you were saying," Takouhi impatiently wanted to hear the rest of the speech.

"Just know that you are extremely close to me and always will be."

Takouhi just smiled.

"But I will tell you this, if you think I'm emotionally constipated then what do you think of my friend Heros in LA?"

"Don't even get me started on him" she rolled her eyes and continued "Arka you are my focus right now and I just want you to express yourself in a trusting environment knowing that everything will work out in its right time place and sequence!"

"C'est vrai?"

"Absoulement!"

# 19

# THE BS OF BUSINESS

It was another long weekend in November, Remembrance Day. Last year she had flown to LA for a business trip and had met Arka in Las Vegas. In her mind she had seen more than twelve full moons since she had met him and yet it had only been one year. It was so interesting that Takouhi was now seeing him what seemed like once a month. She did her routine. Morning flight, rental car, check in at hotel, text and pick up downstairs.

"Are you okay with taking me to chemo again?"

"Of course I am."

He was very quiet. Once again, he didn't let her come inside the treatment room. She sat patiently in the waiting room as always. For once she had no energy to write. She was tired. Not from the flight but from work. There was something brewing and she couldn't put her finger on it. She was quite aware that there were forces working behind the scenes with the other companies they had aligned themselves with. For the first time she was so overwhelmed with the little details as there was so much of it that she didn't have time to step back and look at the big picture.

When Arka came out of his treatment she could tell that he was exhausted. He was walking very slowly and holding on to the walls or nearby chairs for support. He had to lean on her and put his arm around her shoulder for support as they made their way to the car. Had she asked him for them to go to the beach or have carrot cake he wouldn't have said no because he wouldn't want to let her down. She knew better. She took him home. He needed to rest, no questions asked.

The next day, Takouhi and Arka went to Old Pasadena. She could tell there was something on his mind. He was acting the same way he had back in July when he felt awkward about the friendship talk.

"What are your plans for Christmas?" he asked.

"I suppose either you come to Vancouver or I'll come to you."

"Well that's what I want to talk to you about."

"Ok, you look stressed out again. What's up?"

"Well it seems like a group of us and our families are either going to our local ski resort or we're going to go on a cruise."

"I'm not welcome. Is that what you're saying?"

"Well I don't know how the families would handle you and who they would think you are."

For the same reason Takouhi had avoided staying with family in order so that they wouldn't ask about Arka. Now it was happening to her. The difference being was that she would be protecting him from their negative BS. She wasn't sure how her presence would harm them or hurt her.

"They're just not open minded, Takouhi. They wouldn't understand who you are and what you have to offer and would just judge you. Is that what you really want?"

Takouhi was not afraid of their BS and them judging her, but something bigger was happening here. He wasn't worried about their reaction to her because he was quite aware that she could take care of herself. He was pushing her away.

"Arka, whatever makes you the most comfortable. My friendship with you is to help you get better, not to create a stressful situation."

"Thanks for understanding Lil M."

Her biggest concern was that he was pushing her away because he wasn't thinking of a tomorrow anymore. The medication, the frustration, and his BS that he was dealing with on a day-to-day basis were getting to him.

The last day, Arka, Takouhi and Asbed went to Marina Del Rey to have the traditional goodbye puffs. Arka was not well at all. He barely had the energy to be there.

"You don't look the same," said Asbed to Takouhi "you really look tired. I was going to say something in Vancouver in October. The last time I saw you before that was back in July. What happened to you over the summer?"

"Work happened to me. The summer months have always been crazy. This year my boss left again for two months but what made it different was that we had a huge contract that was way over our heads. It took four companies to make it happen."

"What's in it for you?" he asked.

"I don't know what you mean?" she asked puzzled.

"Why are you working so hard for him?"

"For who?"

"Your boss!"

"I'm not working hard for him. I'm working hard for the company. If it has my name on it then I am going to give it my best!

"Does it have your name on it?" continued Arka.

"No not in writing but that's not what I meant by my name on it."

"Tell her Asbed, tell her she's being naïve and wasting her time with people who will drop her in a heartbeat!"

"Oh stop it! We're not like that. I just meant that if I am responsible for something I am going to give it my best! I'm my own boss!"

"Ok so if that's your belief system then why are you so stressed out."

"Well the work load is huge and my boss's behavior has changed. He brought in a consultant to help us organize and become more efficient but since then I have lost touch with him. We used to have morning chats and he would say he couldn't start his day without our chats but it's stopped. He won't talk to me anymore. His emails are actually sent by the consultant but with my boss's name on it. Something strange is going on."

"Takouhi, get ready. It's coming!" Asbed said.

"What's coming?"

"They are getting ready to get rid of you."

"Oh, what BS you have. For someone so smart you are so naïve!" Arka jumped in.

"No, you follow your belief system and I'll follow mine. I am operating with shero principles. You are operating with scarcity, paranoia, and the concept that everyone is out to get each other. I trust people. I have seen so many amazing business models that aren't like that. A company's greatest assets are its employees! You can make money and have satisfied employees. You can have a win-win situation. The only difference is having a will to do it."

"Talk to me next year this time, let's compare notes then!" said Arka just nodding his head.

This comment made Takouhi happy. It meant that Arka believed he was going to be around next year.

"Is your boss married?" asked Asbed.

"No why?"

"Does he have a girlfriend?"

"Yeah he is dating."

"That's another thing. Has she met you?"

"Yeah a few times."

"Do you get along?"

"What does that have to do with anything?"

"She might be whispering thoughts in his ear about you. There's always jealousy and the ability of another women to get rid of you especially if she feels threatened" continued Asbed.

"Do you guys walk around with these suspicious BSs all the time? They are all negative and destructive. How do you function?"

"I told you before Lil M, it's all about the Benjamins!"

Takouhi was too tired to continue. Okay she thought. She had been in business for 17 years, and in that time she had opened another business on the side. She was quite aware of the Benjamins. Her greatest satisfaction was engaging with people. She didn't want to look down when her moral compass told her to look up. Some people may be the way the brothers described. However, it didn't apply to her. Her world was different. Wasn't it?

# 20

# WHEN A DOOR CLOSES

While she was on the plane flying back from LA she kept remembering the conversation she had just had with her abers.

"Get out of there."

"They don't appreciate you."

"It's not yours."

"You're just an employee and they will get rid of you."

At the same time she was thinking back to the conversation she had had with her employer in August, suggesting to him that if her position in the company was going to effect the future of the company's alliances and revenue generating opportunities then for the sake of the company she helped build she would step aside. Her employer had responded by saying absolutely not and that one of the main reasons he brought in the consultant was to fine tune things. Takouhi was all for cleaning things up and creating a stealth-like environment where everything moved forward like a finely oiled piece of machinery. She had been outstretched in different directions that year, especially between May and November. She oversaw all aspects of the company from operations, logistics, human resources, accounting and numerous others without much assistance. Yes, she was exhausted but she always believed in the bigger picture.

Her abers didn't understand her employer. He wasn't even her employer. They were a team. She had his back and he had hers.

Arka and Asbed didn't understand or know the history, the sacrifices, and the feeling of a workplace as a family. She had been young when she started there and so was the company so they grew up together. Now the stage was set where changes were coming. The company had grown and pressure had been dangerously building like a nuclear power plant about to explode.

She was about to clarify her role and make peace with the alliance members but nothing had prepared her for the consultant that was sent in. The consultant eloquently convinced her employer to abdicate his throne and took complete charge of the company. Originally he befriended her as he was trying to assess the key players in the company. He began to take away her responsibilities and soon, Takouhi herself was on the chopping block. She was invited into the conference room. The man across from her pulled his glasses down and peered from over the top of the rims at her calmly. She knew what was coming. When she walked out of the board-room her back seized. Her mind was numb and her body was reacting. She felt she was in a horror movie where she was so overcome with emotion that her throat had seized. She was screaming but nobody could hear. Her employer offered nothing but silence. She was so tired and exhausted she could not make sense of what happened. Why had they chosen this method of termination when only months ago she had told her employer that she would willingly depart for the greater good in a win-win situation. After 17 years, after 17 years!

So now what? Opportunity wasn't just knocking: it was striking at the door. 'Takouhi get into shero state now,' she thought. 'Go and don't look back. You are being presented with an opportunity to leave. Okay, you may not like the way in which it was handled but go. You're not a victim. Whatever you have done for the company you have done so by choice. You did it because it's who you are. You have been true to yourself and gave what you knew you were capable of giving. You are and always will be your own boss operating on the highest possible frequency.' The opportunity was to see what's out there. The opportunity was to leave the safe harbor and explore. Maybe this was meant to be so she could move her life in another direction. How would she know if she didn't go?

It was time for her to fly. She had come to learn one very precious lesson from Arka. Although it was something she spoke about daily, the reality of it didn't hit home the way it did now. The realization was the importance of the present moment. All those years she had focused intensely on the future, while the present was slipping through her fingers. It was time that Takouhi reeled in the anchor and set sail.

The best way for Takouhi to get into shero state was on a road trip. Her drug of choice was gasoline. When opportunity came through the door she thought 'time to detox in the city of botox.' Thinking win-win her plan was to rent a studio in Marina Del Rey for a couple of months and mentally cleanse herself by writing as much as she could and also spent as much time as she could with Arka. Her dash stashed with her favourite CDs; Napoleon Hill, Norman Vincent Peale, James Allen, Dale Carnegie,

John Maxwell, Daniel Goleman, Deepak Chopra, Stephen Covey, Wayne Dyer, Michael Beckwith, and Anthony 'main man' Robbins. She had heard him speak about mentorship and surrounding yourself with people who you can learn from. In the absence of people she admired, books and CDs were the next best thing. Having experienced that things can change at a moment's notice, she didn't want to waste any opportunity. She was excited and nervous at the same time. She had spent time with Arka and Asbed but never day-to-day for two months. Plus, Arka kept telling her that he wasn't the same anymore. Last time she had seen him was in November. Two months had passed since then. In his situation a lot could happen in two months. He felt increasingly weak. Time was of the essence and opportunity was indeed knocking.

While she was driving down the Pacific Coast Highway, her soul, spirit, and thoughts were travelling the world. She would catch herself and come back and laugh. If someone was tracking her on GPS they could physically find her but it would just be the outside shell as she wasn't really there at certain moments. In spite of listening to inspirational, motivational, leadership, and spiritual CDs, she was squirrelly, a little insecure and unable to stop the chit-chat of thoughts and doubts. Some of her squirrely thoughts had to do with what had just taken place at work. 'Most people would have killed to have a position like mine and finally get paid the money I was making. What went wrong?' she thought which was followed quickly by 'what happened was that my time at that place was finished. It was a hurtful way to go but the only way. I saw them as family and felt too responsible for them to be able to leave in any other way. Similar to when a mother has a difficult time letting go of her children. It was like pulling off a band-aid: really quickly. In a weird way they did you a favour.' The more she thought along those lines the more empowered she felt. So what if the money was great when she knew that she wasn't reaching anything near her potential and was emotionally and physically taxed on a day-to-day basis. 'Imagine,' she thought 'if I can make more money than before doing what I love doing and surrounding myself with like minded, solution focused, constructive people leading their lives with shero principles. Wow! It is possible and this is my opportunity. If not now, when? If not me, who? Did the consultant do me a favour? Maybe I should write him a thank you letter. After all Satan was once an angel too!' She laughed out loud in her car and would wonder if other drivers passing by thought she was nuts. She wasn't nuts; she was having a squirrelly episode!

When she had tackled the squirrelly work thoughts, her thoughts jumped to money concerns, missing her immediate family by going away, and Arka. She started doubting, 'Who am I to think that I can make a difference in Arka's life when I'm sure he's already surrounded by loving friends and family?' One by one she talked her way through each squirrelly scenario to empower herself and take responsibility. Her belief system was that everything happens for a reason which empowered her, as opposed to 'Why me? Why does the wind always bring spit my way?' She focused on the opportunity to spend time with Arka. That was important. She needed to get to him, take him out of his present environment and give him a change of scenery. Marina Del Rey had significance for them as they had had great memories there. Last year, they had visited Marina Del Rey numerous times. Wasn't it funny, she thought, that back then she could see herself living in Marina Del Rey and now she was heading down there to stay. 'What your mind can conceive, you can achieve if you believe!' All her Guru's repeated that over and over again and it had become her mantra. Although the fear of an unknown path was alive within her, there was a greater fear that she was embracing. The fear of regret far outweighed the fear of the unknown. Had she not taken this opportunity to make a difference for her friend, regret would have eaten her alive for years to come. If it was true that life was defined by the opportunities presented to her she didn't want it to be defined by the ones she didn't take. She was of the opinion that in life people don't regret things they did as much as the things they didn't do. She didn't want to regret the latter. Not walking through the door of opportunity would have meant failure in her mind. Taking the risk was an automatic success because it meant she had moved herself forward in life with positive intentions. There was no regret when a person did something with good intentions and shero principles. The regret came when a person stood still and did nothing but watch the world go by just as her boss had done with his silence. By the time she was close to her destination, her resolve was absolute and her commitment complete. She thought 'Yes, I have decided to willingly and wholeheartedly enter this chapter in my life by choice. Nothing and no one will stand in my way. Other people's opinions will not matter nor shake me. I am determined, I am steadfast. I have left the safety of the harbour and am sailing towards the rewarding unknown.' When Takouhi's mother was being over-protective and worried about her, Takouhi would tell her the following phrase to put her mind at ease: "Mom, imagine if Columbus listened to his mom when she said 'Honey, don't go. They say that the world is flat, you will fall off! What if they're all right?" to which Takouhi envisioned Columbus's response to his mother "And what if they're all wrong?"

# 21

# MARINA DEL REY

It took her two days to drive down to the Los Angeles area. She had been driving very slowly as there were storms in Northern California. It was the first time ever that she was more focused on looking at her dash to check the temperature as opposed to looking to see how fast she was driving. Her car was not suited for winter weather and she knew on this trip the last thing she had to worry about was a speeding ticket. It slowly warmed up until she was in sunny southern California. She headed straight to Marina Del Rey to grab the keys to her two-month home away from home. The next day, Takouhi jumped out of bed, and took a good look at the beautiful California coast. The waves of the Pacific were steps away from her studio. 'So this is what waking up by the water in California looks like. Hmm, I can get used to this!' she thought. She grabbed her journal and went for a walk by the beach. Completely inspired by the glorious morning, she sat down and began to write in her journal.

*February 5, 2008*

*I am overwhelmed with gratitude and thankfulness. I am overwhelmed with the beauty of nature that surrounds me, the sunshine, the ocean, the blue sky, the majesty of the horizon. Before me awaits the totality of possibilities. I am so thankful that I have been able to organize myself in such a way and more importantly blessed that I am able to be sitting here writing this. I see snow covered mountains in the distance and yet I sit here warm and protected under the sun's glistening rays. I walked down Marina Del Rey's pier this morning and said hello to passersby, which I think caught them off guard. I forgot how Canadian I am, eh? There was an old man sitting at the end of the pier surrounded by pigeon's. A simple good morning and you should have seen how his face lit up.*

She was so lost in thought that she didn't realize there was someone standing over her watching her write. She became aware of his presence when there was a shadow over her blocking her sun.

"May I ask what you're writing about?" asked a gentleman who reminded her of her grandfather.

"Just various thoughts of appreciation."

"Interesting. Are you a visitor?" he asked with curiosity.

"To Marina Del Rey yes, but not to California. I've been here many times before."

"So what brings you here this time?"

"A different chapter in my life and I want to be here for my friend who isn't well!"

"Good for you for being there for your friend. "

"Actually it's a win-win situation. I've learned a lot from him. I'm learning about spirituality, humanity, enlightenment, responsibility, and opportunity. Or, as I like to call it, shero!"

The man's eyes lit up.

"Wow!" and he sat down next to her and continued.

"I was watching you walking down the pier and I saw you say hello to that man surrounded by pigeons. Do you know that he sits there everyday and nobody says anything to him"

"That's a shame. I wonder why people don't acknowledge each other sometimes."

"Well let's not talk about why they don't, let's talk about why you did."

"OK, that's easy. To quote one of my favourite people named David Hawkins he's a psychiatrist, spiritual author, and lecturer "Make a gift of your life and all mankind by being kind, considerate, forgiving and compassionate at all times in all places and under all conditions with everyone as well as yourself. This is the greatest gift anyone can give.'

"I understand that but how does this apply to you saying hello to a stranger."

"I get great satisfaction and feed off the positive energy that I get from a smile. In a way I'm being selfish. But I see it as a win-win situation. I make them feel good and acknowledge their presence with genuine heartfelt hello, and in return I feel good and am propelled with positivity when I see them smile. There is nothing more beautiful to me than when a person smiles. I do this all the time in elevators. In my building at home I am usually the first one on as I live on the top floor. Each time someone walks in especially in the mornings they do so with their head hanging down and there are those awkward moments of silence in a vertical box that hangs from a cable. Nine out of ten times you should see how people react when you say good morning to them and acknowledge them. It's a beautiful thing. "

"What about the one person who doesn't acknowledge it?"

She started laughing as she thought of her father at that very moment.

"Why are you laughing?"

"You just sounded like my father. I would come home with 98% on my report card and he would say where is the other 2%?"

The man realized her point and started chuckling himself.

"I missed the point huh?"

"No you understand. Just like my father, you have good intentions and want the best possible result. There's nothing wrong with that. Hard work is a great principle. Being your best at any given moment is a great principle. The belief that it has to be perfect otherwise it doesn't count or it's a failure is what I question. Appreciating the process and the people along the way is what's valuable."

"Well my new friend, for whatever it's worth, I'm one of the nine out of ten people who valued this conversation. I'll leave you to your writing!" and he walked away with a huge smile.

Takouhi grabbed her journal and went to her apartment so she could get ready to pick up Arka. She hadn't seen him yet and was anxious to see what condition he was in. She drove up to his parents' building as per usual hoping to see him standing below waiting for her. For the very first time he wasn't standing there waiting for her by himself. He was leaning on an older gentleman at the door of the apartment. Right away Takouhi knew that this was his father. The resemblance was uncanny. But she saw something else that made her feel like someone had put their hand on her heart and was squeezing it. There was a big difference between the Arka she had seen in November and now. He was completely dependent on his father to lead him to the car. He was so pale she could see the blood vessels under his skin. By the time he reached her car he was breathing as if he had just ran around the block ten times. She knew right then that the walks she had envisioned with Arka on the beach at Marina Del Rey were not going to happen. It was too late... The most she could do was hope to have great conversations while eating puffs as they had done before.

The sun reflected off his pale face and his exposed white teeth and almost blinded Takouhi as he got into the car with the help of his father. She could tell by that giant smile he was happy. His father invited her to their house for dinner in a few days, an invite which she graciously accepted. She didn't ask for directions as she headed straight to their favourite carrot cake restaurant in Burbank.

"So you made it" he said with a big smile but his voice was muddled, as if he had just come back from a visit to the dentist.

"Ain't no mountain high enough, ain't no valley low enough, ain't no river wide enough to keep me from youoooooooo…" she started singing as if she was one of the Supremes.

He was half embarrassed at her whacky behaviour but couldn't help to crack up laughing.

"She's back! As if my patch and my appearance doesn't draw enough attention now you have to sing too!" is all he could get himself to say and they were once again in tears of laughter.

"So why are you here again?"

"To get away from it all. To start fresh. To decompress as they say in the diving world after all the craziness lately."

"Oh I thought you were here to see me."

"Ah what the heck, if I see you I see you…"

"Don't mess with my head; I'm too tired."

He was suddenly serious. In an instant his mood had changed. Something was very different about him. He took things very seriously now. More than she had ever seen before. The mood and tone had changed in comparison to all the weekend trips last year. Takouhi realized at that moment that the next two months would be nothing like she had imagined. Nothing!

The proceeding days were spent with Takouhi taking Arka to doctor's appointments, chemo sessions, MRI's and anything else that needed to be done. At one point, Takouhi watched as Arka had to make phone calls to different MRI offices asking for prices. His choice depended on how much money he had in his pocket. She valued the Canadian medical system and realized how much she had taken it for granted up until then. How sad that a person who was sick had to bargain for their treatment. It didn't make sense to her, especially in a country considered a super power. They were world leaders in their own mind's eye yet they do not take care of the basic needs of their own citizens. The day finally came when Arka asked Takouhi to join him inside the chemo-treatment room as opposed to sitting outside in the waiting room as she had done in the past on numerous occasions. Takouhi didn't say much during the entire process, and neither did he. The doctor was cold and clinical. Takouhi couldn't look at Arka. She wanted to grab Arka and ran as far away as she could from there. Takouhi pulled herself together for Arka's sake and took him to the next room where they would be administering the chemo. In this room, lots of people were getting chemo for various different kinds of cancer. During the process of administering chemo to Arka, he had fallen asleep. She needed to vent. She couldn't to him thus came out the journal and Jules Verne and she wrote…

> *Sitting at the chemotherapy centre with Arka. I've been here in the past but never like this. I always sat outside in the waiting room for two hours wondering what went on behind the doors as soon as he walked through. The most I had been able to determine in the past was they took a blood test when he walked in. Today I saw the rooms. What struck me the most was the way in which his doctor was speaking to us about the condition saying things like "You may be delaying the inevitable." Are you kidding me? As humans we die everyday. We age, we slow down, and yes, death is inevitable. He may outlive me for goodness sake. What if I get breast cancer and die in a year? Or what if on my drive back home I get into a horrific car accident and become a vegetable. I'll be alive but will I be living? The point is that the doctor looked at him as if it was game over. He's a fighter I know him he won't give up. He will fight harder than before. All I know is that I have to do everything in my power to pull him through this. We were wondering if he should continue chemo and the answer for the time being is yes. I wish I knew what he was thinking. He said it's the one thing he doesn't have the answer for. In the past apparently he got himself into predicaments or even everyday challenges and he always knew how to work around them. That's exactly where I am so connected with him as I felt the same about myself. However, when he said that he didn't have the answer for this it makes*

*me realize just how much health is wealth when you're sitting in a cancer ward. I still don't know how I got here. How the events in life have unfolded such that I am sitting next to a man who is so much like me. How I met Asbed and Vrej. How I enjoyed my time in a foreign yet familiar land. How I met Arka as a direct result of the other two. How his ex-wife left him. How I became his good-will ambassador. How he helped me and put work in perspective for me in spite of the adversity he was facing. How I was able to get away from work five times last year to spend time with him. How after 17 years of building a company it all came to an end within a few months. How I made a decision to leave my home and come and spend at least two months with him. And here I am. Rented a furnished place in Marina Del Rey and he is here beside me. He and his brother are exactly the way my brother and I are. We are bantering, insultin and childish but in a playful way. We never hurt yet tease and uplift. Are we like this because we are members of the same tribe? I don't think so. I have lots of tribal members but we don't connect like this. We just happen to get along like puzzle pieces that fit together. I would laugh if somewhere down the line we find out we are related. We tend to do that don't we? He is so and so's brothers uncles wife's sisters daughters grandchild! Oh they are family!*

Takouhi stopped for a moment and took a good look at him. She realized she was being squirelly with her thoughts going all over the place because she was very hurt over the doctor's behavior. Arka's eyes were moving as if he was dreaming. She wondered what he was dreaming about. Was he scared? Was he thinking game over? She thought of a question she wanted to ask him when he woke up. In the meantime she picked up the pen again and continued to write.

> *If I could tell him anything it would be don't give up. I've already told him how valuable he is and how so many people love him. The question remains, does he believe me when I tell him these things? I really don't know. How would I feel if the tables were turned right now? What if it was me sitting in the chair with chemo pouring into my veins and he was staring at me? Would I accept his words if he told me how valuable I am and don't give up? Would I acknowledge it, accept it, and verbalize it back? Or would I be so worried about myself and my future and not want to burden him with my troubles? I hope he doesn't think that he is burdening me.*
>
> *Many things have changed and I have learned much from him in such a short time. He is smart, clever, wise, intelligent, charismatic, and funny. I don't care what he says, he has been hurt and internalizes everything. I can imagine the stress he put himself under and the expectations he had of himself and the expectations others had of him. There's no bigger burden than great expectations. That's where the tribal BS must have kicked in for him. I still can't believe that his wife just left him while he was going through the cancer because "it wasn't what she had signed up for." When he was fresh out of law school and healthy she had signed up for that. She was going to be the wife of a lawyer. And now that the lawyer could no longer be a lawyer and was in need of support... Sorry... I'm out! I will always wonder who she sees when she looks in the mirror. I know one thing. She doesn't see a person operating with shero principles! If she knew better she'd do better right? Yes, therefore I cannot*

*judge nor should I judge. This has nothing to do with her being Armenian or a woman. This has everything to do with where she is in her evolution as a person. What her values and beliefs are. Arka's ex-wife may consider shero principles at some point in the future. However, the first step is to look in the mirror, acknowledge your authentic self, and take responsibility for your actions and not make excuses. By authentic self I mean acknowledging who you truly are; not what someone wants you to be or thinks you are. By being completely honest with yourself and acknowledging your strengths and areas that you need to improve. Money comes and goes, status comes and goes, but mutual respect, connections, admiration, and loyalty are priceless and are harder to come by than a pink diamond. My parents had lots of money and dad had a great status as a university teacher. Well paid, summer homes, you name it. All that went away when they pretty much ran away due to a revolution. But they were united. Love isn't just about gazing into each others' eyes but looking down the road in the same direction. Can you imagine if my mother had said "Sorry I didn't sign up for not having money?" Or later, when dad had cancer "Sorry I didn't sign up for this?"*
*Divorce tore me apart. It challenged my way of looking at my tribe and for many years it sent me in a tail spin of wondering who I was and where I belonged. How would I have felt if on top of all that pain I also had inoperable and possibly fatal cancer? She had the power to give to him, as difficult as it may have been. We can destroy or build, improve, give, and live with shero principles. Usually this path requires sacrifice and some growing pains. And yet most of us choose the path of least resistance. It's easy to leave it's harder to stay. It's easy to*

*be bad, it's harder to be good. It's easy to give in to the tribal mentality; it's harder to stand up for your values. Change is not easy. With great change comes great pain. But is it worth it? Absolutely! We all go astray at times, including me. I wish I could just wave a magic wand and take his pain away, take all the negative memories away. But then I realize I can't do that because those memories and events of his past made him who he is today. Just as my past has made me who I am today."*

Her hand was hurting as the thoughts were flowing. She had to put the pen down. Just as she finished the last sentence his eyes opened.

"Good morning sunshine! You were asleep for the last two hours."

"Takouhi guess what?"

"What?"

"I prolonged my life for another two hours," he said and started to chuckle.

The doctor's cold words had impacted his core like a meteor hitting the earth. She helped him to the car. He was getting weaker and weaker. He refused to use a walking stick or a wheelchair. He wanted to fight and not get lazy. Takouhi became his walking stick. She didn't mind. As they were driving away she remembered the question she wanted to ask him while she had been writing in her journal.

"Arka, do you ever ask yourself why me or that it's not fair?" she said in a quiet voice.

He opened his eye and looked at her with a smile.

"Whoever told you life is fair Takouhi?"

She bit her lip.

"One of my favourite moments in law school was a philosophy class I once took. The instructor was usually very cordial and collaborated with his students on deadlines and extensions. One day however he decided that he was going to give us a surprise test and it was going to count for 30% of our mark. Right then and there. At that level, 30% is a lot. When he announced that the students in the class began to grumble and one of them had the guts to call out: 'That's just not fair!' And this is where it left an impression on me. The instructor was silent. The class was dead silent for five minutes. The instructor didn't look up from the podium, he just closed his heavy book. The sound of the book made everyone jump as it echoed between the auditorium walls. At which time he pulled his glasses away from his face and simply said "Whoever told you life is fair, Mr. Steinbeck?" As he finished his story there was a smile of contentment on his face because he had travelled back to a time where he felt good about himself and all the memories brought him to life. Takouhi thought that as long as he was happy then he was helping his immune system. She could wish for nothing more at that moment.

Takouhi had finally met the parents during those weeks. She had heard so much about the mother from Arka, Asbed, and even Vrej and she now realized why she was so loved. Although her main focus was Arka, Takouhi started wondering what it was like for the mom. She was giving, loving, compassionate and Takouhi knew she would be absolutely devastated if she were to outlive her child. There were days that Takouhi would take Arka to Marina Del Rey for a change of scenery. She felt selfish about it sometimes because she thought maybe it would be better for him to be around his family. Not necessarily for him but for them. Takouhi took the mom and Arka to church on a Sunday once. Arka never in the past professed to be religious but now as he had already mentioned he was asking for all the help he could get. The family and Takouhi tried everything for him. They even drove to the Mexican border, to a man who claimed he was a healer and had performed miracles. Desperate times and desperate measures. Despite all these efforts, Arka was fading fast and spent most of his time sleeping. For every ten days between chemo treatments he would spend the first five in bed. He began to question the quality of life. He was losing the ability to speak clearly. The great conversations that they once had were now only present in the pages of her old journals. He was either sleeping or trying his best to text his ideas with his right hand. The only hand that was functioning. It was almost time for her to go back to Vancouver. Two months had flown by with doctor's appointments, chemo, and just hanging out with his parents and family. But she had to go back and organize her life and work situation. How would she leave?

# 22

## D DAY

It was almost the end of March and Takouhi was getting herself mentally ready to go back home. Her days were spent driving to see him at his parent's house in the mornings and driving back to Marina Del Rey in the evenings. She felt that being surrounded with family and friends was far more beneficial to Arka than the change of scenery he would experience in Marina Del Rey. He would just sleep and in the back and forth process he would get tired. It was much easier for her to go to him than to trouble him. As time had passed she had grown attached to his family and had adopted them as her own.

The last week in March as per their every ten day routine Takouhi took Arka for his chemotherapy. This time he was really weak. Takouhi was not a petite person but even she could not carry his weight on her shoulders. As per routine they did the blood test first and Takouhi helped Arka into the consultation room to speak with the doctor.

"How are you feeling today?" said the good doctor.

"I think I've made a decision," he said.

Takouhi was startled as she wasn't expecting that.

"I've decided to stop the chemotherapy."

"Are you sure that's what you want?" said the doctor "If in two weeks you change your mind, I don't think the chemo will help you anymore."

There was silence in the room. Takouhi had bit her lip so hard she tasted blood, but it was useless. Her eyes were flooding. She knew what this meant.

"Arka, while you still can, I seriously suggest you get your affairs in order," continued the doctor.

Takouhi finally had the courage to look at him. He was looking at her and his eye welled up but he didn't say a word. Even in this state he was fully engaged with the BS that men don't cry. As painful as that moment was, she was thankful that he wasn't alone. This was bare bones fragile humanity. She couldn't imagine what he was thinking. What is a person's belief when mortality looks them in the eye? Knowing this is it. It could be any day now. Takouhi helped him up from the chair and whereas before they would walk into the room to grab the two-hour chemo Martini, this time they walked out the front door right away. He was so powerless and so weak she almost dropped him. Hot tears were streaming down her face. They made it to the car and proceeded to drive to his parents place.

"*Kyank,* dear one, I won't be here in June when you come back for your cousins wedding." He barely got his words out.

"Don't talk like that. How can I leave in a week when you say those things?"

"I will never forget what you have done and I hope you know what you mean to me. You are beside me when I can't even walk. She left me when I was still able to drive. You've challenged my belief system about selfishness and humanity. You have no idea how much I love and respect your ability to talk the talk and walk the walk."

"The only thing I want is for you to get better so we can learn all those languages we wanted to learn by travelling to all those different countries as we talked about."

"I'm not giving up. I'm going to try the holistic stuff so it can strengthen my immune system but…"

"But what?"

"I'm tired. I'm tired of inconveniencing everyone. It's been almost three years of this. Everyone's life is on hold because of me."

"Are you kidding? They, we, would do anything to get you better. How can you even think that? What kind of belief system is that? That we only want you when you are healthy and get rid of you when you're not?"

"Takouhi" he said in a soft voice and took a deep breath, "mom is going to have a very hard time with this. Can you..."

Takouhi took her hand and put it on his and squeezed it as much as she could. She was squeezing it the same way she felt someone was squeezing all her internal organs at the same time. She couldn't breath. Pain scratched at her chest. He didn't need to finish his sentence. She knew exactly what he was asking. He finally let go of his BS. In silence they both cried very silent and hot tears driving down the 405.

One morning prior to her going to the family's house she got up and decided to go for a walk on the beach, her second one since arriving there. The original plan was that she and Arka would walk on the beach as much as they could. She thought about how different everything had worked out. When her mother had called her that morning, she chocked up and couldn't speak to her.

The only words she could get herself to say to her mother were, "Mom he can barely speak anymore." She started walking close to the water this time. This is where Takouhi always felt connected with the spiritual world. Where she knew that she was just a pebble in the big scheme of things and was always humbled yet in tune. The tribal he said, she said, who owns what, how much money do you make, what car do you drive etc was so far removed from her even though she was in the lair of the tribe. In a rare Takouhi moment, she didn't want to mingle with people. She was talking and tapping into a higher power and needed its attention.

"If you're listening I want to ask you one thing. You took grandma two years ago and as much as I loved her I'm okay with that because she lived a life she can be proud of. I can't be selfish and ask you to make him better or fix him. All I can ask you is whatever the plan is please do not make him suffer. It's enough. If he was supposed to learn certain lessons I'm sure he has aced them. I am sure he will get 100% not even 98% if you were to test him. If this was all about the lessons other people were to learn from his example I hope they have learned it but don't let him suffer if they have not. As for me, I assure you I get it. And if you think I don't that's okay but I am a willing and eager lifetime student. But not at his expense. Please, please give me a sign that you are listening to me!"

Takouhi suddenly stopped walking. She looked down on the sand and right in front of her foot was a beautiful red ladybug. She picked up the ladybug and placed it on her hand and fell on her knees. Takouhi's sobbing could be heard on the pier but she didn't care if anyone was watching. All she knew was that she was heard. The ladybug was her way of knowing that Grandma was listening just like when they did when all this started with the letter. What were the chances of a ladybug being there right in front of her shoe on the sand by the beach where there are no trees. She turned around and walked back to her apartment. Just before Takouhi walked in the main doors the ladybug gently flew away. Divine spiritual intervention. Message heard loud and clear!

Although she was scheduled to head back home on March 31, she kept prolonging her departure. After all those conversations, especially the very last one at the chemotherapy centre, how could she leave him? But she knew she had to. Asbed was back from his trip overseas. When he had left, his brother could somewhat communicate but at this point he could not converse at all. He had absolutely no power. He would just sit there and with the minimal texting ability say things like 'I am one with the couch.' His humour was still there. The night before she left, as the entire family was sitting in the living room surrounding each other with love and laughter, Takouhi received a text from Arka sitting across the room.

"You need to know something."

"What's that?"

"You were a gift in my life."

Takouhi just looked at the floor. She couldn't look at him, she couldn't look at the family. It took all of her will power to control a flood of tears that would drown all of those sitting near her. She was still for five minutes.

"Hello?" Arka texted again, wanting her to look up.

"I hope you kept the receipt!" is all she could get herself to type. As she got the courage to look at him she saw that his head was bobbing around uncontrollably with laughter.

"Do you realize this is the last time we will be together?"

"You wish you can get rid of me that easily!" she replied trying to turn a heavy moment into something light and fun.

"Smartass."

"Leave my ass alone."

"How can anyone avoid that 5 x 7 by 5 x 7 fixture!"

"Have you looked at yourself lately?"

"Look at me; I'm gorgeous!"

"Indeed you are!" she said and bit her lip yet again. The dreaded moment finally came where she put all her bags in her car and had to leave. She was up early in the morning to say goodbye to the mother as she was on her way to work. They both hugged and held each other. Takouhi watched as she drove away with tears in her eyes. She wasn't just leaving Arka, but the entire family. She went back into the house. After breakfast it was time. She told him that she would be back for his holistic doctor's appointment in two weeks time. This time she would fly down she said. He just smiled. He couldn't get up. All she could do was sit next to him and he hugged her with the one arm that still had some strength. He didn't want to let go and she didn't want to go. Finally she let go and started to walk towards the door. Asbed and the father were right behind her to walk her to the car. She looked back one more time at the man that had meant so much to her during that two-year period. So fragile, so helpless but stronger than she could ever imagine herself to be. Sitting on the couch was class, dignity, nobility, and grace. He smiled at her and didn't care if his father or brother saw his tears. She walked out with the other two to the elevator and couldn't care less if they saw her tears either.

The drive back home was a complete blur for her. Takouhi wished someone would have created windshield wipers for eyes. California, Oregon, Washington connected by Interstate Five. At moments she felt she was in one of those old movies where the focus was on the driver and the changing scenery was surreal and unfocused. She cried from the moment she started her drive home to the final moments where she composed herself at the US–Canada border at two in the morning.

"Anything to declare" said the bored customs agent.

"I declare that I have learned life lessons no government can put a price tag on and tax me on!"

"That's a clever answer; I can't say I've ever heard that!"

"Unless of course I write a book about it and the government taxes me on that."

# 23

# THE LAST DOCTORS VISIT

During the two-week period since she was back in Vancouver, Takouhi was restless. She knew she had to focus on her future and the next steps she had to take. What would be her new job? What new adventures was she to partake in Vancouver? Or should she move? Was this the time? Was LA her new harbour? Her thoughts were everywhere. The only constant was her thoughts of Arka and his family. What is he doing? Is he weakening? There were no more texts. She made a decision.

She had promised. So she flew back to LA within two weeks of being home. The plan was for her to fly down Thursday night and fly back home that following Sunday. She packed a small carry on with a pair of jeans and two t-shirts. She knew she would be staying at Arka's parents house and they would not be going anywhere except for the doctor's appointment. Her parents were confused and didn't understand her ways. But there was no time to argue or explain. Time was of the essence. She knew that she had very intelligent parents and they would eventually understand what she was up to by watching her in action. There was no time for tell time, it was show time. One of her favourite saying was that in order to lead the orchestra, you might need to turn your back on the crowds. This saying applied. She had to trust that they would get it because the risk of not proceeding was far more painful than the risk of perplexing her parents. She also had to trust that she was who she was because some of their DNA had trickled down to her. She had taken their values and was applying them to a new and improved belief system. That it didn't matter what others thought when her intention was for good.

Asbed was at the airport to greet her. For once she didn't have a rental car. She didn't realize until that moment how much she had missed him. The conversations with Asbed were very different than the conversations with Arka. Two very amazing people, brothers yet entirely different belief systems. Takouhi remembered conversations she had had with Arka in the past where he had admitted that it used to affect him what others thought and it would influence his decision. Whereas the cancer changed that. But Asbed was a different soul. It wasn't that he didn't care what others thought; in fact he was very sensitive to the world around him.

"So you're back!" Asbed said with a smile.

"Yup, I promised him!"

"Is that why you came just because you promised him? Lots of people promise lots of things but they don't follow through you know."

"I suppose there are people like that out there but I keep my promises. I know it's a cliché but I say what I mean and mean what I say. It's seems like we are living in a society where people take for granted that we lie and they are okay with it. When did lying become the norm? When did being fake become the norm? It took a long time to convince Arka that not everyone is selfish. He had a belief system that everyone is selfish and he proceeded to live his life and interpret the events that happened around him based on that system."

He just smiled. Takouhi took a look at him as he was driving. So much had happened since the first moment she had seen him at Gate 22 in London. She wondered if he was responsible for bringing her to be his brothers' friend in some mysterious way. She also knew that she couldn't voice that opinion out loud because some people would think she was nuts. The universe was full of magic for all those who knew how to tap into it.

They made it home finally and there he was. He had asked for his hair to be shaved so his bald head was glowing. He was no longer wearing the patch on the eye. It didn't matter to him. He was seeing double but he didn't care. Arka couldn't talk at all and could barely sit without falling over but Takouhi knew how happy he was. She couldn't believe that after that emotional departure two weeks prior she was back again to see his glowing face.

"Hi stranger," the text.

"What's up homie?"

"So you brought your size 10 feet back here huh?"

"If the shoe fits!"

She was sitting close to him to help him sit up straight. He pointed to his mom and the mom jumped up. She grabbed a little box and gave it to Takouhi. She opened the box to find a cute little porcelain rabbit jewelry box. Arka knew how much she loved little rabbits and the one she had had passed away while she was in LA for those two months. He remembered enough to get the mom to get her something to acknowledge to her that he understood. Takouhi was touched. There was no conversation just texting back and forth. In those two weeks he had taken a turn and was much weaker than before.

The next day Arka's father, Arka and Takouhi sat in the car and drove to Orange County to visit with his new holistic doctor. Arka was not feeling well at all. The two of them sat in the back of the car as the father drove.

"Why is God punishing me?" Arka's text.

She was shocked.

"You're not being punished. This is not punishment."

"What is this then? I haven't been so bad in my life. Maybe a few things here and there but I have been good for the most part."

Takouhi knew the last thing he wanted to hear at that moment was that everything happens for a reason and that the universe works in mysterious ways. It occurred to her that he was panicking. He was dying.

"I don't believe in him anymore. Why am I hanging all these crosses around my neck?" He proceeded to take off his crosses but couldn't as his arm was so weak. The more he tried the more frustrated he became until finally he rolled over to his side and his head fell on her lap and began sobbing.

*"Kyank,"* she whispered in his ear "He loves you. He's not punishing you. If anything he's giving you a choice that if you want to go home, you can. While the rest of us still have lessons to learn you have the option to graduate. But it's still up to you. You make the decision."

She calmed him down as she stroked his smooth head. He fell asleep and she looked outside the window and cried silent tears.

By the time they drove to the doctor and back home Arka was physically and mentally exhausted. When they got home he fell asleep on the couch. By this time, the mother and Asbed had come home. While Arka slept on the couch, the four of them went into the other room to quietly watch tv. She looked at them and wondered how loving they all are. What was coming was going to tear their hearts out. When Takouhi went to check on Arka an hour after they had arrived she realized something was wrong. He wasn't breathing the same. It appeared as if he was hyperventilating. He was fully awake. They tried to communicate with him to take him to the hospital but his eyes bulged up and he tried to shake himself as if to say no. As much as he refused, his parents decided to call 911 and take him to the hospital. In the past he had mentioned that he didn't want to go to the hospital because he had always thought that once he was hospitalized that the doctors would not help him fight, they would create a situation where he would leave. It was at that moment that Takouhi realized it was time to put on the army gear as she was about to engage fully in the trenches.

She rode with him in the ambulance. Despite oxygen, he was breathing very rapidly. Takouhi was the front person to explain what was going on to the paramedics. The family did not question her. They trusted her enough to let her take over.

Arka was taken to the ICU. They had to put him on a breathing machine in order to regulate his breathing. She worried about his pain when they forced the tube down his throat. They gave him lots of medication to sedate him. Although it appeared that Arka was sleeping his heart monitor showed that his heartbeat and rate of breathing was very high. The medication slowly started to take effect yet it took his system the entire night to become in sync with the breathing machine. The initial panic amongst his immediate family and close friends was slowly fading as he was calming down. The irony was that Arka's breathing was slowing down whereas his family and friends were beginning to breath again.

He was to be held in ICU indefinitely until they ran a series of tests to determine the best course of action. Takouhi was now the liaison between the family and the nurses and doctors. She had originally scheduled to fly home Sunday night and it was already Sunday morning. She didn't have to think twice about what she had to do. The entire family including her started taking shifts being with him. He was never alone. His immediate family and extended family were either taking turns going into the ICU or they were outside in the waiting room. Usually two people would go in to be with him and one of the two was his mother. On a rare occasion Takouhi was alone with him in the ICU. She was standing at the foot of his bed and thought, 'here we are. There's so much left to say but now there is no voice. You may be yelling out your thoughts but I can no longer hear you.'

During the course of the days doctors would come in and out of his room. They were all specialists in their own fields. One doctor came up to Takouhi and said, "You have to let him go, you are torturing him. You know the tumour is not going to go away and yet you are keeping him on the breathing machine." The doctor expected Takouhi to take that information straight to the parents. Takouhi in turn took that information straight to the social worker and said, "I want another doctor to be in charge of Arka's case. I do not want the other doctors to follow his lead and start prescribing him things based on their belief systems that will bring his life to an end." The social worker was in agreement with her. That particular doctor kept a safe walking distance from Takouhi from that moment on. Takouhi was defending Arka and fighting off belief systems. They were coming at her from all sides. At one point she went to the waiting room. She noticed that one of the older women who had come there in support of the parents was wearing black. Takouhi wondered who had died. She wondered if that lady's husband had died in the past and thus she was still wearing black. Sometimes the belief system was that as a sign of respect they should wear black for mourning for as long as it took. She didn't understand why she was so focused on that woman. Takouhi quietly asked around who the woman was and if she had recently lost someone in her family. She finally asked the woman directly. The older women said she was wearing black out of respect for Arka and what was about to happen. What kind of belief system is this? Takouhi snapped. She got up in front of the unsuspecting crowd sitting in the ICU and in a firm and clear no nonsense voice said, "If you want to wear black as a so called sign of respect do so at your own home. Do not show up here wearing black and proclaiming game over when this family is doing everything in its power to help him fight this." Takouhi was so angry she was shaking but she continued, "I don't want any negativity here. You are not supporting this family if you come here with your negative, fatalistic beliefs. Stay home." She said it and she walked back into the ICU. She only wished she had a camera to see what the reactions of the people were and the aftermath after having dropped the bomb. She almost felt bad. Almost.

Days turned into weeks and pretty soon a month had passed, and a routine made. Around 8:00 a.m. they would walk to the hospital. Around 5:00 p.m. they would go home for a break, come back around 6:30 p.m. and stay there until 11:00 p.m.. During those days many people came and went. Many people who Takouhi had never heard of nor did they know who Takouhi was. Who was this person that was going back and forth between the doctors? Who was this person who was going into the medical library at the hospital and doing further research in desperation to help her friend? At one point she was phoning other medical institutions where they were experimenting with certain types of brain tumour therapies. Asbed and Takouhi were willing and able to fly to wherever it was to figure this out.

It was incredible how she could tell they were trying to figure her out through their belief systems. How old was she? How come she could be here for so long? Did she live with her parents? She's here all the way from Vancouver? Is she the girlfriend? What, she was once married? She met Asbed first? Takouhi could hear all the questions but she simply walked in and out of the ICU with her head held high.

Takouhi and Arka's mother had become very close. In fact they were now sleeping in the same bed together like mother and daughter. They were under each other's noses the entire day and in spite of the circumstances they loved each other's company. One day Takouhi noticed that one of the visitors was wearing a beautiful bracelet that had blue eyes on it. In their culture and in many other cultures in the Mediterranean and Middle East having some sort of a blue eye ornament mean that you were warding off evil. It wasn't that Takouhi necessarily believed in that BS but she loved the colour blue and its connection for her to spirituality. Takouhi and the mom were sitting there and she mentioned the bracelet in passing to the adopted mom. "Maybe we should get you one so they don't jinx you" she said. So that's where the son had learned it from. That took her all the way back to when Asbed had said she had jinxed the plane. Maybe the plane should have been covered in blue too. She started chuckling to herself.

During those days, Asbed and Takouhi spent more time together than they had done in the past. It was as if everything was coming full circle. This journey had started with Asbed and here they were again. On one occasion Takouhi was over tired. She was tired of all the opinions. Everyone was an expert at something. It just overwhelmed her. It was 5:00 p.m. and time to go home for a break. Usually she would walk home with the family but she really needed alone time. She hadn't been on her own for so long and she really needed to recharge. She had no idea that Asbed had seen her take off by herself. He called her on her cell phone but she didn't pick up. She had nothing to say. She was spent. She barely made it home and ran into the shower, which took almost an hour as she didn't want them to hear her sobbing. As she was getting dressed there was a knock on the bathroom door.

"I'll be right out!" she said.

"I know you're going to come out. I just want to know if you're okay," is all he had to say and Takouhi started crying silently. She did hear him eventually walk away and she came out. That night she came home earlier than usual and went straight to bed after kissing her adopted family goodnight. She was so exhausted that she fell asleep right away. When she woke up she turned to the bedside table to see what time it was as she didn't want to oversleep. She froze and thought she must have the same look on her face as when Arka had when she had given him his favourite pen. On the bedside table in the little rabbit jewellery box that was hers was a beautiful white gold bracelet with blue eyes. She looked up and there was her adopted mom with a big smile on her face. She jumped up and gave her a huge hug. Just like she supposed Arka wanted to do when he took off his seatbelt to get out of the car. Takouhi felt at home. It was the feeling she was looking for when she had sat on the plane to go to Armenia. It dawned on her at that moment. It wasn't the location or where you come from but it's when every fiber of your being is in tune with itself. Takouhi was very proud and humbled to observe someone living life with shero principles.

As time passed in the hospital Takouhi became more and more exposed to tribe and the BS. She was becoming fascinated with the BS surrounding her over this entire situation. The questions Takouhi was constantly hearing in the waiting room by the visitors was 'why him'? He is such a nice guy. So many bad people like drug dealers and criminals around. Why did he get picked? Why is the grandmother who is in her late 80s who smokes still alive and kicking but his guy at this young age suffering the way he is? Depending on who the visitor was she would get a very different and in her opinion interesting answer. Achkov Dvan, literally translated meant someone gave him the evil eye. The idea behind that BS was that he was such a catch in so many people's opinions that their jealousy created bad vibes. Takouhi knew this belief system was not unique to this particular tribe. After all, many cultures were constantly using the term you jinxed me which meant exactly the same thing. Most of them saw themselves as religious people and would wear a cross and go to church. The irony was that the same people would believe in things like the evil eye and tookhd oo geer. That literally translated to some sort of voodoo. Apparently it was something that was done even during the reign of the Tudors in England. Where you make a wish and write it on a piece of paper and some kind of witch doctor does their magic. Takouhi admitted that was something she had never heard of. The other thing that struck Takouhi was how much everybody was concerned about what somebody else would say or think. She thought if only they were concerned with living up to high standards and values then why would it matter what others would say. To her it was as crazy as say a runner at the Olympics in one way looking ahead at the finish line but in another way constantly looking over their shoulder seeing where the competition is. That would be suicide. What kind of life would that be? she thought. The only people who look over their shoulders constantly and should worry about stuff are those who have done something that are not in line with shero principles. Takouhi couldn't see the logic. On the one hand, they claimed to be religious and following the will of God. On the other hand, they had the audacity to proclaim and judge who should die before Arka. If you truly believe in that belief system about religion and that God's will is good then why do you question what is going on? If they were so religious and believed in the amazing afterlife why weren't they happy that Arka was going to a better place? The answer was simple to Takouhi. Religion does not equal spirituality just like capitalism does not equal democracy. She had this vision that what if Jesus, Muhammad, Ghandi, Buddha, Moses and all who were in between were sitting around a round table having a discussion about the people on earth interrpreting their words. They would probably be shaking their heads in disbelief.

"I never told them to kill another human being if their thoughts are different."

"I never told them to have six wives."

"I never said just hang out and be one with the world."

"I didn't part the water, a Tsunami pulled the water back."

"I never said man is better than a woman and she has to obey."

Takouhi chuckled because she thought the only thing they would constantly say is 'that's not what I meant, you're twisting my words' as they heard the people on earth put words in their mouth. It was like the telephone game, by the time the first person said the message and it got to the last person on the line the message was completely different. The spirit had disappeared from religion.

Just when Takouhi thought she had heard all the belief systems she could possibly hear over this entire situation she was once again taken off guard. One day one of Arka's friends came to visit him in the ICU. Arka was still on the breathing machine and asleep most of the time. Takouhi and the friend walked outside the hospital for some fresh air. Takouhi had no idea what conversation was about to take place.

"I'm glad I got to meet you because we were all worried that Arka had gotten himself in trouble again! You are nothing like we had imagined. In fact you don't even fit any kind of mould we were thinking about."

"What do you mean?" asked Takouhi puzzled.

"Well, I'm sure you know that Arka has gone through a lot lately and we were all worried that maybe you were some kind of vulture that was coming in for the kill to take things from him. We had heard that you are older than him and you were once married so we figured you would have baggage like two kids and were hanging out with him because it was the best that you could do."

Before Takouhi could get in a word the friend continued.

"Now that we've seen you in person and in action it's amazing. You're not even bad to look at. We thought you would be ugly or plain."

Takouhi was hoping that that was the caboose to this person's train of thought. She didn't know which was more painful, Arka fighting for his life in the ICU or the pain of this persons beliefs firing towards her like a machine gun.

Takouhi's jaw dropped. Who were these people? Did they even think before they expressed themselves? Their belief system questioned why someone would come all the way to be with their friend during this time of need unless there was something in it for them. Takouhi had admitted that yes what was in it for her was sheer satisfaction of spending time with a kindred spirit and knowing by unconditionally giving she was also getting, but this explanation? Well I guess Takouhi should have been ever so thankful that they came to meet her and she was so accepted. Needless to say Takouhi did not spend too much time with that bunch after those comments. Arka had always had the ability to be friends with people from all walks of life. Thus even these friends were valuable, if only for the purpose of showing the difference between a constructive way of thinking as opposed to a destructive way of thinking.

As time passed, it became clear to Takouhi that Arka was not going to come home. She spent as much time with him in the ICU as possible to make sure that he was comfortable. There were moments where she was extremely exhausted. Between speaking with the family and speaking with the doctors she didn't have much time to regroup. The best she could do was disappear in the hospital's cafeteria take out her journal and write. It was her only savior at the moment. The only place to vent. She didn't understand why people didn't understand the lessons they were supposed to be learning. Why was this amazing person in the ICU struggling for his life and they were sitting in the waiting room still focused on he said she said. She just wanted to snap and yell at them. Just at that moment she received a text on her phone. She jumped up because she hadn't received a text since Arka had been admitted to the hospital. It was from her girlfriend with whom she hadn't conversed with for months but she was close to her nonetheless. The text simply said "Get into shero state now!" That's all she needed to hear. She got herself back into an empowered state and walked right back into the ICU to be with Arka.

# 24

# TO CODE OR NOT TO CODE

She knew it was time. She had dreamt about him the night before where he said he was tired just as he had done the last day in the car. One thing was very clear to her. If he was going, now was the time for her to show her humanity in another way. Now, it was all about the family, the ones he was leaving behind. She began to put the seeds of thought in the unsuspecting family's minds. Arka was being transferred for another procedure in the arm. The doctors in charge always went to Takouhi to discuss situations and procedures. The one she liked and admired for his friendliness and positive bedside manner pulled her aside that morning.

"Do you know he's on full code?" he said with a very concerned and daunting look.

"Yes, I'm afraid so." For once she allowed sadness to come through in her voice.

"Don't you think given the circumstances as of today and all that has happened in the last month and a half it should be reconsidered?"

Takouhi took a deep heart wrenching breath and looked directly in his eyes. "I agree. Had you asked me that a month or so ago I would have said no, he's a fighter. But I now know that he is telling me something."

"Can't you convince the parents by explaining how traumatic a full code is to a person's body. His lungs are already not functioning on their own, his kidney is failing, his stomach isn't processing food. If his heart stops we'll have to pull all the tubes out and potentially break ribs to get his heart started again. This isn't like television. It's pretty traumatic. Is that what they want? More pain and anguish for their son?"

Takouhi with hot tears streaming down her face barely came up with her words. She knew however, that she needed to change the doctors' point of view.

"They don't want him to go. Don't you think they already know in their hearts? Can there be a greater pain in life than outliving your child? Please do not think that the parents are being selfish and please do not judge them. They will be left behind with the pain of missing him now and the loss of a future they saw for him in their mind's eye, and they are the ones we need to look after at this moment. The code is pretty brutal I agree but chances are he won't feel it. It's time to focus on the family and the aftermath."

The doctor looked at her amazed. His belief system changed in a few sentences. He went from thinking they were being selfish to wanting to reach out to them.

"Let me know if there is anything I can do for you and the family."

With that he left the room and the preparations began to move Arka to the ICU again.

Takouhi went looking for Asbed.

"You need to see you brother today."

"What's your problem? Have you been crying?"

"Yes, but it doesn't matter. I'm telling you something. Please go see him!"

"You know Takouhi I don't understand you sometimes. They did this last time, and nothing has changed. They said his heart rate was weird but then he fixed himself."

"Brother, I'm telling you something! Don't just listen to my words or voice. Please hear me!"

Asbed took a serious look at Takouhi. Something about her eyes made him change his mind. He decided to go into the ICU with his mother while Takouhi waited outside. Fifteen minutes later he came outside.

"What was the big deal? He's the same like last time just like I told you."

It was okay that he didn't understand she felt good that he at least saw him. Every fiber of her being knew the road ahead. It wasn't about visualization. At that moment, it wasn't about her conscious mind telling the subconscious what to do. It was about common sense. If only people saw things for the way things were and not better or worse.

She could hear Arka. They could not. She barely made it to the nearest bathroom and started convulsing and vomiting. Then a tsunami of tears hit her without any warning. In a moment her face turned pomegranate red and she started to hyperventilate. Then she took a good look at herself in the mirror and started laughing. If Arka could see her now, she knew what he would say. "Even when you are a mess you can't get away from being Armenian huh? I like your pomegranate colour! Takouhi managed to calm herself down. She lost herself and brought herself back all in private all in five minutes. She didn't want the others who were so dependent on her emotionally to see that she was coming undone. She gathered herself together and walked out of the bathroom.

Although she had calmed down and cooled off her face with cold water, her puffy red eyes were a dead giveaway to the man who noticed every single detail.

"You were crying in there again weren't you? I won't let you go inside and see him if you keep this up." Asbed tried to sound stern.

All of a sudden Takouhi turned to him with such a physical stand and eloquent force that made him take two steps back. "Try to keep me away from him! Just try it!" And she proceeded to walk into the ICU.

The hours were passing by and all she could do was stare at the monitor. Heart rate going down, going up and simply being erratic. Arka was communicating but nobody had the translator to figure it out. He was heavily sedated. His right eye was stitched shut due to a scratch on his cornea. His left eye was closed. Was he sleeping? Was he preparing? His mother was sitting at his feet while Takouhi was massaging his head to relax him. The moment was right.

"Mom are you ready?"

"For what?"

"He wants to go. Do you want to be here when it happens or would you rather be outside? It's not going to be peaceful unless you change the code."

"No I don't want to see it. But I can't leave him."

The audacity of Takouhi to be so tenacious to tell a mother that the son is leaving. She never doubted it. It was as crystal clear to her as her decision to come spent time with him in Marina Del Rey. Despite the uproar, disapproval, dismay, and concern about her leaving from her family and friends, she didn't blink. She knew what she had to do back then as she knew now. Their BS was theirs. They had positive intentions in that they wanted to protect her from physical and emotional harm but it did not matter.

The mother stayed. The father walked in and Takouhi thought that maybe she could convince him to change his mind about the code.

"No. My son is a fighter."

"I know he is a fighter. He's fought all this time but his body is not what it used to be two months ago when we first walked in. Dad, you have to let his soul pass in peace."

The answer was still a firm no.

At least she could say that she tried and she would have no "what if" moments in the future.

Takouhi kept looking at the heart monitor and it was close. She had seen her grandmother take her last breath two years prior in an ICU ward similar to this one but in Vancouver. She knew it was coming. She took a deep breath and walked over to stand by Arka's head. She started massaging his temples and the bits of his hair that had grown in the two months as he was lying in ICU. She tried to see how best she would be able to remember this moment for a lifetime. His lungs were rising and falling too fast. A cold sweat was over him. One eye was sown shut yet the other popped open and he was staring directly at her. She was taken off guard and noticed one tear streaming down the corner of his eye. Takouhi matched his tear with hers. One hot single tear rolled down her cheek. She finally did what she knew she had to do the entire day. She leaned into his left ear and gently whispered.

"Arka, thank you! Thank you for everything. Thank you for all the lessons you taught me. Thank you for allowing me into your life at such a vulnerable time.

Thank you for allowing me to witness your humanity in its purest form. I hope I have made a difference for you in the last two years. It was my honour, pleasure, and privilege to get to know you. You have proven yourself. You have put up a valiant fight. You don't have anything else to prove to anyone. Go in peace. You will always be loved and missed. You will never be forgotten. But we will meet again. Say hi to grandma for me. Don't be scared. You are graduating to an amazing place. Just one request. Please wait until I leave the room."

With that she kissed his forehead and stared at his one eye one more time. He gently closed his eyes as if to signal. He was breathing but his eye was closed.

Takouhi was frozen. She couldn't believe she had done that. What if he was going to be around for months. How dare she say goodbye. But, no, she knew!

She walked outside of the doors of the ICU. Everybody had left and Asbed was sitting by himself. He took one look at her and knew she was serious. She sat next to him and didn't say a word.

As soon as she sat down the emergency intercom sounded.

CODE BLUE ICU Room 113

CODE BLUE ICU Room 113

Asbed looked at Takouhi in shock.

Takouhi's tears were hotter and louder than the burning lava and thunderous explosion of a volcano that had been dormant for years.

Arka kept his promise and waited for her to leave the room so he could leave too.

# 25

# AN ELOQUENT FAREWELL

For the next few days, the parents' house was full with people who paid their respects. Yes, now was the time to wear black if your belief system was such that you equated black with showing respect at the time of mourning. The point was not to let the family alone in troubled times. The mother was shattered but surrounded by her sisters and family. Takouhi's focus turned to Asbed. He was the strong man, taking care of business. He was also surrounded by his family and friends but Takouhi looked at him differently. Whereas all the others were crying and hence releasing some of the pressure, he wasn't. He was taking care of the arrangements for the funeral and all the details. Takouhi felt numb, motionless, and speechless, the day she saw him walk into Arka's bedroom with a beautiful suit. It was the last suit that Arka was going to wear.

'He would like this tie don't you think?' he said.

Takouhi had wondered if either brother knew how much they meant to each other. Asbed had told her during the two months they had been in the hospital's ICU ward that none of his accomplishment would mean anything if he didn't have his brother next to him. Whereas Arka had once told her that he would do anything and everything for Asbed. She wondered if there was a way she could unite the thoughts of the two. She wished she had something solid and concrete.

Now that Arka had passed, Takouhi no longer slept with his mother. Instead, she slept in his room. In spite of it being his room and him not being there she didn't have trouble sleeping as she was so exhausted. One night she dreamt about him and woke up suddenly. She turned on the lights and looked straight at his bookshelf. There was a series of books, some of which she had given to him. But something caught her eye. The journal that she had given him last year. The one he had sworn he had written in. She was torn. Her thoughts took over 'Should I open it? It's private, he will get upset! But wait, he's not here anymore. Nobody needs to know! Is there a reason I just found this after being in the house for over four months? It has been in front of my face all this time but I guess I wasn't ready to see it.' She opened it and read it. She cried and smiled at the same time. She put the journal away.

The family and friends did many great things during that entire period, but the one thing they could not get themselves to do was the eulogy. They were just too hurt. Takouhi was close enough to Arka to be able to pull it off yet far enough that she wouldn't break down. Or at least she hoped she wouldn't.

She needed a place to be able to sit still and think about what she wanted to say about him. Something that wasn't too personal but that did him justice. She wanted to focus on the good and not what the tribe considered as him being wronged and shortchanged. She wanted to make sure he was honored and rightfully respected and in doing so respecting his family. She finally found a place on the roof. She climbed to the roof to lie down and stare in the California sky looking for inspiration. Four hours later she came downstairs, lost in thought.

The day of the funeral this is what she read to over 200 people who were there, crowding the church.

> *I would like to share a few thoughts in English for our dear non Armenian family and friends who are sharing this heart wrenching day with us today.*
>
> *Life isn't measured by the number of breaths we take, yet by the moments that take our breath away. That is how I felt when I met Arka for the first time in November of 2006. Sitting drinking tea with this complete stranger who had a patch covering his right eye. Three hours of conversation flew by as if they were three minutes.*
>
> *In those three hours he told me a brief summary of his life. I learned about where he was born all the way to what courses he had taken in university and all that was in between like a resume. Somewhere in that conversation I asked him about his illness and he spoke of it as if it was no big deal. To him it was like having the flu, nothing he couldn't handle and overcome. He did not have a victim mentality, of thinking why me? I knew right then and there a very strong spirit was sitting across the table from me.*
>
> *Yet rather than continuing on with a resume like version of his accomplishments I want to speak about the character of the man that impressed and inspired me so much.*
>
> *The thought of helping others is compassion, knowing how we can do it is wisdom, doing something about it is courage, writes Sakyong Mipham. This was also Arka's mantra and conviction. He did not like injustice. He wanted to help those he could, as much as he could, no matter what it took and he went out of his way in child custody cases, fighting for the well-being of the child.*

*Arka's name best describes his innate characteristics. Arka to me stands for Authentic, Regal, Kind, and Aspiring. Who sitting in this room can deny the authenticity of this man? Authentic in terms of his word. He meant what he said and said what he meant. His word was his bond. If he promised he would follow through. Regal in the way in which he carried himself with class and grace. Rarely did I see Arka lose his temper. Arka was kind and befriended everybody from every walk of life never judging based on ethnicity, race, culture, and so called materialistic class standings. And finally the last letter in his name, A for aspiring. He aspired for greatness in himself and humanity. He believed that all things were possible. He was a man who was wise beyond his years. He was an old soul, a scholar, and a gentleman.*

*The confusion lies when we ask the question why? Why did this happen to a person who had the ability to touch so many lives in such a positive way? Why was he taken? It's not fair! But this is where Arka would look to me and say 'Takouhi, whoever told you that life is fair?'*

*Being that as it may, I had the privilege and honour to spend the last few months with him and share some incredible philosophical conversations. As hard as it was, we discussed the possibility of today's events. And the only thing we could come up with was a quote from our favourite Stoic Philosopher Epictetus.*

*'Ask not that events happen as you will,*
*Yet let your will be that events happen as they do,*
*And you shall have peace'*

*And this is what Arka would wish for all of you today. He wouldn't want anybody in this life to focus on the word why, or blame events in his past. Rather, the best way to honour this man is to speak of him throughout our lives with pride. Remember all the memories as if they happened yesterday. Carry his legacy of caring, loving, understanding, and compassion.*

*I only met him a year and half ago and I am humbled and honoured to have known him. And although we would speak about how wonderful life would have been had I met him five years ago, I think how tragic it would have been had I not met him at all.*

*God rest your soul, my valiant fighter. We will miss you every minute of everyday but we will take comfort in knowing that you are working for God now as he was a bit short staffed with good people. We love you and always will.*

She was amazed at how well she had kept her composure throughout the whole reading. But when she heard herself say valiant fighter her voice cracked and the hot tears rolled down her face. She took a moment to look at the crowd in front of her. There wasn't a dry eye in the room. Shero was there in all of them. The entire church along with all those who could not find room to sit and were standing outside the wide open church doors were touched in one way or another by one of the five principles of shero. Takouhi realized that something huge happened. A big part of her just wanted to smile because she knew he was there and probably saying in his smartass tone. 'Takouhi you made me sound really good and I'm impressed.' As she walked by the casket she looked at him and knew it wasn't him. She went up to his ear and whispered. 'I know you are watching me as I'm doing this and I know you're probably just standing beside me and smiling but my human side wants to be close to you in this way just one more time!' At that moment there was nobody in the church as far as she was concerned. Her hand stroked his forehead one last time as she had done the last night in the hospital. It was just the two of them just like in the restaurant in Las Vegas, just like the walks on the beach, just like when they ate puffs, just like when they went for drives in the car. Just the two of them until something made her look up as if someone had tapped her on the shoulder.

Asbed caught her attention. He was seated in the corner of one of the pews by the wall. It reminded her of a little boy who was sent in a corner to do time out. The weight of his entire upper body was supported by his clenched hands as they rested on his knees. His head, heavy with grief, was hanging down, his eyes fixed to the ground. His jaw was tightly clenched and throbbing, perhaps in an effort to take away the anguish in his heart. She realized at that very moment that there was one thing left to do.

# 26

## SHEROVISION

The days following the funeral reminded Takouhi of the things that she truly admired about her tribe. It was customary for Armenians to commemorate the seventh and fortieth day after passing. During the forty-day period it was common for friends and loved ones to spend as much time with the grieving family as possible and to support them during that difficult time. The house was full of people from the moment Takouhi would wake up until the moment she would go to bed. The door of the house only closed when they went to bed. People would walk in bringing food and drinks so the family would not have to concern themselves with such things. There was always a group of people sitting next to her adopted mother and just being with her. Sometimes the group would talk, sometimes it was silent but for the most part it was their presence that comforted her. It was a touch on the hand, a hug, a smile, or a story they shared about her son that made all the difference. Takouhi would often look at the mothers posture as she was sitting in her chair. Fully cloaked in black, her face hanging down, her shoulders hunched forward, her hands on her face covering her puffy eyes. She was so young and so beautiful and so broken. Her shell was there but Takouhi wondered where was she really?

There may have been solid reasons within Armenian religious practices for the observation of the forty-day period. However, this ritual had taken a life of its own in the modern sense. It had become a modern social support network. Arka's network was coming together, Armenians and all. Whatever their differences of culture, religion, race, age, gender, and everything in between, they had Arka in common. But, Takouhi wondered; where had they been before he passed away?

One day as Takouhi was making Armenian coffee in the kitchen, she looked up to see an entirely new set of people walk in the door that she had never met before. In spite of not having met Takouhi the newcomers hugged her and she did feel the genuine love and warmth coming from them as they squeezed her tightly. She didn't know who they were but she supposed they knew who Takouhi was as she had done the eulogy. But what surprised Takouhi was her own reaction to them. Her body was tense and not so forthcoming with hugs in return. She could not help wondering why it takes death for people to come together. She went to the living room and served coffee to the new comers and proceeded to sit in a corner close to the door. She wanted to be close to an exit because with the wave of people coming and going she felt she was always riding an emotional tsunami wave. Just when she had control over the waves, a new group of people would come in and another tsunami would have to be tamed. There were moments where she could not control her emotions anymore. If they cried, she cried. Knowing in that state she was no use to anyone she would try to get out of the room. She would exit in stealth like fashion without anyone noticing. This was one of those moments. She slowly got up and backed out of the room when the crowded room was focused on Arka's mom. Just as she headed towards her new hiding place, the roof, she was caught off guard.

"Where are you going?" asked Asbed.

Where did he come from? She had her back to him and her shoulders dropped as if she was caught doing something she wasn't supposed to be doing.

"I just need some time on my own."

"No you don't. You need to come with me to get some food for everyone," he said.

At least it would get her away from the house for a bit, she thought to herself. They quietly rode in the elevator and proceeded to go to the garage. She had nothing to say.

"Wow" he looked at her with his big brown eyes enlarged as he took a step back. She swore she could see his pupils dilated.

"Wow what?" She said in a stern and short voice as she got in the car and slammed the door.

"I have never seen you like this." He said smiling and they drove off. His smile was so genuine it made his eyes sparkle and little crow's feet appeared. Her tense body softened up in a flash. She took a deep breath and matched his smile with hers.

"I'm sorry. I'm just frustrated!" she said in a shy voice as she looked away to hide her new tears.

"Tell me why?"

"All these people that are coming in to pay their respects to your family and help them during the grieving process..."

"Yeah?"

"I have been here for over four months now and I never saw most of them. Why is it that in this forty-day period all these people are making time to come and spend with the family but when Arka was alive, they were too busy to visit or call him?"

"People are busy I suppose." replied Asbed in a low saddened voice realizing what she was saying. He didn't sound to convincing to her.

"Most of these people live in the LA area right? Where were they? Why did they just start showing up at the hospital, funeral, and now here? Do they all value death more than life?" Her voice was cracking as she was trying to be articulate yet controlling a new storm being formed. She looked outside the window at the rush of traffic on the 101 freeway. All these cars speeding and changing lanes as if everyone was always an hour late for something!

"To me, the most precious thing one person can give to someone else is their time. I am allergic to people saying I'm too busy. I wouldn't want someone to show up at my funeral after not seeing me for a long time. I won't be there. It wouldn't mean anything to me. And I wouldn't want someone to make up time lost by buying me things. I'm not going to take stuff with me. We are all valuable. I just want a persons time and I am willing to give mine especially if I consider someone a friend. People are valuable, not things. When did we forget this? When did we take each other for granted and explain it all away by saying we're busy?"

"So if I understand you correctly you're saying I should have let you go to the roof?" Asbed was trying to alter Takouhi's emotional state with sarcasm. Her frustration led to tears, and she had started gasping for air in mid sentences. Asbed's comment worked. She took a deep breath and smiled. There was silence again as she took a long look at the man driving with his tired and unshaven face. She wondered what was going on internally having lost his best friend, his brother. Her eyes welled up again and she quickly looked out the window as if there was a life-altering message on the freeway sign.

"I drive you nuts with all these thoughts huh?" she said with a calm voice and turned to face him again.

"I just think you're a female B2G! The Peacemaker and keeper" he said and gave her a quick playful wink.

"Where did that come from? And how do you know about B2G?" she was pleasantly surprised and her already large cow eyes grew bigger with excitement.

"Boutros Boutros-Ghali the United Nations Secretary General? Doesn't everyone know who he is?" He replied as if he was singing.

"Correct me if I'm wrong but he was the UN Secretary General from 1992 to 1997 and presently it's 2008!" Amazing how sad tears could turn into joyful tears in a split moment.

"Oh just give me credit for at least knowing the name of one of them!"

She was gasping for air again but this time it was because her ribs were hurting from laughing so hard. They eventually calmed down enough for her to continue with her gripe.

"Asbed I know what you're trying to do and I appreciate it. But it doesn't take away from the facts of how we behave as human beings toward each other."

"But we do get busy Takouhi, it's a fact! There are bills to pay, mortgages, car payments. In this fast paced society we are always behind in some way it seems."

"That's my point. Don't you see? We claim we are busy yet we sit and watch four hours of television to take away from the stress of the day-to-day which we in fact have created ourselves. If we were to spend thirty minutes of the fours hours with a loved one and value them then not only are we making a difference for them but we change our state as well. As opposed to watching television why don't we practice sherovision?"

"Sherovision? I've heard you speak about living with shero principles but you've never mentioned sherovision!" They had exited the freeway and his mischievous brown eyes were probing her thoughts like x-ray vision.

"It's no different than the principle of shero. It's basically looking at life through shero eyes. As opposed to thinking I want to shut my brain off by watching television to avoid stress you embrace shero principles to make a difference for yourself and people around you. Your busyness should include your friends and people you love. The fact that you're busy is because you have not utilized your resources properly or you're not in tune with yourself and your beliefs."

"I'm not quite sure what you mean?" His forehead wrinkled up confused as he proceeded to drive.

Hmm... Takouhi thought of an opportune way to reach him. They both loved cars... "Well you know this car with its dual barrel double exhaust V8 engine 0 – 60 in 3.2 seconds that you are driving right now? It has the potential to go up to what? 300 mph?" The machine gun that was Takouhi was fully loaded. She took a deep breath and sat upright in her seat. She was in her element. The engine was revving and her pistons were firing.

"Yeah?" He looked at her with the corner of his eyes with that smile that said oh, oh... here we go!

"Well imagine if you have your foot on the gas but you have not released the emergency break. And to make matters worse as opposed to looking down the road ahead you are constantly looking in the rearview mirror. In that state, your tires will be spinning creating smoke. You may want to move forward but you're not moving an inch."

His perplexed look made her describe the scene further. She spoke with her hands as she pointed out the components she was referring to.

"Okay picture this. Imagine if the car is your body and the driver is equivalent to your brain. By brain I don't mean the white matter. I'm referring to your wants, desires, beliefs, and all the things that shape you to be who you are. Let's call it your consciousness. The driver, your consciousness, is constantly pushing the car, the body, to do things. The engine, the transmission, and all that makes your body run are working very hard. It gets fixated on a certain belief not questioning its effectiveness or validity and causing the gas pedal to be fully engaged. Your wheels are spinning because it's the intent of the consciousness to move the car forward. But somewhere within your beliefs something is holding you back and that's equivalent to the driver holding on to the emergency break. The emergency break is your consciousness' security blanket that is made of beliefs intricately woven together, giving the world outside the windows a meaning. The car is driven with the emergency break engaged most of the time. Thus the car and driver never realize their full potential. Not to mention the damage that's being done to the entire being." She paused for a moment and looked at him. He was driving yet focused on her words trying to picture it for himself.

"Are you with me?" if her grin were any wider you would have seen her tonsils.

"Yeah. My consciousness is driving this car isn't it?" The crow's feet appeared again.

"Okay but there's more." She jumped in her seat and pointed to the road ahead and the rearview mirror. "The driver, the consciousness, is caught in a paradox of looking forward to go down the road ahead but looking in the mirror at the past and old beliefs as well as seeing how it fits in with the rest of the tribe. The driver keeps pushing the car wanting things to change but not comprehending that nothing is going to change unless he changes the way he drives. As you're spinning your wheels, you're creating smoke and all of a sudden you can't tell where the road is anymore. The car is busy but it's not going anywhere. The driver doesn't see the road anymore. Doesn't know what it originally set out to do. And it has now exhausted the body, the car. At this point some people give up and say this is my life. It's just the way it is. Others think it's because they had the wrong car. So they go for external changes. They think they're not getting anywhere because they're too fat, too thin, to old, too young, wrong race, wrong time, or it's someone else's fault. They change things externally yet ultimately things stay the same. Why? Because only when you realize that the change comes from the inside out by changing you beliefs and thought patterns then you can drive the car to its full potential. There is no quick fix. Living a life with shero principles it's my example of living a constructive, healthy, and enjoyable life. For the car I'm driving, shero is equivalent to premium unleaded fuel. There's no substitute because I love my car. I value the roads I came from to get here as they have shaped me but my focus is this moment and the road ahead. We all have different roads and paths but what we all have in common is the ability to maximize our potential. When the rubber hits the road and you can drive forward without the emergency break on that's when you can say you have lived!"

"So that's what you mean when you say people have great cars, thus a great tool but their resources are out of place. If I understand you correctly you're saying it's not what we do that's making us busy it's the beliefs and the chaos we create in the depths of our minds that make us busy."

"You got it! So why not try sherovision?" as she reached over and gave him a high five!

"And with that ladies and gentlemen, she rests her case! You should have been a lawyer!"

"Nah, I would have had more fun as a mechanic or a race car driver!" she looked out the window to find the driver in the car next to them smiling back at them. The animated explanation and laughter within their cockpit was contagious.

"Takouhi?" Asbed's chest dropped as if suddenly he lost the air in his tires.

"What?" she was taken aback by the sudden change of mood in the car and her body tensed up again fearing the worst. They had pulled into the parking stall at the restaurant where they were to pick up the food.

"When are you leaving? Do you have to go?" his eyes began to glisten as the sun brought to light the moisture in his eyes.

"Soon. I have to go back. But not before I do one more thing." Darn that sun and its ability to focus on the moisture even in her eyes.

"What's that?"

"You'll see!"

# 27

# IN WRITING

Takouhi had decided that she would be heading back home soon after the fortieth day memorial of Arka's passing. She and the immediate family had visited the gravesite everyday for forty days. On the fortieth day however, it was like the funeral yet again. Everyone had gathered at the cemetery to pay his or her respects one more time. Takouhi wondered if Arka was looking at them. Was he thinking what she was thinking? Like a murder of crows, all dressed in black, gathered around a plot of land with nothing but white flowers. During the forty day period she had slowly began to move to the background of events. As much as she had been at the centre of things during the two months in the ICU and especially during the eulogy, she was now a Hollywood extra by her own will. She thought that this was the best way to prepare the family for her departure. It was also the best way to prepare her as well as she had become so attached to the family.

With her black and white polka dot dress, she was standing on a staircase in close proximity to the gravesite, having somewhat of an aerial view. She looked down at the crowd. It appeared as if a black hole had come to that corner of the world. She thought 'if this is the view from me standing four steps higher than everyone, I wonder what the view is if I were looking from above where Arka is.' Instantly she had to turn and face away not because she was tearful but quite the opposite. She was concerned that the bright California beams of light would reflect off her white enamel. Why? Because she knew exactly what Arka would be saying at that very moment. He would be wondering how many people are there for him, how many people are there because they are truly religious, and how many people were there because they were sheep, in that they had to be there for fear of raising eyebrows. But to Takouhi, if this is what people needed to satisfy the need in them to think that Arka is now in the hands of God then so be it. If this was their way of being at peace with themselves for thinking that they had done what was needed to lay him to rest in accordance with tribal beliefs then so be it. She took a deep breath and looked at the sea of black slowly dispersing as the memorial had come to a close. As they were dispersing she wondered how many of them would come back again. How many would continue to remember him? She went back in time to the moment where they had left the oncology centre and he had decided to stop chemo. He had said that in time, nobody would remember him and life would go on. Was this the moment where life went on where everyone had completed the obligations of the forty-day memorial?

Everyone gathered in their cars and headed towards the restaurant for another memorial luncheon in Arka's honour. The cars followed each other like a long black centipede crawling to its destination. Takouhi had a car at her disposal that day. In fact, it was Asbed's car as he would always let her borrow it knowing how much she loved to drive and explore. He knew it was her space and time out. She cherished the car because it was her way of transporting herself to different galaxies and helping her change her state. It was her time machine, her state machine. As everyone headed out of the cemetery, Takouhi followed a sudden urge to pull away from the crowd. She did a U-turn and headed back to the gravesite.

She was able to drive the car very close to the gravesite as all the people and their cars had left. She stepped out of the car and went to the trunk. She opened the trunk and picked up the flowers she had for him. It was one of her favourites Daisies. She loved them because they were very simple and reminded her of her childhood. Every time her mother had put her hair in ponytails or braids she would place a daisy pin to complete the look. They were white with a beautiful yellow centre. Takouhi didn't know or understand why she had left the flowers in the trunk when everyone was there. She realized that some people might have wondered why she didn't show up with flowers, as it was customary to do so. It almost seemed like she was being stubborn and resisting. She wanted to prove to herself that she wasn't doing something like a sheep because it was expected of her. The flowers were for him, not so people would see that she brought them to satisfy tribal beliefs. It was between Arka and her. She walked towards Arka's spot very slowly. It was only moments ago she had left the familiar peaceful scene but this time it was different. She approached the gravesite and viewed the amazing amount of flowers that had been brought by the attendees. Would her daisies make a difference? There was only one way to find out. She placed the flowers close to where his heart would have been in the casket six feet below. There were no chairs to sit on. The grass was dry so she sat down next to him. However, she felt uneasy sitting on the grass. The last thing she wanted to do was look down towards him when she knew he was up there somewhere. Lying on the grass looking towards the sky with her head close to where she imagined his would be seemed like a much better option. Her left hand reached out to touch the place where his right hand would be. She lay there for a moment lost in time and not concerned if anyone was there to watch. Takouhi looked directly to the blue sky above as hot tears streamed down her face. For the second time since his passing she felt immense pressure in her chest. It almost felt as it did the night she had heard the phrase ICU Code Blue. She didn't fight the tears, the floodgates were open and no dam would have been able to hold them back at that point, not even Hoover...

She recalled the conversation she had had on the beach in Marina Del Rey asking the powers that be that whatever the plan was for Arka to not let him suffer. And here they were almost two months later. Takouhi had been told during the entire hospital time and during the forty days after passing that she should have met Arka when he wasn't sick. That he was such an energetic man, full of life. And although part of her wished that she had met him when he was healthy and physically able to move about and do things and travel and all the stuff a young man should do, she wondered. Would he have been the same man she got to know and admire for his openness and candor? Without the illness, he may have taken things for granted, and the level of conversation might not have been as in-depth as it had been. Takouhi took a deep breath and looked to see if there were any clouds that she could make shapes out of but she could see nothing but an indescribable shade of blue. She wondered about her own attitudes.

Did she take people for granted or did she really practice what she preached? Did the people around her know that they were loved? If she were to join Arka today, would she have made a difference for anyone? Did she inspire, touch someone's heart, or leave a legacy? She looked over to her left and thought this was the final destination for the physical chapter in this man's life. Had he enjoyed the journey? Was he aware while he was on the journey or was he too busy thinking about the finish line? There was nothing left for him to do. No smiles, hugs, calls, or laughter. That chapter was completely closed. Would Arka have been as open to share his thoughts the way he had done if he wasn't facing illness and mortality? Would he have allowed himself to be vulnerable to the thoughts he had shared with her? Would he have valued their friendship or would he have been too busy at work? Somehow she knew the answer. The answer was that most people closed not just themselves yet their real selves to the world. Takouhi thought that people spent so much time protecting themselves from the world that they lost touch with it. She would never know what Arka was really like without his illness. But she liked the Arka she knew. She had seen the fragility of life, that in a moment they could all be whisked away to another dimension. In her time on this planet, she wanted to make sure people realized that they could be committed and loving, and in tune with their true selves all the time, and not just pencil it in when it suited them. Arka's condition had reminded some of the people that shared his atmosphere of the preciousness of life, yet most went right back to routine and business as usual.

She had observed that the ones who had the hardest time with Arka's departure were those who had things left to say to him, or those who wished they had treated him a different way. The ones at peace were the ones who knew that Arka knew how much they loved him.

Takouhi wanted to talk to Arka one last time but she couldn't make a sound. It was her head doing all the talking. She stopped for a moment and wiped off her tears with her right hand. She still hadn't moved her left hand from his. But she had to let go. Takouhi sat up and looked at his heart. On her daisies there was a bright little ladybug. Again? She put her hand on her heart and began to gasp for air as she sobbed. It wasn't because of the thoughts she had just had. It wasn't because she missed him and was leaving. It was simply because she knew she had been heard. She slowly walked away down the path towards her car. She looked back one last time so she could remember it all in her mind's eye. The perfectly manicured fresh cut grass and the smell of the flowers had become part of her day-to-day for forty days. She was sure that it would be with her for days to come. She sat in her car and rested her forehead on the steering wheel as both hands held the steering wheel tight. She felt so dehydrated and thought she must have looked like a shriveled raisin. But it didn't matter. It didn't matter what she looked like on the outside. It was all about what she was feeling on the inside. She had one last thing she needed to do before she could leave the next day.

Takouhi drove off and joined the rest of the family at the restaurant for one last memorial lunch. It was a great opportunity for her to say her goodbyes to everyone, which included Arka's immediate family, friends, and colleagues. They had all become a very important part of her life. She had learned so many things simply by observing and listening. And maybe just maybe they had picked up a few things here and there from her. Every day and every moment was an opportunity for her to practice, improve upon and build on the shero principles she believed in so much. Every day there was an opportunity to transform and re mould tribal beliefs and make them constructive, efficient and positively intentioned. Nothing in life done by force lasted, positive change took time and leadership was not just talk yet by example. At the end of the forty days Takouhi had seen a shift in her tribe's attitude and beliefs towards her. Some of the tribal members stopped inquiring, measuring themselves to or caring about Takouhi's past, where she was from or what she knew, they simply knew that she cared and that's all that mattered. She knew the hardest person, other than Arka's mother, to say goodbye to was Asbed. But she wasn't done with him yet, one last thing to do in the morning before she left for the airport.

Breakfast at the table was very somber the next morning. There was really nothing that could be said. Takouhi looked across the table at her adopted parents wearing black with the picture of their beloved son on the credenza behind them. A parent's nightmare she thought, outliving their child. Takouhi went to the bedroom to grab her suitcase and she reached for something from Arka's bookshelf and placed it in her handbag. Asbed appeared as he had promised the night before to take Takouhi to the airport. His house was close by to his parents and it had always reminded Takouhi of the same closeness she had with her parents. She lived close enough to them that she visited often during the week sometimes twice in a day. Her family was as close as Asbed's and she had always been fond of that. The fact that Takouhi had been away from her family for so long was rare but it was necessary.

Finally the time had arrived to depart. She looked at Arka's mom and wondered if she was thinking her son was gone and now her adopted daughter was leaving. The tears that hit the cold cement floor of the garage deafened their ears. Finally, Takouhi sat in the passenger seat as Asbed set a course for the airport. One final wave goodbye was all she could muster as she looked at the two parents now standing by the roadside with their heads hanging down. She continued looking out the window. It was easier than facing Asbed with her tears.

The ride to the airport usually took over an hour with traffic but on that day it was unusually fast. Or did it feel that way because she was anxious and uneasy?

"So you're going huh?" he finally broke the silence

"Yeah, it looks that way doesn't it!" she said in a very low voice.

"Any last words, Guru?" he attempted to get a smile out of her. As usual it worked!

"Sort of!" she said as she tried bringing herself back to the moment.

"No, it was a figure of speech. Really it's all good!" and his crow's feet showed again along with a deep chuckle from his belly. She couldn't help but join in his laughter as she reached over and punched his arm.

"Hey show some respect for your sister!" her voice was chocking up.

Again the cockpit was quiet. Takouhi was looking outside her window as they passed all the familiar exit signs. The exit to the Getty Museum, Wilshire Boulevard, where she had exited to take Arka to the Oncology centre, exit to Marina Del Rey which had become a temporary home. She was passing by all of them. She knew she would see the signs again but she would never feel the same way. Just like reading a history book, the signs would be there but the emotions would be different. What an amazing two year period it had been. In fact it was almost two years minus one month. She had met Asbed in August of 2006 and now she was heading back home in July of 2008. She began the journey wanting to discover the root of the belief systems that had helped shape her and then evolving it to a global principle of shero. She was able to silence her questions with constructive answers. In doing so she applied it not only to her tribe but globally. Surely all tribes would appreciate the many applications and dimensions of living shero principles. And everybody had beliefs that could be shaped and adjusted to make their lives much easier and healthier; both mentally and physically. The more everyone related to each other the easier for everyone to work together, be together and share together. Takouhi never expected or thought that people should be the same but underneath the differences of customs and practices was a nervous system that everyone shared. A smile was as universal as love!

They arrived at the airport and he parked the car. She had thought he would simply drop her off outside by her airlines designated area. His plan was to walk into the ticketing and baggage area with her. She panicked for a moment as there was something she had wanted to do quickly and run. It would have been perfect had he just simply dropped her off by the curb. She didn't want to run because she was afraid of his reaction towards her. Simply put, she had planned to run so he would have time to react in private. Asbed, like his brother, was very private and she hadn't really seen him show that much emotion during this entire tragedy. Plan B, Takouhi thought, 'looks like I have to do this right here and now and see where this path takes me.'

Asbed was about to get out of the car.

"Can you wait a minute?" she whispered in a shy trembling voice as she reached over to grab his arm to pull him back in the car.

"Yeah sure what is it?" he was startled and his body tensed up as he sat back in his seat and looked directly at her.

"You know he loved you right?"

"What are you talking about?"

"Arka loved you very much! You know that right?"

"Yeah of course. We never said it but it was understood!"

"Well I just want you to know that a day didn't go by that he didn't tell me how much he loved you!" and her eyes started glistening.

He bit his lip so hard and looked to the left outside the driver's side window.

"But there's more my dear Asbed. First of all I want to thank you for bringing me here. And I don't mean the airport" she tried to muster a smile with her small joke but it wasn't working.

"This journey has been amazing and I am so much richer for it. I want to make sure you know how much he adored you. I saw you both interact in Vancouver and I saw the unspoken respect and rapport. It's important that you know that the spoken is just as real as the unspoken."

"I don't understand Takouhi" he was finally able to look back at her.

"I know he hugged you that one time before we went to the hospital and that spoke volumes to you but I'm about to give you something that you will have forever. It's his voice and it's about you!"

She reached into her handbag and brought out the journal that she had given Arka a year ago. The journal he had promised her that he had written in. The journal that she had found after he had passed away. The journal that she had read and had known in whose trusting hands it belonged.

His eyes were trembling with waves of tears. She had hoped that she wouldn't be there at the moment so he would not resist and be himself.

"I can't!" and he turned beet red in two seconds. "I can't read it."

"When you're ready you will! I won't read it for you. Let it be his voice you hear the way you remember him!"

She reached over and kissed his cheek as a tear was rolling down his face. He sat their motionless. He looked like a perfectly chiseled statue. She wanted to disappear and let him be. Grabbing her suitcase and handbag she walked over to the driver side door.

"Give me a hug and I will let you be with him! The sooner I go the sooner you can hear his voice!" she said with her voice and body trembling.

He got out of the car and as soon as they hugged each other the tears just flowed. There was no shortage of liquid in their reservoirs. They were both hugging and grasping for air at the same time. If either of them had let go the other one would have fallen. She finally let him go and walked away. All she could think about was that she had given Asbed something tangible yet invaluable by way of a journal. She brought the brothers' words and emotions together. Was there anything more solid or concrete than the journal? She kept walking and didn't look back. She walked to the ticketing agent. She walked through the security check. She walked to the gate. She sat down. There was nobody at the airport at that moment. It was just her with notebook and pen. On the clear page she wrote, *shero; principles of leadership.* The next chapter was about to commence.